BANKING AND INDUSTRIAL FINANCE: THEORY AND ANALYSIS

Banking and Industrial Finance: Theory and Analysis

Data Ram Joshi

CYBER TECH PUBLICATIONS
4264/3, Ansari Road, Daryaganj, New Delhi-110002 (India)
Ph.: 011-23244078. Fax: 011-23280028
E-Mail: cyberpublicationsdelhi@yahoo.com

BANKING AND INDUSTRIAL FINANCE: THEORY AND ANALYSIS

Data Ram Joshi

First Edition 2009

Published by :

G.S. Rawat for **Cyber Tech Publications**
4264/3, Ansari Road, Daryaganj, New Delhi-110002 (India)
Ph.: 011-23244078. Fax: 011-23280028
E-Mail: cyberpublicationsdelhi@yahoo.com

Printed at : Asian Offset Printers

Preface

The system of Development Banking being a global issue is the basic approach in the global business. Hence, in this book the authors' presents a comprehensive and an analytical picture of the development banking in India in industrializing the country. The text contains objectives of the study with review of researches in development banking, new vistas in development finance, operational policies and practices of development banks in general and a case study of IDBI in particular. Keeping in view, the research norms a brief chapter end-summary and suggestions and number of figures and tables have been designed in order to make the script more informative illuminating and insightful.

In the era of globalization, liberalization and world trade treaties, the role of government is changing from a participant to that of a facilitator in creation of infrastructure/institutional mechanism for rapid economic growth. Such a change cannot be abrupt and has to be planned properly. The Commission has made an attempt to chalk out a road map for Punjab Government to withdraw itself from the role of a participant and to play its part through its institutions as facilitator so that social sectors like education and health, including disability benefits etc. get their due in the State Budget.

This book will make a significant contribution to the existing literature on development banking sector in the changing business scenario. The book is intended to be useful for business professionals, researchers, financial executives and business educators of the world.

— *Author*

CONTENTS

1

Introduction

The Indian banking can be broadly categorized into nationalized (government owned), private banks and specialized banking institutions. The Reserve Bank of India acts a centralized body monitoring any discrepancies and shortcoming in the system. Since the nationalization of banks in 1969, the public sector banks or the nationalized banks have acquired a place of prominence and has since then seen tremendous progress. The need to become highly customer focused has forced the slow-moving public sector banks to adopt a fast track approach.

The unleashing of products and services through the net has galvanized players at all levels of the banking and financial institutions market grid to look anew at their existing portfolio offering. Conservative banking practices allowed Indian banks to be insulated partially from the Asian currency crisis. Indian banks are now quoting al higher valuation when compared to banks in other Asian countries (viz. Hong Kong, Singapore, Philippines etc.) that have major problems linked to huge Non Performing Assets (NPAs) and payment defaults. Co-operative banks are nimble footed in approach and armed with efficient branch networks focus primarily on the 'high revenue' niche retail segments.

The Indian banking has finally worked up to the competitive dynamics of the 'new' Indian market and is addressing the relevant issues to take on the multifarious challenges of globalization. Banks that employ IT solutions are perceived to be 'futuristic' and proactive players capable of meeting the multifarious requirements of the large customers base. Private banks have been fast on the uptake and are reorienting their strategies using the internet as a medium The Internet has emerged as the new and challenging frontier of marketing with the conventional physical world tenets being just as applicable like in any other marketing medium.

The Indian banking has come from a long way from being a sleepy business institution to a highly proactive and dynamic entity. This transformation has been largely brought about by the large dose of liberalization and economic reforms that allowed banks to explore new business opportunities rather than generating revenues from conventional streams (i.e. borrowing and lending). The banking in India is highly fragmented with 30 banking units contributing to almost 50% of deposits and 60% of advances. Indian nationalized banks (banks owned by the government) continue to be the major lenders in the economy due to their sheer size and penetrative networks which assures them high deposit mobilization. The Indian banking can be broadly categorized into nationalized. private banks and specialized banking institutions.

The Reserve Bank of India act as a centralized body monitoring any discrepancies and shortcoming in the system. It is the foremost monitoring body in the Indian financial sector. The nationalized banks (i.e. government-owned banks) continue to dominate the Indian banking arena. Industry estimates indicate that out of 274 commercial banks operating in India, 223 banks are in the public sector and 51 are in the private sector. The private sector bank grid also includes 24 foreign banks that have started their operations here. Under the ambit of the nationalized banks come the specialized banking institutions. These co-operatives, rural banks focus on areas of agriculture, rural development etc.,

Capital Market

Stock market volatility touches every participant directly/ indirectly in the capital market. General feeling is that the stock markets worldwide have become very fragile in the recent past on account of various developments such as Asian crisis.

Brazil Real fall and Russian debacle. Many far-reaching stock reforms have been introduced in the Indian market for the last few years. These reforms, in turn, changed market structure. Changing market structure influences nature of stock price behavior.

Primary Securities Market

The primary capital market (PCM) plays an important role in the overall functioning of securities market. Despite several measures the primary market remained lackluster till recently and the pick up is gradual. According to the SEBI annual report fewer number of issues accessed the primary market during the year and the significantly lower than that of the Previous financial year. Share of the equity issues, in terms of number and amount Mobilized, however, was higher in this financial year compared to the previous one. More than three-fourths of the total amount was occupied second and no resources were in the previous years, banks and financial institutions continued for 84.5% of the resourced mobilized compared to 68.1% in 2001-02. All other industries shared the remaining portion.

Capital Raised During 2002-03

During the financial year 2002-03, primary market witnessed a decrease of 46.0% in the amount raised and also a decrease of 25.7% in the number of issues launched compared to the same period in 2001-02. A total of 26 issues (14 public issues and 12 rights issues) opened during the financial year 2002-03 raising Rs. 4070.29 crore (Rs. 3638.6 crore through public issues and 431.6 crore through rights issues). In 2001-02 a total of 35 issues opened for raising Rs. 7543.0 crore (20 public issues-Rs. 6501.8 crore and 15 rights issues-Rs. 1041.2).

Industry Wise Capital Mobilization

Three industries viz. Banks/Fls, Engineering and Telecommunications accounted for 93.2 per cent of the resourced mobilized in 2001-02. In the current year, the same three industries accounted for 84.7 per cent of the funds raised. With the banks and Fls, increasing their share from 68.3 per cent to 84.5 per cent and companies in the Telecommunications sector and raising any resourced. In 2002-03 the three industries which accounted for 95.3 per cent of the resources where Banking/FIs, Information Technology, Paper and Pulp.

SECONDARY MARKET

During 2002-03, performance of Indian Stock market was, by and large, a lackluster one, S&P CNX NIFTY and BSE Sensex both registered

INTRODUCTION

Duration

In exercise of the powers conferred under Section 5 of The Foreign Trade (Development and Regulation Act), 1992 (No. 22 of 1992), the Central Government hereby notifies the Export and Import Policy for the period 2002-2007. This Policy shall come into force with effect from 1st April, 2002 and shall remain in force upto 31st March, 2007 and will be co-terminus with the Tenth Five Year Plan (2002-2007). However, the Central Government reserves the right in public interest to make any amendments to this Policy in exercise of the powers conferred by Section-5 of the Act. Such amendment shall be made by means of a Notification published in the Gazette of India.

Transitional Arrangements

Any Notifications made or Public Notices issued or anything done under the previous Export/Import policies, and in force immediately before the commencement of this Policy shall, in so far as they are not inconsistent with the provisions of this Policy, continue to be in force and shall be deemed to have been made, issued or done under this Policy.

Licence/certificate/permissions issued before the commencement of this Policy shall continue to be valid for the purpose for which such licence/certificate/permission was issued unless otherwise stipulated.

In case an export or import that is permitted freely under this Policy is subsequently subjected to any restriction or regulation, such export or import will ordinarily be permitted notwithstanding such restriction or regulation, unless otherwise stipulated, provided that the shipment of the export or import is made within the original validity of the irrevocable letter of credit established before the date of imposition of such restriction

FOREIGN TRADE POLICY

Objectives

Trade is not an end in itself, but a means to economic growth and national development. The primary purpose is not the mere earning of foreign exchange, but the stimulation of greater economic activity. The Foreign Trade Policy is rooted in this belief and built around two major objectives. These are:

(i) To double our percentage share of global merchandise trade within the next five years; and

(ii) To act as an effective instrument of economic growth by giving a thrust to employment generation.

Strategy

These objectives are proposed to be achieved by adopting, among others, the following strategies:

(i) Unshackling of controls and creating an atmosphere of trust and transparency to unleash the innate entrepreneurship of our businessmen, industrialists and traders.

(ii) Simplifying procedures and bringing down transaction costs.

(iii) Neutralizing incidence of all levies and duties on inputs used in export products, based on the fundamental principle that duties and levies should not be exported.

(iv) Facilitating development of India as a global hub for manufacturing, trading and services.

(v) Identifying and nurturing special focus areas which would generate additional employment opportunities, particularly in semi-urban and rural areas, and developing a series of 'Initiatives' for each of these.

(vi) Facilitating technological and infrastructural upgradation of all the sectors of the Indian economy, especially through import of capital goods and equipment, thereby increasing value addition and productivity, while attaining internationally accepted standards of quality.

(vii) Avoiding inverted duty structures and ensuring that our domestic sectors are not disadvantaged in the Free Trade Agreements/Regional Trade Agreements/ Preferential Trade Agreements that we enter into in order to enhance our exports.

(viii) Upgrading our infrastructural network, both physical and virtual, related to the entire Foreign Trade chain, to international standards.

(ix) Revitalising the Board of Trade by redefining its role, giving it due recognition and inducting experts on Trade Policy.

(x) Activating our Embassies as key players in our export strategy and linking our Commercial Wings abroad through an electronic platform for real time trade intelligence and enquiry dissemination.

Partenership

The new Policy envisages merchant exporters and manufacturer exporters, business and industry as partners of Government in the achievement of its stated objectives and goals. Prolonged and unnecessary litigation vitiates the premise of partnership.

In order to obviate the need for litigation and nurture a constructive and conducive atmosphere, a suitable Grievance Redressal Mechanism will be established which, it is hoped, would substantially reduce litigation and further a relationship of partnership.

The dynamics of a liberalized trading system sometimes results in injury caused to domestic industry on account of dumping. When this happens, effective measures to redress such injury will be taken.

Roadmap

This Policy is essentially a roadmap for the development of India's foreign trade. It contains the basic principles and points the direction in which we propose to go. By virtue of its very dynamics, a trade policy cannot be fully comprehensive in all its details. It would naturally require modification from time to time. We propose to do this through continuous updation, based on the inevitable changing dynamics of international trade. It is in partnership with business and industry that we propose to erect milestones on this roadmap.

FUNCTIONS OF COMMERCIAL BANKING

A commercial bank is a type of financial intermediary and a type of bank. Commercial bank has two possible meanings:

- Commercial bank is the term used for a normal bank to distinguish it from an investment bank.

  This is what people normally call a "bank". The term "commercial" was used to distinguish it from an investment bank. Since the two types of banks no longer have to be separate companies, some have used the term "commercial bank" to refer to banks which focus mainly on companies. In some English-speaking countries outside North America, the term "trading bank" was and is used to denote a commercial bank. (After the great depression, the U.S. Congress required that banks only engage in banking activities, whereas investment banks were limited to capital markets activities. This separation is no longer mandatory.)

  It raises funds by collecting deposits from businesses and consumers via checkable deposits, savings deposits, and time (or term) deposits. It makes loans to businesses and consumers. It also buys corporate bonds and government bonds. Its primary liabilities are deposits and primary assets are loans and bonds.

- Commercial banking can also refer to a bank or a division of a bank that mostly deals with deposits and loans from corporations or large businesses, as opposed to normal individual members of the public (retail banking)

WHAT ARE CENTRAL BANKS?

The central bank has been described as "the lender of last resort", which means that it is responsible for providing its economy with funds when commercial banks cannot cover a supply shortage. In other words, the central bank prevents the country's banking system from failing. However, the primary goal of central banks is to provide their countries' currencies with price stability by controlling inflation. A central bank also acts as the regulatory authority of a country's monetary policy and is the sole provider and printer of notes and coins in circulation. Time has proven that the central bank can best function in these capacities by remaining independent from government fiscal policy and therefore uninfluenced by the political concerns of any regime. The central bank should also be completely divested of any commercial banking interests.

The Rise of the Central Bank

Today the central bank is government owned but separate from the country's ministry of finance. Although the central bank is frequently termed the "government's bank" because it handles the buying and selling of government bonds and other instruments, political decisions should not influence central bank operations. Of course, the nature of the relationship between the central bank and the ruling regime varies from country to country and continues to evolve with time. To ensure the stability of a country's currency, the central bank should be the regulator and authority in the banking and monetary systems. Historically, the role of the central bank has been growing, some may argue, since the establishment of the Bank of England in 1694. It is, however, generally agreed upon that the concept of the modern central bank did not appear until the 20th century as problems developed in the commercial banking system. Thus, the central bank's modern function emerged in response to an already present commercial banking structure.

Between 1870 and 1914, when world currencies were pegged to the gold standard (GS), maintaining price stability was a lot easier because the amount of gold available was limited. Consequently, monetary expansion could not occur simply from a political decision to print more money, so inflation was easier to control. The central bank at that time was primarily responsible for maintaining the convertibility of gold into currency; it issued notes based on a country's reserves of gold.

At the outbreak of WWI, the GS was abandoned, and it came apparent that, in times of crisis, governments, facing budget deficits (because it costs money to wage war) and needing greater resources, will order the printing of more money. As governments did so, they encountered inflation. After WWI, many governments opted to go back to the GS to try to stabilize their economies. With this rose the awareness of the importance of the central bank's independence from the political machine.

During the unsettling times of the Great Depression and the aftermath of WWII, world governments predominantly favored a return to a central bank dependent on the political decision making process. This view emerged mostly from the need to establish control over war-shattered economies; furthermore, countries with newly-acquired independence opted to keep control over all aspects of their countries-a backlash against colonialism.

The rise of managed economies in the Eastern Bloc was also responsible for increased government interference in the macroeconomy. Soon after the effects of WWII, however, the independence of the central bank from the government came back into fashion in Western economies and has prevailed as the optimal way to achieve a liberal and stable economic regime.

HOW THE BANK INFLUENCES AN ECONOMY

A central bank can be said to have two main kinds of functions: (1) macroeconomic when regulating inflation and price stability and (2) microeconomic when functioning as a lender of last resort.

Macroeconomic Influences

As it is responsible for price stability, the central bank must regulate the level of inflation by controlling money supplies by means of monetary policy. The central bank performs open market transactions that either inject the market with liquidity or absorb extra funds, directly affecting the level of inflation. To increase the amount of money in circulation and decrease the interest rate (cost) for borrowing, the central bank can buy government bonds, bills, or other government-issued notes. This buying can, however, also lead to higher inflation. When it needs to absorb money to reduce inflation, the central bank will sell government bonds on the open market, which increases the interest rate and discourages borrowing. Open market operations are the key means by which a central bank controls inflation, money supply, and price stability.

Microeconomic Influences

The establishment of central banks as lender of last resort has pushed the need for their freedom from commercial banking. A commercial bank offers funds to clients on a first come, first serve basis. If the commercial bank does not have enough liquidity to meet its clients' demands (commercial banks typically do not hold reserves equal to the needs of the entire market), the commercial bank can turn to the central bank to borrow additional funds.

This provides the system with stability in an objective way; central banks cannot favor any particular commercial bank. As such, many central banks will hold commercial-bank reserves that are based on a ratio of each commercial bank's deposits. Thus, a central bank may require all commercial banks to keep, for example, a 1:10 reserve/deposit ratio. Enforcing a policy of commercial bank reserves functions as another means to control money supply in the market. Not all central banks, however, require commercial banks to deposit reserves. The United Kingdom, for example, does not have this policy while the United States does.

The rate at which commercial banks and other lending facilities can borrow short-term funds from the central bank is called the discount rate (which is set by the central bank and provides a base rate for interest rates). It has been argued that, for open market transactions to become more efficient, the discount rate should keep the banks from perpetual borrowing, which would disrupt the market's money supply and the central bank's monetary policy. By borrowing too much, the commercial bank will be circulating more money in the system. Use of the discount rate can be restricted by making it unattractive when used repeatedly.

Transitional Economies

Today developing economies are faced with issues such as the transition from managed to free market economies. The main concern is often controlling inflation. This can lead to the creation of an independent central bank but can take some time, given that many developing nations maintain control over their economies in an effort to retain control of their power. But government intervention, whether direct or indirect through fiscal policy, can stunt central bank development. Unfortunately, many developing nations are faced with civil disorder or war, which can force a government to divert funds away from the development of the economy as a whole. Nonetheless, one factor that seems to be confirmed is that, for a market economy to develop, a stable currency (whether achieved through a fixed or floating exchange rate) is needed. However, the central banks in both industrial and emerging economies are dynamic because there is no guaranteed way to run an economy regardless of its stage of development.

BANKING IN INDIA

Banking in India originated in the first decade of 18th century with The General Bank of India coming into existence in 1786. This was followed by Bank of Hindustan. Both these banks are now defunct. The oldest bank in existence in India is the State Bank of India being established as "The Bank of Bengal" in Calcutta in June 1806. A couple of decades later, foreign banks like Credit Lyonnais started their Calcutta operations in the 1850s. At that point of time, Calcutta was the most active trading port, mainly due to the trade of the British Empire, and due to which banking activity took roots there and prospered. The first fully Indian owned bank was the Allahabad Bank, which was established in 1865.

By the 1900s, the market expanded with the establishment of banks such as Punjab National Bank, in 1895 in Lahore and Bank of India, in 1906, in Mumbai-both of which were founded under private ownership. The Reserve Bank of India formally took on the responsibility of regulating the Indian banking sector from 1935. After India's independence in 1947, the Reserve Bank was nationalized and given broader powers.

Nationalisation

The next significant milestone in Indian Banking occurred on July 19, 1969 when the then Indira Gandhi government nationalized the 14 largest commercial banks. A second nationalization of 6 more commercial banks followed in 1980. The stated reason for the nationalisation was to give the government more control of credit delivery. After this, until the 1990s, the nationalised banks grew at a leisurely pace of around 4%, closer to the average growth rate of the Indian economy.

Liberalisation

In the early 1990s the then Narasimha Rao government embarked on a policy of liberalisation and gave licences to a small number of private banks, which came to be known as New Generation tech-savvy banks, which included banks such as UTI Bank (the first of such new generation banks to be set up), ICICI Bank and HDFC Bank. This move, along with the rapid growth in the economy of India, kickstarted the banking sector in India, which has seen rapid growth with strong contribution from all the three sectors of banks, namely, government banks, private banks and foreign banks.

The next stage for the Indian banking has been setup with the proposed relaxation in the norms for Foreign Direct Investment, where all Foreign Investors in banks may be given voting rights which could exceed the present cap of 10%.

The new policy shook the Banking sector in India completely. Bankers, till this time, were used to the 4-6-4 method (Borrow at 4%; Lend at 6%; Go home at 4) of functioning. The new wave ushered in a modern outlook and tech-savvy methods of working for traditional banks. All this led to the retail boom in India. People not just demanded more from their banks but also received more.

Currently (2007), overall, banking in India is considered as fairly mature in terms of supply, product range and reach-even though reach in rural India still remains a challenge for the private sector and foreign banks.

Even in terms of quality of assets and capital adequacy, Indian banks are considered to have clean, strong and transparent balance sheets-as compared to other banks in comparable economies in its region. The Reserve Bank of India is an autonomous body, with minimal pressure from the government. The stated policy of the Bank on the Indian Rupee is to manage volatility-without any stated exchange rate-and this has mostly been true.

With the growth in the Indian economy expected to be strong for quite some time-especially in its services sector, the demand for banking services-especially retail banking, mortgages and investment services are expected to be strong. M&As, takeovers, asset sales and much more action (as it is unravelling in China) will happen on this front in India.

In March 2006, the Reserve Bank of India allowed Warburg Pincus to increase its stake in Kotak Mahindra Bank (a private sector bank) to 10%. This is the first time an investor has been allowed to hold more than 5% in a private sector bank since the RBI announced norms in 2005 that any stake exceeding 5% in the private sector banks would need to be vetted by them.

Currently, India has 88 scheduled commercial banks (SCBs)-28 public sector banks (that is with the Government of India holding a stake), 29 private banks (these do not have government stake; they may be publicly listed and traded on stock exchanges) and 31 foreign banks.

They have a combined network of over 53,000 branches and 17,000 ATMs. According to a report by ICRA Limited, a rating agency, the public sector banks hold over 75 percent of total assets of the banking industry, with the private and foreign banks holding 18.2% and 6.5% respectively.

DIRECT FINANCE PAYMENT

Definition

Direct Finance Payment refers to payment service where the finance authority issues payment instruction according to fund application by eligible department and ICBC pays the fund directly to the payee account through the treasury's single account system according to the payment instruction.

Products' Target Client

The service mainly serves the finance authorities at each level included in the treasury centralized payment reform and is applicable for the wage expenditure, project procurement, and goods and service procurement of the budgeting units.

Features and Strengths

Large Business Network

ICBC not only has large number of Business Offices in wide distribution, but also possess the largest customer group in the domestic banking sector. It has shaped the banking competitive advantage of highest ratio for efficient fund allocation within system and lowest ratio for cross-bank payment.

Advanced Payment System

All transactions are centralized in one data center for processing. The fund is linked to accounting entries, which effectively prevents the criminal attempts by internal and external personnel taking advantage of time lag between fund activities and accounting entries. The leading "Bank-Finance Link" system in the sector synchronizes the fund flow and information flow. The transaction information is transmitted through encrypted mode.

The system achieved the electronic State treasury fund payment clearing, standardized information transmission, and informationalized reporting system management. The system makes ICBC at the leadership position in China in terms of agency State treasury centralized payment service. Therefore, ICBC is capable to promptly respond to the variety of large batch, inter-region, and inter-bank fund payment requests from the finance authorities and budgeting units.

Diversified Information Feedback Platform

In response to the special requirement by finance authority's centralized payment service, ICBC launched automated processing for fund settlement, accounting, information transmission, and reporting.

It realized real-time enquiry, collection and sorting, and summary and analysis of information and ensured timely, accurate, and secure feedbacks to the finance authorities and budgeting units at each level.

Furthermore, ICBC takes full advantage of its IT and electronic service and makes use of special-line networking, Internet Banking, and other channels to break through the limitation of Business Offices and the business hours. It provides a 24-7 electronic real-time enquiry system for the finance authorities and budgeting units at each level and provides multi-function, convenient and prompt, and safe and reliable electronic enquiry service.

Service Channels

"Bank-Finance Link" system.

Application Condition

The finance authorities at each level that are included in the Treasury centralized payment reform are eligible to apply for direct payment services.

Service Procedure

(I) As per finance authority's notification, ICBC opens the zero-balance account for direct payment and Treasury single account clearing.

(II) The finance authority issues Finance Direct Payment Voucher to ICBC or sends the electronic direct payment instruction to ICBC through special line.

(III) ICBC transfers the fund to the payee or the eligible unit's account on real-time basis through "Bank-Finance Link" system.

(IV) ICBC timely delivers the payment slip to the finance authority and upload the electronic return slip to the finance authority through special line and deliver the Finance Direct Payment Deposit Advice to the budgeting units. It presents the finance direct payment 10-day (monthly) report to the finance authority as per stipulated time and enables the dynamic monitoring service to the finance authority to cover Treasury fund payments.

FINANCE AUTHORIZED PAYMENT

Definition

Finance Authorized Payment is service arrangement where the finance authority allocate the monthly fund limit to the zero-balance account of the budgeting units according to the budget and fund usage plan, whereas the budgeting units make their payments within the allocated fund limit.

Product's Target Client

The service mainly targets to the budgeting units at each level included in the Treasury centralized payment reforms. It is applicable for the procurement payment and random expenditures not yet included in the Finance Direct Payment.

Features and Strengths

Automatic Line Distribution: "Bank-Finance Link" system automatically receives the authorized payment limit transmitted from finance authority to ICBC through special line or other methods and automatically diverts it to the intermediary service platform of each first-tier (direct control) branches and automatically prints the line deposit advice for the budgeting units.

Automatic Line Control

"Bank-Finance Link" system is managed centrally as per first-tier budgeting units for the authorized payment limit. It automatically renew the line after the new line granting or line drawdown; for over-the-limit payment, it automatically stops payment and sends feedback to the budgeting unit; it automatically reinstates the relevant limits when the funds are returned to the Treasury.

Automatic System Resources Retrieval

The teller user only needs to input the few key elements such as receiving account number and is able to retrieve the budgeting unit name, account code, and other voucher data pre-stored in the system, thereby minimizing the data entry volume.

Dynamic Monitoring Service

The system retrieves the finance payment details from the database and retrieves the back office system per minute on real-time basis to generate the real-time monitoring file saved under the designated folder for real-time monitoring by the finance authority.

Automatic Generation of Various Payment Information

The "Bank-Finance Link" system automatically generates electronic return slip and all sorts of reports that are fed back to the finance authority through special line or other means and automatically print the reconciliation breakdown and monthly reconciliation sheet for the budgeting unit.

Service Channels

"Bank-Finance Link" system.

Application Condition

The budgeting units at each level that are included in the Treasury centralized payment reform and who holds approval by the finance authority permitting the unit to open zero-balance account and relevant materials stipulated in Administrative Methods on Bank Account are eligible for Authorized Payment services.

Service Procedure

(I) ICBC opens zero-balance account for the budgeting unit.

(II) The finance authority passes the electronic Detailed Finance Authorized Payment Limit Advice through special line or other means to ICBC's "Bank-Finance Link" system.

(III) "Bank-Finance Link" system automatically breaks down the authorized payment limit and the administering Business Offices enquires and prints Finance Authorized Payment Line Deposit Advice to be sent to the basic budgeting units.

(IV) The budgeting unit presents the payment application and the administering Business Office generates the authorized payment transaction through "Bank-Finance Link" system. For over-the-limit payments, the system automatically stops payment and provide payment stop feedback to the budgeting unit. For payment within line, the system transfers the fund to the payee account on real-time basis.

(V) "Bank-Finance Link" system automatically generates the Finance Authorized Payment electronic return slip and daily, ten-day, and monthly report to be fed back to Ministry of Finance, the People's Bank of China, and the budgeting units; the system automatically generates monthly reconciliation sheet and detailed reconciliation sheet to be delivered to the budgeting units by administering Business Offices.

NON-TAX REVENUE COLLECTION

Definition

The Non-Tax Revenue Collection refers to service where ICBC opens non-tax revenue special account, fund collection, remittance and transfer clearing, and information feedback for the finance authorities, State authorities, public utilities, and non-government organizations at each level.

Product Target Client

The service is applicable for the collection and payment management for State authorities, public utilities, and non-government organizations at each level including: administrative fee collection, centralized receipts by supervisory department (incl. sector organizations with government function), and other non-tax revenues.

Features and Strengths

Large Business Network: ICBC has a large number and wide distribution of Business Offices. Its Business Office distribution pattern can match with the non-tax income-receiving units' characteristics of wide distribution, highly systematic organization, and wide dispersion of payers. It is capable to provide services for the payers and the receiving units all over China. All its Business Offices accept the finance non-tax fund collection requests and formed powerful network coverage advantage.

Advanced Business System

All transactions are centralized in one data center for processing. The fund is linked to accounting entries, which effectively prevents the criminal attempts by internal and external personnel taking advantage of time lag between fund activities and accounting entries. The leading "Bank-Finance Link" system in the sector synchronizes the fund flow and information flow. The transaction information is transmitted through encrypted mode. The system achieved the electronic State non-tax fund payment clearing, standardized information transmission, and informationalized reporting system management. The system makes ICBC at the leadership position in China in terms of agency State treasury non-tax revenue collection service.

Diversified Information Feedback Platform

In response to the special requirement by finance authority's non-tax revenue information feedback, ICBC launched automated processing for fund settlement, accounting, information transmission, and reporting. It realized real-time enquiry, collection and sorting, and summary and analysis of information and ensured timely, accurate, and secure feedbacks to the finance authorities, supervisory departments, and the receiving units at each level. Furthermore, ICBC takes full advantage of its IT and electronic service and makes use of special-line networking, Internet Banking, and other channels to break through the limitation of Business Offices and the business hours.

It provides a 24-7 electronic real-time enquiry system for the finance authorities, supervisory departments, and the receiving units at each level and provide multi-function, convenient and prompt, and safe and reliable electronic enquiry service.

Convenient Service Process

It adopts the leading and revolutionary technology in the sector that optimizes services procedure, shortens the hierarchy of accounting, realizes the flat management, and simplifies the system search and visit procedures to the maximum extent, thereby increasing the speed of service processing.

The teller only needs to input the few key elements such as amount and receiving account number, the system can retrieve the corresponding voucher element resources pre-stored in the system for automated data processing, thereby minimizing the data entry volume.

Diversified Fee Payment Platform

ICBC takes the full advantage in Internet Banking to enable customers' fee payment services through Internet Banking. The administering personnel of the supervisory departments or receiving units and the payers may pay fees and enquire relevant information behind the doors. The payer may also enquire fee payment information at any time through Telephone Banking or cell phone SMS.

Service Channels

"Bank-Finance Link" system.

Application Condition

The finance authorities, supervision departments, and receiving units at each level who holds relevant materials stipulated in Administrative Methods on Bank Account are eligible for Non-tax Revenue Collection services.

Service Procedure

Account Opening: ICBC sets up finance special account for the finance authorities as per the finance authority's notice and relevant regulations. ICBC opens the finance remittance and payment special account at ICBC branch institutions for the receiving unit as per the stipulated procedures.

Payment

The payers or the receiving units make payment at ICBC Business office and presents General Non-Tax Revenue Payment Advice ("Payment Advice" hereinafter). ICBC's Business Offices that accept non-tax revenue payment include finance special account bank, finance payment special account bank, and the associate bank (all Business offices other than remittance and payment special account banks).

Fund Remittance and Transfer

ICBC Business Office double-checks the key elements in Payment Advice and input the relevant information into "Bank-Finance Link" system. The system automatically verifies the check code and transfers the non-tax revenue to the finance special account of finance remittance and payment special account on real-time basis through real-time clearing system. It then passes the key information in the Payment Advice to the special account bank on real-time basis through "Bank-Finance Link" system.

Fund Sweeping

By the close of each working day, each finance remittance and payment account sweep the fund deposited in the finance remittance and payment special account to the finance special account through real-time clearing system. It also passes the relevant non-tax revenue collection information to the finance special account bank through "Bank-Finance Link" system. The finance remittance and payment account balance is back to zero after sweeping.

Diversion to Treasury or Fund Allocation: ICBC finance special account bank diverts the fund in finance special account to the Treasury unified account or fund allocation as per instruction of the finance authority.

Feedback

Electronic Feedback: By the end of each day, ICBC "Bank-Finance Link" system pools the non-tax revenue collection information and sends feedback to the finance authority as per stipulated format through data transmission special line or other methods and deliver Non-Tax Revenue Reconciliation Statement to the finance authority upon the next day. The "Bank-Finance Link" system's dynamic monitoring system can also provide the finance authority with ICBC's real-time monitoring and control service for all non-tax revenue collection accounts. The finance authority can enquire the combination information for non-tax revenue collection details, total, and number of payments as per department, account, time period, and other criteria. Meanwhile, ICBC Internet Banking system provides feedback to the supervisory departments for the non-tax revenue collection of its subordinate receiving units and provides feedback to the receiving units for account information of finance remittance and payment special account.

Report Feedback: "Bank-Finance Link" system can automatically generate all sorts of income reports and accounting statements. ICBC finance special account banks double-check the fund data each day and present the finance special account fund collection, payment, balance daily reconciliation statement to the finance authority in the next day and reconcile the finance special account fund account with the finance authority by the next day following the close of the month. Each account bank will print ICBC Ten-Day (Monthly) Statement of Agency Non-Tax Revenue Collection as per stipulated format to the finance authority, supervisory department, and receiving units within 2 days after each ten-day period of the month and within 4 days after each month and reconcile accounts with the finance authority, supervisory department, and receiving units within 4 days after each month

Revenue Refund

As per instruction from the finance authority, ICBC finance special account bank inputs the relevant revenue refund information in "Bank-Finance Link" and process the revenue refund through finance special account. ICBC transfers the fund into the payer's account bank and sends feedback to the finance authority through "Bank-Finance Link" system. The revenue refund is generally completed through account transfer, and there is no cash refund. For refund needing cash, ICBC processes the refund strictly as per relevant regulations by the finance authority.

More Money in Circulation Means more Trade

Many of the mercantilists, some of whom also used the arguments already discussed, wanted more money because they regarded money, not merely as a passive medium of exchange, but as a force acting through its circulation from hand to hand as an active stimulus to trade. An increased amount of money in circulation, they believed, meant (or caused) an increased volume of trade, and since men would produce only what they could sell a quickening of trade meant an increase of production and therefore a wealthier country. Here, it should be noted, money is valued as an instrument or stimulus of trade rather than for its own sake. The writers who stressed "circulation" as the valuable service of money often shifted, however, from the concept of money circulating as a medium of exchange to money passing from the hands of a lender to those of a borrower, and rarely distinguished clearly between them. The underlying reasoning is often presented in the form of analogies, especially with the circulation of the blood, which William Harvey had discovered not long before.

Stress on the importance of an abundance of money in circulation if trade was to flourish is already to be found in very early writers. The most elaborate expositions of the "circulation" argument were made by William Potter and John Law. Potter's argument seems to reduce to this: The wealth of a country is equal to the value of the goods of all sorts therein, money being valuable only as it serves to bring about the production of more goods. The more money men have, the more they spend and the faster they spend it. If men acquire more money and spend it as fast as they receive it, the sales of merchants and manufacturers will increase proportionately. If they sell five times as much in money value, they will produce five times as much, and even more, in physical quantities, since they can afford to charge lower prices on the greater volume of sales.

In reference to a commonwealth, or any society of men, the greater quantity there is amongst them, of money, credit, or that which is taken by them for commodities, the more commodity they sell, that is, the greater is their trade. For whatsoever is taken amongst men for commodity, though it were ten times more than now it is, yet if it be one way or other laid out by each man, as fast as he receives it, it must needs come to pass, that (resting nowhere) it doth occasion a quickness in the revolution of commodity from hand to hand, that is trade, proportionable to the greatness of its quantity.

John Law's argument is essentially the same, although stated more conservatively. The most enthusiastic advocates of the circulation argument, Potter and Law included, were advocates of paper money. But if paper money were accepted as of equal value to metallic money, the great reason for desiring a favorable balance of trade, that it results in an inflow of bullion, should lose its force. Such in fact was the case with some of them, as the following extracts show:

For whether a nation have any silver amongst them or no, yet if they can trade as well without it, what need they care? for their estates in vendible commodities (and consequently their credit) is of as real value as if it were in money.

Whatsoever quantity of credit shall be raised in this office, will be as good, and of as much use, as if there were so much money in specie added to the present stock of the nation...'tis more prudent and advantageous to a nation, to have the common standard or medium of their trade within their power, and to arise from their native product, than to be at the mercy of a foreign prince for his gold and silver, which he may at pleasure behold.... Credit can neither be hoarded up, nor transported to the nation's disadvantage; which consequently frees us from the care and necessity of making laws to prevent exportation of bullion or coin, being always able to command a credit of our own,...as useful, and as much as shall be necessary. The only necessity of a foreign trade for England is because we make a foreign commodity (gold and silver) the standard of all ours, and the only medium of commerce, which (as long as it continues so) if we want, all trades must cease; but if we can find out another and safer medium of exchange (as this credit) appropriated to the place where we live and not subject to such obstruction as the other, why should we not readily embrace it?

And if the proprietors of the bank can circulate their funds of twelve hundred thousand pounds, without having more than two or three hundred thousand pounds lying dead at one time with another, this bank will be in effect, as nine hundred thousand pounds, or a million of fresh money, brought into the nation.

Whether in any one year half a million is brought into a commercial country by trade, or issued out by banks, in notes, upon good security, it will serve for the same purposes.

Some advocates of paper money made little or no reference to the balance of trade or to trade policy in their tracts. This freedom from the prevailing obsession with the state of the balance of trade may have been due to a loss of interest in a policy of securing laboriously through the complicated regulation of trade the increase of money which could be secured more quickly, with greater certainty, and with less effort, by means of the printing press. But some of the advocates of paper money displayed loyalty to the current belief in the importance of a favorable balance of trade, either because of blind acceptance of traditional doctrine, or on the basis of the store of wealth argument or the analogy from personal finance that one should buy less than one sells, and these writers claimed that an increase of paper money would not drive bullion out of the country, but on the contrary would make the balance of trade more favorable through its beneficial effect on production and trade.

THE QUANTITY THEORY OF MONEY

Those mercantilists who sought an increase in the supply of money because they wanted more circulation or more invested capital clearly wanted genuine physical increases in trade or capital and not merely nominal increases in terms of a depreciated monetary unit. Their doctrines, therefore, would seem to come into sharp conflict with any theory of the value of money which makes it vary inversely with its quantity, whether proportionately or not. Only for those mercantilists who wanted an increase of money for use as hoards or stores of wealth would acceptance of a quantity theory of money involve no problem of reconciliation. Many of the mercantilist writers gave no evidence of recognition of the dependence of the value of money upon its quantity. A few of them, in fact, wanted more money as a cure for the evils resulting from high prices. But, although Locke is sometimes credited with the first clear English formulation of the quantity theory, many of the mercantilists, from the beginning of the seventeenth century on, did present, in one connection or another, some simple version of the quantity theory, although in most cases they failed to incorporate it as an integral part of their foreign-trade doctrine and failed also to show any concern about its consistency with the rest of their doctrine. There follow quotations from writings antedating Locke by some forty to ninety years which present some form of quantity theory of the value of money:

> Plenty of money maketh generally things dear, and scarcity of money maketh likewise generally things good cheap. Whereas things particularly are also dear or good cheap according to plenty or scarcity of the things themselves, or the use of them.

> Even as plenty of money maketh things dear, and scarcity of money maketh things good cheap: even so plenty or scarcity of commodities maketh the price thereof to rise and fall according to their use more or less. It is a common saying, that plenty or scarcity of money makes all things dear or good or cheap. Gold and silver...in the intrinsic...are commodities, valuing each other according to the plenty or scarcity; and so all other commodities by them; and that is the sole power of trade. Money through want or plenty raises or diminishes the price of all things. In those countries where monies are scarce, there the lands and native wares are cheap, so likewise where money doth abound, there the lands and wares are dear.

Several mercantilists faced squarely the apparent conflict between the quantity theory of money and their doctrines and attempted to meet the issue either by arguing that they could be reconciled or by denying the truth of the quantity theory. Apparently the first of these was William Potter, who has not received the attention which he deserves in this connection. Potter, as has been shown, claimed that an increase of money in circulation would result in an even more than proportionate increase in trade and production, or in goods in circulation. In order to refute it, he states a quantity theory of money in its simplest one-sided form:

> If then, in opposition to what is thus undertaken to be proved, it should be objected, that an increase of money would occasion an increase in the price of commodities, proportionable to such increase of money, (that is, if the money were twice as much, commodity would be twice as dear) consequently (going never the further in commodity by the increase thereof) would not occasion any increase in the sale of commodity: therefore not any increase of trade; and yet (by causing the price of commodities to rise) incur an inconvenience, contrary to what is before affirmed.

His answer is elaborate and not always intelligible. He assumes the basis of the theory of money he is attacking to be that an increase of money increases prices by increasing the (physical) volume of sales (by increasing the demand for commodities). He replies that if, when money is doubled, the prices of commodities are also doubled, there will be no increase in the (physical) amount of sales. The theory therefore involves a contradiction. He then attempts to meet it by another line of reasoning. Quick trade permits of a small profit, and therefore a lower price. Quick sales enable artisans and others to produce more quickly, and if they sell more they can afford to charge a lower price. The increase in the amount of commodities resulting from the stimulus to trade of an increase in money, instead of raising prices, will therefore lower them. Prices will rise only if the increase in commodities is proportionately less than the increase in money, which is not likely to be the case. But even if prices should rise somewhat, it is better to have an abundance of comforts, though dear, than a smaller amount thereof, though never so cheap.

Another advocate of paper money, John Asgill, denied the truth of the quantity theory of money on different and exceedingly slender grounds: an increase in money would lower the rate of interest and therefore raise land values, but not the prices of commodities in general, because "the price of corn and cattle don't rise and fall with the interest of money." John Law attacked it, partly by arguments closely resembling those of Potter, partly on reasoning peculiarly his own. The stimulus to trade and industry resulting from an increase in money would result in an increase in commodities. Because money would be easier to borrow, merchants would be able to increase the extent of their operations and to sell at lower rates of profit, and therefore the value of the money would not fall, *i.e.*, prices would not rise. Money falls in value only when given to a people in greater quantity than there is demand for; if the money is issued only as there is demand for it, its value will not depreciate, "the quantity and demand increasing and decreasing together. Law concedes that if the quantity of money in any particular country "should increase beyond the proportion that country bears to Europe," prices would rise there, but the rise of prices would spread elsewhere, so that the value of money would become the same, or about the same, everywhere. The country which had acquired the increase of money would profit greatly thereby, "for that country would have the whole benefit of the greater quantity, and only bear a share of the lesser value, according to the proportion its money had to the money of Europe. What would make the prices rise elsewhere, he does not explain.

Another writer, James Hodges, who complained of scarcity of money, wanted plate called in and coined and the monetary value of the English standard coin raised as a remedy for this scarcity. He claimed that these measures would result in higher prices only after they resulted in an increase in the number of coins in circulation. The effect on prices would therefore be gradual, and meanwhile there would be a stimulus to trade. After a short time the value of the coin could be gradually lowered, and the surplus bullion returned to be made into plate again if its owners so desired. His argument is interesting as an anticipation of Hume's doctrine that rising prices are a stimulus to trade, and for its endeavor to find a method of obtaining this stimulus without involving a permanent increase in the price level. The difficulty with the scheme, granting its logic, is, of course, that the period of stimulus would be followed by a period of at least corresponding depression.

Both Potter and Law claimed that an increase of (paper) money would make the balance of trade more favorable and would lead to an inflow of bullion. Potter argued that the beneficial effects of an increased quantity of money would enable England to outsell other countries, for "the greater trade of one country hath a capacity of undermining and eating out the lesser trade of other countries. For reasons not explained, unless it be the fall in English prices alleged to result from an increase in the quantity of money, both foreign and English commodities would fall in price in England, but not abroad. Exports would therefore be paid for with bullion (and presumably imports would be paid for with English commodity exports), and the bullion could be coined into English money without loss.

But with unusual consistency Potter admits that when paper money or credit is available as a substitute, metallic money would be of little importance to England. Law showed more concern than did Potter about the state of the balance of trade, but he also claimed that an increased amount of money through the issue of paper money would make the balance favorable: "Most people think scarcity of money is only the consequence of a balance due; but 'tis the cause as well as the consequence, and the effectual way to bring the balance to our side, is to add to the money." More money, by employing more people, would make a surplus of goods available for export, and if sufficient money was issued production would reach a level at which more would be exported than imported. Conversely, if the amount of money was reduced, some of the laborers would be rendered idle, the domestic output would shrink, exports would fall, and an unfavorable balance would result. These results of a change in the quantity of money he would apparently expect not to be transitory but to persist as long as the new quantity of money persisted.

The Mercantilists on Hoards and Plate

Because the mercantilists differed among themselves as to the character of the benefit which resulted from an increase in the amount of bullion in a country, they also differed in their attitudes toward the miser, the collector of gold or silver plate, the usurer, and the spendthrift. Those mercantilists for whom the chief virtue in an increased supply of bullion lay in its stimulus to circulation condemned private hoards as an evil, and also regarded other practices which kept bullion from circulating as money, such as its use in the manufacture of plate, as objectionable. Vaughan condemned hoarding and the use of plate as contributing factors to the scarcity of money, and recommended sumptuary legislation to check the melting of money and its manufacture into plate. An anonymous writer criticized the Established church on the ground that it hoarded riches which should circulate, so that "the money that before ran current in trading, is dammed up in their coffers."

Another pamphlet, written as an answer to this one, condemned the excess of silver plate for the same reason, but claimed that there was no occasion for alarm about hoarding, as there was not much of it, and urged in the defense of the church that it could be charged with responsibility for the prevailing scarcity of money only if the clerics kept "banks of money dead by them, which was not the case. Complaint against the usurer as a hoarder of money was likewise without basis, since "his money walks, though upon other legs, either serving the tradesman or the gentleman, for preparing commodities to export, or to buy what is imported for his expenses.

Manley found fault with the miser, because "money locked up in the miser's coffers is like dung in a heap, it does no good, but being dispersed, and orderly disposed abroad, enricheth the land." An anonymous writer wanted misers' hoards taxed, in order to draw some of their money into circulation, especially in time of war when trade was slack. "I know no difference," he wrote, "betwixt bringing treasure out of an iron chest by a good law, and plowing the seas by long and dangerous voyages" in order to secure bullion through foreign trade. One of Locke's objections to the reduction of the interest rate by law was that it would result in men keeping their money "dead" by them, instead of lending it, with resultant loss to trade. Petty expressed a preference for money over plate, because it served trade better, as did also Hugh Chamberlain: "Money is living riches, plate but dead; that being capable of turning and improving trade, when this is not."

Hodges's scheme for a forced three-year surrender of plate in return for "raised" money, with prohibition of ownership of plate in the interval, in order for a time to secure relief from the prevailing scarcity of money, and to obtain the stimulus to trade of slowly rising prices, has already been referred to. Another writer urged a similar scheme for raising money 5 per cent, in order to draw hoards of the old, and therefore undervalued, coins into circulation. One writer made the same sort of contrast between hoarded and circulating money, hoarded credit being the exchequer bills which, because of the high rate of interest they carried, were held instead of being used as money: "...in the frequent passing of credit from hand to hand, consists its great usefulness in trade; for when either money or credit is hoarded up, it may more properly be said to stagnate, than to circulate." Postlethwayt, in a curious argument, claimed that lending of money at interest involved hoarding and therefore on circulation grounds was to be condemned. If some money is hoarded, the volume of trade will fall. In order to bring the hoarded money back into trade, those in great need of it will offer interest ("profit") for its loan. The result will be that other moneyed men, instead of "circulating their money" in trade, will "lock it up," while awaiting the opportunity to lend it, preferring to get their income by usury instead of by trade. Eventually the money so withdrawn from trade would be lent and would thus return to trade, but bearing an interest charge which would act as a restraint on trade.

Some writers objected, on similar grounds, to the establishment of banks, holding that they monopolized money, and kept it from circulating. Child, for example, maintained that "principally this seeming scarcity of money proceeds from the trade of bankering, which obstructs circulation." Strangely enough, considering his views on the effect of lending at interest on monetary circulation, Postlethwayt made the most effective rejoinder to this argument which I have found:

> It may be here requisite to take notice of that erroneous notion entertained by some, that banks and bankers engross the money, hoard it up, and hinder its circulation in trade; but, if such will consider this matter in its true light, they will easily be convinced, that the money lodged in banks, and in the hands of bankers, is the most constantly employed of any; for, though the specie should lie still till called for, yet the notes given out for its value, are continually circulating; whereby is done abundantly more service to trade, than if the same lay dormant in private hands; and yet the necessities of the depositors are effectually answered.

Once hoarding and the use of coin or bullion in the making of plate were attacked, there were few to come to their defense, and the use of gold and silver in the making of thread or in gilding met with almost general condemnation. Mun, however, opposed restrictions on the melting-down of coin into plate on the ground that gold and silver were more apt to be carried out of the kingdom in payment of purchases of foreign goods if in the form of coin than if kept in the form of plate, and Misselden before him, while conceding that too much plate in the kingdom would cause scarcity of money, nevertheless held that it was better to have bullion kept in the form of plate than to turn it into coin and thus turn it out of the kingdom because of the undervaluation of coin which he alleged then prevailed in England. A sixteenth-century writer condoned the use of bullion for plate, because it resulted in the formation of a sort of secondary national reserve for emergencies, upon which the king, in case of a great war, could draw "without any grouching of the Commons." The same argument is to be found occasionally in the later literature, and is made by Briscoe to serve as a defense of private hoards. Hoarded treasure, bullion and coin, is part of the "capital stock of national treasure" and can be drawn upon in a national emergency. Private hoarding is as good as having treasure stored by the king.

Toward the end of the seventeenth century there appeared a new doctrine of the existence of a "due proportion" between money and goods, and therefore of the possibility of excess of money as far as trade needs were concerned. The quantity theory of money also tended to lead to the conclusion that an increase in the amount of money by increasing prices would reduce exports and thus eventually be lost to the country. Writers who on "due proportions of money to trade" or on quantity-theory grounds conceded that there was under any given set of circumstances a maximum amount of money which could be kept in circulation, and who still attached special importance to the precious metals, were likely to approve of turning the money into plate or of its hoarding as a means either of stimulating the further import of bullion or of, checking an outflow. It was doubtless such reasoning which led John Houghton to the conclusion that "if the King should hoard up much money, it would for the present make it dearer, that dearness would make it be brought in more plentifully, and that would make it more plentiful than it was before." Petty wrote: "For there may be as well too much money in a country, as too little. I mean, as to the best advantage of its trade; only the remedy is very easy, it may be soon turned into the magnificence of gold and silver vessels."

On similar grounds another writer would tolerate the increased use of plate if there was more money than was necessary to carry on trade and "defray the expense of living," and Vanderlint, who accepted the quantity theory and wanted low prices but at the same time wanted a favorable balance of trade payable in specie, recommended as a means of attaining these apparently conflicting objectives that the private hoarding of gold and silver and their use in plate, and even in gold and silver cloth and gilding, be encouraged. He cited with approval the practice of the East Indians of hoarding the silver they receive, with the result that prices remained low there, exports continued to exceed imports, and the balance was paid in still more silver. Harris presents a similar solution of the same dilemma. If the inflow of bullion resulting from a favorable balance of trade is kept: as a dead stock, either by turning it into plate or by any other method, so as to prevent its getting into trade as money; it may continue to go on increasing in more bullion, which in this case will be a real increase of wealth.... Let an increased stock of bullion get out again into trade, and it will soon turn the balance the other way.

But gold and silver can be best stored up in the form of plate: But people in general will not hoard up cash; all like to display their wealth, and to lay out their superfluities in some costly things. There seems then no method so effectual for the securing of a dead stock of treasure in any country, as the encouraging the use of plate, by making it fashionable, preferable to more brittle or more perishable commodities. Plate would be a national resource in case of emergency, and not the less so, because the precious metals had not as yet received the shape of coins.

Hume in 1752 claimed that state hoarding was the only expedient by which a country could raise its supply of the precious metals above the equilibrium level, but commented that this was "a practice which we should all exclaim against as destructive, namely, the gathering of large sums into a public treasure, locking them up, and absolutely preventing their circulation."

Henry Home accepted so whole-heartedly the lesson of the quantity theory of money that he looked upon an export surplus alike with an import surplus as dangerous to the country. The latter meant an outward drain of money, with a consequent fall of prices and stoppage of industry. The former meant an influx of specie, extravagance, rise in prices, and finally a fall in exports, rise in imports, an unfavorable balance again, and a recurrence of the drain of specie. What was to be desired was an even balance. Therefore, "let the registers of foreign mints be carefully watched, in order that our current coin may not exceed that of our industrious neighbors." But it was not the quantity of gold and silver in a country that determined the price level, but the quantity of money in circulation. Still retaining some traces of the mercantilist attachment for the precious metals, he therefore advocated the conversion of money into plate and even, under favorable circumstances, the formation of a state treasure.

2

Double Digit Growth of Industrial Banking

The role of banking in growth of the economy is sizeable and significant. Economic history indicates that banks have played a stellar role in supporting economic growth across a broad spectrum of countries.

Countries such as the United States and Japan have enormously benefited from strong banking systems which not only helped the domestic economic systems to grow and prosper but also pursue international ambitions and business expansion. Among the mature economies such Germany and France, even today, banks are majorly responsible for financing growth. The recent evidence of dramatic growth of south East Asia that now enjoys the distinction of rapidly growing economic region is also on the back of massive role played by the respective banking system.

There are several indicators that show the importance of banking system in the world of finance. Bank assets account anywhere upto to 50 percent of the total size of the world capital markets. Banks and Bonds account anywhere upto 85 percent of the total activity in the capital markets worldwide today The size of activity of banks is more than the size of the economy in several countries experiencing rapid economic growth. For instance, for the world as whole, bank assets to the gross domestic product is as high as 132 percent. In some regions such as the EU, it is as high as 212 percent. Several mature countries have very high bank assets/GDP ratio and these include; United Kingdom (262 percent), France (255 percent), Japan (168 percent), and Canada (152 percent) For the emerging markets, the bank/GDP ratio is subdued at about 95 perent, though, Asia has a very high ratio of 144 percent, followed by Middle East and Africa. The imperative is that banks do play a very important role in financing growth. The issue is how India could take advantage of its banking systems to pursue the desired growth of the economy.

INDIA AND DOUBLE DIGIT GROWTH

All economies that have experienced rapid economic development in the recent period experienced double digit or very high single digit growth for a very long and sustained period. For instance, China has been experiencing an average growth of 9 to 10 percent for almost a decade and following the liberalization of the economy, it had experience double digit growth as well for several years. East Asian economies too experienced prolonged growth of respective domestic economies for a very long period. Double digit growth thus becomes imperative for India too to enable it to join the league of growth countries. An important aspect of the double digit growth is that, notwithstanding the aspirations, which every country has, but also the presence of enabling conditions or possibilities for harnessing the potential and reaching that target.

The possibilities that make India to enter the realm of double digit growth include;

- Opening up of the economy and growing investment from within and outside.
- Increasing international interest on Indian economy
- Growth in infrastructure development
- Promotion of private enterprise and streamlining of the public sector
- Leadership in service sector growth and expansion
- Resurgence of the industry and in particular the manufacturing sector.

Above all, India is viewed a major opportunity and value which the world financial community is keen to unlock for the benefit of the mutual advantage.

BANKS AND DOUBLE DIGIT GROWTH

The recent years have been remarkable for the growth of Indian banking and its role in the domestic economy. First and foremost has been the significant recovery of banks with very less fiscal costs that makes the turnaround of the Indian banking one of the most efficient in the world.

Profitability and productivity of the banks have been rising at rapid pace and so as the stock prices of banks. I think about ten years ago, Indian banking depicted a very disappointing and dismal picture. Today more investors invest in bank scrips than others and I am sure that members of the FICCI must have made sizeable gains from their investments in banks. Which means banks show more confidence than others, which is a matter of great satisfaction for the banking industry in India that was ridiculed as the most inefficient just a decade ago.

While on profitability and productivity the progress has been quite smart and spectacular, on the growth front, Indian banking still could do more. For instance, between 1990 and 2003, domestic credit provided by the banking sector for the world as a whole (average) rose from 139 percent to 162 percent. This ratio for several emerging countries was much more. In Korea, during this period, bank assets/GDP ratio from 63 percent to 106 percent, in Malaysia from 75 percent to 152 percent, in South Africa from 98 percent to 158 percent, in China from 90 perent to 178 percent. In several other countries the growth of bank assets has been very rapid and fast

The experience of India however is very subdued. The domestic credit provided by banking sector in India as a percent of gross domestic product between the last 13 years rose just by 10 percentage points from 52 percent in 1990 to 62 percent in 2004.

The growth of bank assets in India is growing but still not that rapid. For instance in 2004, bank assets in India grew at an average of 16 percent, but that is due to very high growth of 24 percent showed by the private sector banks, since assets in the public sector in 2004 grew at about 14 percent. Compared to this, world wide, bank assets in 2004 grew at an average rate of about 20 percent and regions such as EU showing a growth rate as high as 27 percent. Several transition economies in the Africa and Europe too showed growth in the region of over 25 percent. It is imperative that Indian banks step up growth in the assets that is would be critical from the point of view of supporting the double digit growth of the economy.

As there are several enabling features that could make double digit growth of the economy possible, equally relevant is the enabling features that could enable banking to support such a growth rate in the economy. These include;

- Smart turnaround in Indian banking. They are now more profitable and productive than anytime in the past.
- Efficiency levels are continuously improving.
- Able to function in an intensely competitive environment
- Product range is fast expanding
- Professional competencies and capabilities are growing
- Greater thrust on regulatory compliance and best practices
- Better management of assets and credit monitoring
- Growing international relations and business opportunities

In the background of these, I would now attempt to touch upon a few aspects that would be of significance to Indian banking, that would equip and enable them to meet the challenges of the financing double digit growth of the economy.

Size has a Meaning in Global Context

There was a time when it was considered small is Beautiful. It is true even today, but not so necessarily in banks. Banks worldwide are once again acquiring to growth both in stature and size. Globalisation and deregulation offer banks a host of opportunities for business and growth but smaller banks would not be able in take full advantage of these due to limitations of capital and regulatory restraints. A lot of churning out is happening at the banking systems in a number of regions primarily focused on getting into proper size which could withstand competition and command greater market share.

Indian banks should be able to grow at more than 20 percent a year for the next 10 years that would be relevant to pursue not only their respective growth but also relevant for financing the economy that is aiming at double digit growth. In this context, it would not be out of context to say that banks should seriously examine the issues of right size that makes them competent and capable to meet the emerging challenges.

Need for Innovative Instruments

Capital is the most important constraint for the growth of bank assets. For public sector banks, it is much more important since there is a limit to which the government stake could be reduced. Even today, public sector banks account for about 80 percent of the bank assets in India and these are also the banks which provide a major chunk of bank credit.

To enable to them expand the assets, it becomes important that their capital positions too are boosted and accessing stock markets, though helps, but cannot provide complete solution to the challenge at this juncture. In this background, it is important that some innovative instruments of financing the public sector banks towards capital be evolved to make the growth process much easier and efficient.

Financing Agriculture

Despite predominance of service sector in the Indian economy, and its rapidly growing share in the overall economy,. Agriculture is the sector which will make the success of the reforms more meaningful and relevant. It is because a large proportion of people are still employed in the agriculture sector. In this background, it becomes imperative that this sector attracts large investments. When I say large investments, it does not necessarily mean financing crops and other allied activities.

There is enormous scope for financing agri business and also play a useful role in the development of commodities markets. Commodities futures markets in India are already experiencing rapid pace of growth and banks could play a very important role in stepping financing towards this sector. Financing innovative crops and cultivation techniques also becomes very pertinent in this context. The overall focus should be in improving the both production and productivity of the agriculture sector that would be of great help for the rest of the economy to march ahead.

Reinforce Retail Lending

Indian economy now shows growing signs of being led by consumption which is largely bank financed. Personal loans as a percent of bank credit in India shot up significantly from about 10 percent in 1997 to about 15 percent now. What is more interesting is household balance sheets in India are still robust and household debt as a percent of gross domestic is still at a very low level of about 5 percent, which gives a lot of leg room for the retail lending to boom. Banks should step up this segment, of course with all the precautions and due credit monitoring systems in place, which will be useful for speeding up the momentum of the economic growth.

Resurgence in Manufacturing

For any economy to remain robust for long, it is important that it has a strong manufacturing base. India scores very high on the growth of service sector, but equally important is bringing back high growth in the manufacturing sector. For instance, credit to manufacturing which formed 45 percent of the bank credit in 1996-97 slipped to 33 percent by 2003. The fall has been particularly more in the engineering sector where the share of bank credit fell from 8 perent to 4.5 percent during this period. Banks should look at this challenge with greater intensity and care. Enhancing manufacturing competence and capabilities would strengthen the growth process and also its competitiveness.

Support SMUs

SMU development is critical for any growth process to be robust and sustained. In India several attempts in the past were made to develop SMU development but the need is still large. Banks can play an important role in supporting SMU development. However, to make it a long lasting process, it is important that capital markets too complement the efforts of the banks in this regard. World over, many leading stock exchanges have set up exclusive platforms/exchanges for the SMUs and India also made a beginning with the Indonext Platform, under the aegis of the Bombay Stock Exchange and 18 other regional stock exchanges. It is hoped that a vibrant stock markets exists for the small and medium companies which would fasten the involvement and participation of banks in the process of their growth and development

Product and Service Range

Banks should focus on a continuous development on the product side, particularly for the corporates and other major segments of the customers. Product range enables to banks to offer a wide range of on and off balance sheet services that could increase the overall reach and access, that will be of great relevance for the real economy. Banks could consider interesting collaborations and joint initiatives with institutions in India and abroad for this purpose, subject to the regulatory guidelines and compliance standards.

People to Take Risks

Banks need more professionals who could read, assess and manage risks that are not only domestic in nature but global in reach and perspective. This requirement is more pertinent in the public sector banks. At the same time, it must be added that PSBs are a big repository of skilled people, and what is more relevant is reorientation in approaches, attitudes and skills. Banks should invest in this process to a great length.

Look Ashore

It might not sound too ambitious, if it is said that banks in India could also look with greater intensity opportunities available abroad both for business and growth. Transition economies offer excellent opportunities for making acquisitions, creating new assets and also extending the reach and influence.

Banks in India could keep this at the back of mind, though there might be touch challenges for pursuing them at present. Another aspect of this could be helping Indian companies to acquire and expand business in international markets that would bring enormous benefits to the domestic economy.

INITIATIVES AT DENA BANK

Let me now take this opportunity to outline a few of the initiatives that our bank is taking to play a meaningful and purposeful role in the growth process of the Indian economy and its pursuit of double digit growth. At Dena Bank, we are geared to take advantage of several opportunities that a growing economy offers. Among the various strategies that have been drawn up, Retail, Agriculture and SME have been extended a focused attention. To push the Retail Credit further, the Bank opened 40 FinMarts, a unique concept in Indian Banking, at various centers to provide all retail services to its customers under one roof. These "FinMarts" provide one-stop state-of-the-art customer experience in delivery of the array of Retail Banking products spanning a customer's life cycle. These "FinMarts" which operate in "Branch within Branch" concept have been exclusively designed to present a highly enriched customer ambience for state-of-the-art customer experience. All retail- banking products are available in this one-stop shop where dedicated and smart staff are deployed to deliver.

Dena Bank has over 1123 branches and has a dominant presence in the industrially and economically vibrant Western Region with presence of about 70 percent of the branch network.. About 61% of the branches are situated in rural and semi-urban areas and hence agricultural and related activities remain part of the key business strategies.

Dena Bank has carried out wide ranging initiatives in pushing agricultural credit. Dena Bank was the first to launch credit card to farmers in the name of "Dena Krishi Shakh Patra". To empower the farming community to avail hassle-free credit facilities, the Bank launched "Dena Kisan Gold Credit Card Scheme". A unique feature of this card is that it covers both production and investment credit. As a part of its rural development activities, Dena Bank opened Rural Development & Self Employment Training Centre at Bhuj and Mehsana and the centre imparts vocational trainings to budding entrepreneurs to take up gainful activities in rural areas.

In addition to simplification of procedures, easing of credit terms and incentives for prompt payment, the Bank has established several forward and backward linkages to enable the farmers to reap the benefits thereof. The knowledge services has been given a thrust by setting up Rural Kiosks and this again is a unique and pioneering initiative by Dena Bank. The Scheme envisages loans to the rural youth in collaboration with the service provider for setting up Rural Internet Kiosks and this would provide gainful employment to the educated rural youth.

Recognising the importance of SME in the economic growth and the opportunities that it would provide to the Banks, Dena Bank is in the process of entering into a tie up arrangement with SIDBI for financing of SMEs. A strategic business unit has been set up with a pre-defined role to push the SME credit.

Apart from these, the Bank has also taken several technological initiatives to keep pace with the growing expectations of the industry and customers. In addition to the growing number of ATMs, Dena Bank has launched several technology enabled services like Dena Bill-Pay, Dena M-banking, Dena Internet Banking, Multi-City Cheque facility and value added services through ATM.

THE ROAD AHEAD

The importance of banking systems in many emerging economies stems from a host of factors that include; Prevalence of a high degree of financial intermediation Lack of suitable financial instruments that support and spur growth Regulatory and policy restrictions on range of financial instruments and market participants.

Absence of a vibrant and fully functioning and efficient capital markets Restrictions in access to the international financial markets and global capital flows.

In India however, the situation is rapidly changing with capital markets growing both in stature and size. Today stock markets in India have some of the best practices anywhere relevant in the world, both in terms of practices and procedures. The risk management has been robust and there are no major default in the system.

A debate that has gained enormous influence in the recent period is on the relative efficiencies of the banking and capital markets. Evidence throws up that market based financial systems are found to be emerging more efficient but the underlining message is that a combination of efficient banking systems that provides fast and cheaper payment settlement systems and a capital market that acts as an efficient resource mobilization and allocative mechanism would prove beneficial for the long term growth of the economy.

My message today is that Indian banking should grow more faster but not just alone. Simultaneous with its growth. equally rapid and robust should be the growth, role and responsibility of other segments of the financial sector. Which is when the real economy benefits enormously and it could reach double digit growth and stay there for quite some time.

CONTRIBUTION TO ELECTRICITY SUPPLY INDUSTRY

The two fundamental characteristics of power delivered to a customer are frequency and voltage. The short run supply-demand balance is indicated by frequency. Frequency is a 'public good' having large external effects. Stable operation of the interconnected power system, requires that frequency be maintained within a certain tolerance as defined by the standards adopted in a country.

REAL-TIME BALANCING

Power systems all over the world have to make provisions for achieving a balance between real time demand and supply. Power markets generally have control areas that are prohibited from deviating from scheduled interchange. Concept of Area Control Error (ACE) used to measure these instantaneous deviations takes into account of both frequency and net excess flow out of a control area. Control areas are required to keep their ACE near zero for maintaining a constant frequency in the interconnection. This model for load frequency control used in developed countries may be a good practice but given the techno-economic and socio- political realities prevailing in India, it is currently incompatible with Indian power system.

PRE-ABT SCENARIO

Power system of a country is a manifestation of its society. The indiscipline, lawlessness and absence of accountability prevailing in the Indian society were visible even in power system operation. Till recently regional power system operation was more frightening than an Alfred Hitchcock horror movie. Scholars could be excused for getting a shock of their lives by a mere glance at the daily frequency and voltage profile of any region. System operation was an endless 'jihad' to prevent the system from collapsing.

The central public sector generation incentives were linked to the actual production and not on availability. Generators would continue to pump in as much energy into the system as they could irrespective of the system frequency and still be rewarded for the wastage of scarce resources! The load serving utilities/SEBs would compare the variable cost of their own generators to the composite cost (sunk cost + energy charge) of the external generator causing a skewed dispatch. Ironically, the Regional Grid operators had a harrowing time trying to get generation backed down to protect the turbines of the very generators causing that situation. On the other end of the spectrum, the state utilities could overdraw from the grid with impunity even during deficit and still escape Scot-free by returning equivalent energy to the system during surplus conditions. No wonder there was chaos and despair all around.

THE IMPACT OF UI MECHANISM

The UI mechanism was brought in to perform under such trying circumstances. Although the complexities and contradictions in the system still prevail but there is not an iota of doubt that the scheme has delivered results. The UI mechanism rode on the chariot of floating frequency and the used 'the disease' itself for curing the chronic illness of the power system operation. It is the bedrock on which the foundation of competitive electricity market has been built in India and is flourishing.

Electricity Flows Pricing.' He says, "Unscheduled flows of electricity can contribute more to the reliability of the network than could the establishment of mandatory reliability standards and the fines that would be associated with violating such standards. Pricing unscheduled flows of electricity improves reliability indices without resulting to the draconian policy of mandatory reliability standards and fines for non-compliance.

India has led the way in showing an improvement in reliability indices when it began pricing Unscheduled Interchange. Pricing unscheduled flows of electricity can also improve bulk power competition." UI mechanism has assumed cult-like status in the Indian power sector. It not surprising that the mechanism has split the Diaspora into 'believers' and 'non-believers'. Everyone has interpreted the mechanism in his/her own way and in the process certain misconceptions and misunderstandings have also cropped up. A large section understands UI mechanism to be merely a penal and disciplinary mechanism to deter utilities from deviating from schedule. This view requires reconsideration.

FLOATING FREQUENCY REGIME

Post ABT the power system in India is operated as loose power pools where the state utilities /generators have the liberty to deviate from their interchange schedules as long as the frequency remains within the IEGC specified band of 49.0 to 50.5 Hz. However several experts have expressed reservations on the floating frequency regime adopted in our country. They argue that frequency deviation/fluctuation is problematic for non-digital clocks and rotating machines especially steam turbines.

The IEC standards specify that the steam turbines have to perform satisfactorily within a tolerance of 49.0 to 50.5 Hz. This is precisely what the UI mechanism is trying to achieve in a simple and efficient manner. In the decentralized dispatch scenario, the UI mechanism provides the Automatic Generation Control (AGC) for the Indian electricity grids without employing a vast set of inputs, processing software and last mile connectivity to the generators.

The whole design encourages the utilities to conserve when in surplus so as to provide for when in shortage and thus smoothening the frequency curve. Post ABT the operating frequency band has narrowed down considerably but still sharp fluctuations in frequency do persist. These fluctuations would get further smoothened out only after all the generators sincerely operate on free governor mode of operation as stipulated by IEGC.

Switching in and switching out of hydro units, manual disconnection of large feeders to restrict over drawals and frequent interventions by the system operator results into wide variations in the interchange pattern of the utilities and grid frequency.

UI as Real-time Pricing Mechanism

The design of UI mechanism adopted in India is similar to the one proposed by Arthur Berger & F.C Schweppe in their paper titled 'Real time pricing to assist in load frequency control" (IEEE Transactions on Power Systems, Vol.4, No. 3, August 1989). The paper says - "The plants operate to maximize profits, and the loads operate to maximize a satisfaction index. The energy control centre has perfect information i.e. it knows the models used in the automatic control devices of the plants and the loads. Lastly, all computations take zero time." It further says, "A key feature of this pricing scheme is that the independent power plants can themselves monitor the frequency deviations and thus no real time signal needs to be sent by the electric utility. This eliminates the problem of how the utility could compute and transmit the price faster then the time scale to be controlled."

The UI rate is a frequency-actuated signal available at any wall socket. Every utility reacts to this signal in real time and adjusts its generation/ demand and a new equilibrium is achieved. The UI curve by virtue of its design empowers every utility that has some means to regulate supply/demand to readjust its interchange with the grid and gain from the migration of frequency/UI rate from the earlier level.

The decreasing marginal returns with every additional unit of deviation from the scheduled interchange acts as a counterweight, which forces the utility to seriously weigh the consequences of its actions. Thus the collective action by all the players in this non-cooperative zero sum game, restores the equilibrium to new value, which may or may not be the same as that before the perturbation. What results is a Nash equilibrium at which every player emerges a winner by having maximised his pay-off.

UI FOR MERIT ORDER AND EFFICIENCY

Economists consider perfect competition as an instrument to realize productive and allocative efficiency. A market is considered perfect only when every competitor is small enough to have no discernible influence against the "invisible hand" of the market. This implies that every player in a perfectly competitive market is aware of the market condition and is a price taker. The UI mechanism adopted in India tries to fulfill that design requirement in a rather unconventional manner. Every utility is aware of the UI vector ex ante and in real time (perfect information); the UI rate applies to all inter utility transactions at the regional level (homogeneity); there are no contracts to be signed, no access charges fees; no transmission charges; no losses applicable (no entry barriers); every utility big or small having some control over its generation or load is transformed into a formidable player in real time. All generators connected to the grid can contribute to the unscheduled flow of electricity, dramatically increasing the number of competitors that can serve any customer connected to the grid (atomicity).

The UI mechanism has established a real time balancing market that is workably competitive and provides a powerful force for efficiency and innovation. While the diligent and proactive players have derived rich dividends by being proactive, a large number of players are yet to realize this aspect of UI mechanism. This also explains the unpopularity of UI mechanism in some quarters. Steven Stoft in his book 'Power System Economics Designing Markets for Electricity' says, "Competition is least popular with competitors- every supplier wants to raise the market price, just as every buyer wants to lower it. Perfect competition frustrates both intentions."

Likewise, Larry Ruff while talking about competition in his paper 'Competition in Electricity Markets' says, "Unfortunately, the features that make integrated real-time market/dispatch processes so successful – low transactions cost and market transparency and efficiency – are the very features that are provoking the counterrevolution. A transparent, efficient spot market allows producers and consumers to deal directly with each other with less need for middlemen and market makers, and helps new, small, niche players compete effectively with established, large, diversified players. Not everybody finds these features to their liking or advantage."

TINKERING WITH THE UI VECTOR

The UI Rate at any frequency represents the marginal price of the costliest generator that is expected to be on bar at that frequency that forces players to optimise their exchanges with the grid in order to maximize their profits or minimize their costs. The generators behave as if they are selling their entire output to the pool at UI rate while the buyers behave as if they are purchasing their entire requirement from the pool. The above feature of UI mechanism has brought in efficiency and merit order operation in the grid even in the absence of the centralised scheduling and dispatch mechanism. The UI rate therefore needs to be readjusted whenever the energy costs of generation in the country get revised. The ABT Order dated 04/01/2000 issued by Central Electricity Regulatory Commission recognised this aspect of UI vector and desired that the UI ceiling rate be linked to the energy charge of the diesel generation in the grid.

There have been proposals to change the UI rate to a penal charge but it may not bring the desired effect. Peter Cramton and Robert Wilson in 'A Review of ISO New England's Proposed

Market Rules' say, "Reliance on penalties is highly inefficient and problematic in its workings and is unworkable on a sustained basis in a civilized and competitive market. The whole idea of relying on administered penalties is inefficient, subject to disputes and subject to continual pressure to seek modifications and exceptions. Non-compliance can also be justified by claiming an operating problem, etc."

While speaking about real time balancing mechanism, Sally Hunt in her book, 'Competition and Choice in Electricity', argues that in a competitive market the deviations from scheduled interchanges and the actual flows on the day must be treated and settled as an energy transactions arranged at (infinitesimally) short notice. This strengthens the argument that the real-time deviations have to be appropriately priced to be effective.

CAPACITY ADEQUACY AND UI MECHANISM

The UI mechanism has brought about varying degree of results in different regions. It has been observed that during peak demand situations, the absence of matching generation leads to the weakening of the counterbalancing forces that causes the frequency to hit rock bottom rather frequently. Only augmentation of capacity can resolve this situation. Investors could use the UI duration curve for different regions to arrive at nature and cost of generation that they are planning.

POWER EXCHANGE AND UI MECHANISM

There seems to be some substance in the argument put forth by the proponents of Power Exchange in the country that the absence of an organised day ahead-market is one of the reasons for the lack of investor confidence in the Indian market.

Bilateral trading is being used for increasing the availability of power for a load serving utility especially after the enactment of the short term open access regulations but the exorbitant transaction costs and lack of transparency in price setting are a big deterrent. (Transaction costs are the costs of negotiating, executing and enforcing payment for each purchase.)

The setting up of the Power Exchange could provide another option for power procurement. It could promote further competition on the supply side as well as on the demand side by bringing all sellers and buyers together on a common marketplace with standardized contracts, bid formats, and trading procedures. This would set up a transparent price discovery mechanism in day ahead exactly as UI mechanism is doing in real-time.

The setting up of a PX would in no way diminish the significance of the frequency-linked UI mechanism. It would in fact enhance its relevance as a real time pricing mechanism. The UI market would continue to compete with the long-term and short-term transactions as a means for trading electricity. The price for un-contracted flows underpins all other contract prices. Hence even if they handle only the deviations, they ultimately determine the viability of competitive generation.

The UI mechanism has been a good course correction for the Indian power market and therefore we need to take further steps to reinforce the gains. It is time we started planning for the next step in this initiative. There are other difficult jigsaw pieces that have to be placed rightly before we can entirely solve the Indian power sector puzzle. We need to revisit and probably redesign the transmission pricing and hydro tariff to make it more scientific and effective. Intra state ABT and open access are essential for getting a stronger demand side response.

With the interconnection of the Northern and Central grid in near future we would need to reconsider the reactive tariff to suit the new circumstances. Thus a lot more need to be accomplished to realize the vision of power to all by 2012.

CONTRIBUTION TO INDIAN CAPITAL MARKET

Traditionally, the capital markets in India are more synonymous with the equity markets – both on account of the common investors' preferences and the oft huge capital gains it offered – no matter what the risks involved are. The investor's preference for debt market, on the other hand, has been relatively a recent phenomenon – an outcome of the shift in the economic policy, whereby the market forces have been accorded a greater leeway in influencing the resource allocation. In a developing economy such as India, the role of the public sector and its financial requirements need no emphasis. Growing fiscal deficits and the policy stance of "directed investment" through statutory pre emption (the statutory liquidity ratio – SLR - for banks), ensured a captive but passive market for the Government securities. Besides, participation of the Reserve Bank of India (RBI) as an investor in the Government borrowing programme (monetisation of deficits) led to a regime of financial repression.

In an eventual administered interest rate regime, the asset liability mismatches pose no threat to the balance sheets of financial institutions. As a result, the banking system, which is the major holder of the Government securities portfolio, remained a dominant passive investor segment and the market remained dormant.

The Indian Bond Market has been traditionally dominated by the Government securities market. The reasons for this are:

(1) the high and persistent government deficit and the need to promote an efficient government securities market to finance this deficit at an optimal cost,

(2) a captive market for the government securities in the form of public sector banks which are required to invest in government securities a certain per cent of deposit liabilities as per statutory requirement,

(3) the predominance of bank lending in corporate financing and

(4) regulated interest rate environment that protected the banks' balance sheets on account of their exposure to the government securities.

While these factors ensured the existence of a big Government securities market, the market was passive with the captive investors buying and holding on to the government securities till they mature. The trading activity was conspicuous by its absence. The scenario changed with the reforms process initiated in the early nineties. The gradual deregulation of interest rates and the Government's decision to borrow through auction mechanism and at market related rates. The move towards a market-based economy has a different dimension for resource allocation; here resources are allocated based on the risk return profiles of alternative investments instead of being guided by direct or indirect intervention of the Government. An efficient resource allocation mechanism in turn critically depends upon enabling environment that facilitates efficient asset price discovery.

The need for an efficient price discovery mechanism could be viewed from a different perspective. The fact that the monetary as well as government debt management functions are centralized in the RBI, calls for coordination between monetary and debt management policies. While the objective of the debt management policy is to reduce the cost of debt servicing in the long term, the efficacy of the monetary policy depends upon how efficiently the transmission mechanism works, the basis of which is an efficiently determined interest rates structure. On the other hand, since the sovereign paper acts as a benchmark for pricing corporate bonds, unless the prices of the former reflects its intrinsic worth, markets will not be able to price the latter. All these once again hint at the need to have an efficient price discovery mechanism.

Going by this crucial parameter viz., the system's ability to facilitate asset price discovery and thereby an efficient resource allocation, although the transformation of the debt market could be traced back to the reforms initiated in the government securities market in the late eighties and early part of the nineties, the year 1994 could be considered as a watershed for the landmark decision the Government of India has taken to put an end to the monetization of its deficits through issuance to ad hoc treasury bills to the RBI. Through this land mark decision Government chose to borrow from the market at market related rates – thereby making the beginning of an era which allowed the markets to decide the price of money and thus the development of fixed income securities market.

Efficient price discovery cannot be contemplated independent of an appropriate market micro structure; it needs presence of liquid markets, whereby the transaction costs are minimized and the bid-ask spreads are narrowed. The development of appropriate market infrastructure also requires a supportive regulatory environment. On the other hand, any attempt at reforms also calls for a logical sequencing of the measures and a planned timeframe so that the markets move ahead with such reforms without any friction. The success story of reforms in the debt market is a testimony to the sequencing structure that the concerned authorities meticulously followed.

While that is the motivation and reasons behind the nature of the Government securities market as they exist today, the corporate debt market is still in its infancy, both in terms of market micro structure and market outcome. Traditionally, long term funding was provided by the developmental financial institutions, such as the Industrial Development Bank of India (IDBI). Ever since these development financial institutions changed themselves into banks, there has been a vacuum which logically should have facilitated the development of a debt market.

However, the growth in internal resources and the equity financing averted this. Whatever resources had to be mobilized through the debt market, corporate preferred the private placement route. The absence of well developed derivatives market also hindered the development of the corporate market since there was no way both the issuers and investors could hedge their risks. Meanwhile banks, whose resource base (liabilities) are short term in nature, cannot undertake long term financing making themselves vulnerable to interest rate risk. On the other hand, the need for long term financing, given the investment needs of the infrastructure sector needs no emphasis.

The need to replace bank financing by bond financing was highlighted by the East Asian crisis, since the prevalence of bank financing was quoted as one of the reasons for the crisis. Bond financing is considered a relatively more stable source of debt financing, as bank loans are primarily illiquid, fixed-price assets. In other words, unlike a bond, the price of the loan (the interest rate) does not change with changing interest rates. Thus, whenever there is a sharp movement in interest rates, all the adjustment has to take place by banks adjusting the quantity of lending. This leads to sharp booms and busts in bank flows.

There is thus a need to take a serious look at the issues that come in the way of developing a deep and vibrant corporate debt markets and the authorities, especially the Securities Exchange Board of India (SEBI) and the Government are trying to address the issues.

CONTRIBUTION TO GOVERNMENTAL DEPARTMENTS

Department of Economic Affairs

The reforms undertaken over the last four and half years have led to a revival of strong economic growth, rapid expansion of productive employment, a reduction of poverty a substantial boom in exports and a marked decline in inflation. The full dimensions of the recovery produced by the far reaching reforms initiated in 1991-92 are now becoming clear. Growth of real GDP at factor cost, which had fallen to a mere 0.8 per cent in the crisis year of 1991-92, recovered within a year to reach 5.1 per cent in 1992-93. This represents one of the fastest economic recoveries from a macroeconomic crisis. Fiscal and macroeconomic policies helped in maintaining a growth rate of 5 per cent in 1993-94, despite the disturbing events of late 1992-93. Overall economic growth accelerated significantly in 1994-95 to attain 6.3 per cent and touched 7 per cent in 1995-96. Thus, despite the deep crisis of 1991-92, average growth over the first 4 years of the Eighth Plan at 5.9 per cent is significantly higher than the Plan target of 5.6 per cent. This is a remarkable post-crisis achievement by international standards.

Development in Agriculture and Prices

The year 1995 was the 8th successive normal Monsoon year and the country-wide seasonal rainfall (June to September) was 100 per cent of the long term average. 1995 monsoon made a delayed and sluggish start over most parts of the country, but gained momentum during the second week of July. It set in over Kerala on June 8, 1995 a week later than its normal date. By the end of the monsoon season, 33 out of 35 meteorological sub-divisions and 79 per cent of the districts covering 94 per cent of the country's area had received normal to excess rains. Food grain production in 1995-96 is likely to be 190.4 million tonnes as against 191.1 millions in 1994-95 and 184.3 millions in 1993-94. The expected wheat production in 1995-96 is 64.0 million tonnes as against 65.5 million in 1994-95.

The total oilseeds production in 1995-96 may be of the order of 22.9 million tonnes. In 1994-95 the cane production was 271.2 million tonnes. The likely production in 1995-96 would be around 267.4 million tonnes. The production of cotton is expected to be around 130 lakh bales as against 121 lakh bales produced last year. The production of jute and mesta in 1995-96 is likely to be around 9.0 million bales (of 180 kg. each) as against 9.5 million bales in 1994-95.

During the current marketing season, wheat and rice procurement upto March 31, 1996 was 12.33 million tonnes and 8.26 million tonnes respectively (as against 11.87 million tonnes and 11.95 million tonnes respectively during the corresponding period of last year).

The fiscal 1995-96 started with an annual inflation rate of 10.2 per cent but ended with a very low level of 4.4 per cent at the end of March, 1996. Reasonably good rainfall and comfortable food stock situation together with liberal imports of some of the essential commodities to make up for their shortfall and limit on the monetary growth of 13 per cent to contain excessive demand side pressure on inflation, sustained declining trend in prices.

Development in Industry and Infrastructure

The basic ingredients of the strategy for industrial reforms adopted by the government are abolition of restrictive policy such as licensing, a more level playing field between the public sector and the private sector and freer access to foreign investment and technology.

The stringent conditions for entry of large units in areas reserved for the small scale sector has been relaxed. Several procedural simplifications have been effected to give a boost to the process of liberalisation with full vigour. The new economic policies in the industrial sector, including providing a more competitive environment, inducing higher foreign investment and technology, restructuring PSUs are now bearing fruit and have contributed significantly in terms of industrial growth.

There has been a substantial upsurge in the growth of industrial production during April-February, 1995-96. The latest available Index of Industrial Production (IIP) for February 1996 shows that the overall industrial growth was 13.2 per cent, supported by a growth rate of 15.5 per cent in manufacturing, 8.1 per cent in mining and 5.0 per cent in electricity generation. The cumulative growth of industrial production in April-February 1995-96 was 12.4 per cent, aided by a growth rate of 13.9 per cent in manufacturing, 7.4 per cent in mining and 8.3 per cent in electricity. There are no major constraints to industrial growth and several surveys conducted by industry associations and research institutions indicate a buoyant industrial scenario.

The recovery of the manufacturing industries has been very impressive and broad-based. The performance of the capital goods sector has been most impressive, and it registered a growth rate of 20.4 per cent in April-February, 1995-96. Of late consumer durables have been performing very well.

It registered a growth of 38.0 per cent during April-February, 1995-96. Basic goods, intermediate goods and consumer non-durable goods have also shown good performance during April-February, 1995-96. Amongst others, growth rates of sugar, commercial vehicles, nitrogenous fertilisers, cement, saleable steel have been very high. However, their performance was partially offset by a decline in production of tea, cloth (Mill sector) Pig iron (Saleable), cine films and X Ray films.

Infrastructure

Development of infrastructural services such as energy, transport and power hold the key to the success of economic reforms in the country. International competitiveness of our industry and export expansion strategies are critically dependent on efficient performance of the infrastructural sectors. This calls for greater efficiency and accountability of infrastructure industries. The performance of the core sector, which was quite satisfactory during 1994-95 has been sustained in 1995-96. However few areas of potential concern have emerged. The seven critical infrastructure industries, namely, electricity, coal, steel, crude oil, refinery products, cement and fertilisers which have a total weight of about 31 per cent in the Index of Industrial Production, have achieved an average growth rate of 7.8 per cent in 1995-96 compared with an average growth rate of 8.4 per cent in 1994-95. Electricity generation grew by 8.2 per cent, crude oil by 7.2 per cent, coal by 6.4 per cent, cement by 4.2 per cent during 1995- 96. The rate of growth of coal and cement have accelerated while that of electricity and coal has declined. While railways revenue earnings traffic has shown an improved performance, growth in cargo handled at major ports has marginally declined as compared to last year.

Monetary and Credit Development

Monetary management in 1995-96 was aimed at the twin objectives of reducing inflation and providing necessary credit support for production.The sharp upward trend visible in the growth of money supply in the second half of 1994-95 was reversed in 1995-96. The growth of money supply (M3), declined from 22.3 per cent on March 31, 1995 to 13.0 per cent at the end of 1995-96. It was therefore below the projected growth of 15.5 per cent for 1995-96. The growth of narrow money (M1) has been even lower at 10.9 per cent in 1995-96 as against 27.5 per cent in 1994-95 because of a very weak growth in demand deposits (3.7 per cent) in 1995-96. The modest growth in reserve money (14.8 per cent as against 22.1 per cent in 1994-95) explains this slower monetary expansion.

The unusually slow growth of monetary aggregates in 1995-96 was partly due to the unusually high base on March 31, 1995, resulting from the coincidence of the last reporting Friday for banks being on the final day of the accounting year. With liquidity conditions tightening in the third quarter of

1995-96, the Reserve Bank undertook a phased reduction of the Cash Reserve Ratio between November 1995 and January 1996, which injected more than Rs. 7000 crores of primary liquidity into the system and helped ease credit constraints. Deceleration of reserve money growth started in the second half of 1994-95 and has continued in 1995-96, mainly because of a progressive reduction in the rate of growth of net foreign exchange assets of RBI.

The financial year 1995-96 ended with a little contraction (0.8 per cent) in net foreign exchange assets of RBI which offset in that year the expansion in net RBI credit to Government by 25.1 per cent.

As a result of rising commercial demand for credit on account of high tempo of industrial production the banks which had an excess holding of Government and other approved securities, contributed only Rs. 14766 crore to the borrowing of the Government during 1995-96 as against Rs. 16323 crore in 1994-95. This necessitated sizeable support to market borrowing of the Government from RBI of which in turn increased the growth of net RBI credit to Government. Given the modest growth of Rs. 8485 crore in RBI credit to banks (including NABARD) the marginal contraction in net foreign exchange assets of RBI, the higher growth of RBI credit to the Government did not exacerbate the growth in reserve money.

The up trend in the bank credit to the commercial sector that started in the last quarter of 1994-95 with the recovery of industrial production, accelerated in 1995-96. Between March 31, 1995 and March 31, 1996 other bank credit to the commercial sector grew by 16 per cent (Rs.45654 crore) compared to a growth of 23.7 per cent (Rs.54804 crore) in the corresponding period of 1994-95 and large devolument of Government loans on RBI. Over the same two periods, scheduled commercial bank non-food credit grew by Rs. 43023 crore (1995-96) and Rs. 45775 crore (1994-95). The increase in non-food credit was larger than increase in credit to Government by the banks.

The agreement between the RBI and the Ministry of Finance to phase out ad-hoc borrowings was carried forward. The year end ceiling on borrowing from RBI against ad-hoc treasury bills was reduced from Rs. 6000 crore in 1994-95 to Rs. 5000 crore in 1995-96.

The within year ceiling on such borrowing was retained at Rs. 9000 crore, to take care of the potential monthly mismatch between the revenue and capital inflows and the expenditure outflows. A sharp reduction in Government's market borrowing during the first half of the current financial year has been an important factor in increasing this mis-match. This raised Centre's borrowing against ad-hocs well above the intra-year ceiling. RBI took steps to bring these borrowings down by selling Central Government securities/treasury bills in the market.

Over the past five budgets the fiscal deficit of the Central Government has declined as proportion of GDP from 8.3 per cent in 1990-91 to 5.9 per cent of GDP in 1995-96 (RE). This 2.4 per cent reduction has been brought about by an even sharper 3.2 per cent reduction in the primary deficit. The primary deficit at1.1 per cent of GDP in 1995-96 (RE) is lower than it has been in decades.

Unfortunately, this reduction in the primary deficit has been partly offset by 0.8 percentage point increase in interest payments as a proportion of GDP. This, in turn, is a legacy of past fiscal deficits accumulated as debt and the rise in interest rates.

Non-plan expenditures of the Central Government declined from 14.4 per cent of GDP in 1990-91 to 12.3 per cent in 1995-96 (RE), while Plan expenditures went from 5.3 per cent to 4.5 per cent over the same period. Central Government debt, which reached a peak of 69.7 per cent of GDP in 1993-94, declined to 64.2 per cent in 1995-96 (RE). Gross dissavings of the Central Government show a modest decline to 1.7 per cent of GDP in 1995-96 (BE), from 2.0 per cent in 1990-91.

Reform of the tax system has been one of the key elements of the structural reforms undertaken since July 1991. The basic approach has been to move to a tax structure which is simple, relies on moderate tax rates with a wider base and better enforcement and serves the objectives of equity and efficiency.

Substantial progress has been made in the last five years. The maximum marginal rate of personal income tax was reduced from 56 per cent (inclusive of 12 per cent surcharge) to 40 per cent.

The rates of corporate income tax (inclusive of 15 per cent surcharge), which were 51.75 per cent for publicly held companies and 57.5 per cent for closely held companies were unified and reduced to 46 per cent.

On the indirect tax side reforms have covered both customs and excise. Peak import duty rates which in several cases were around 300 per cent Prior to reforms, were brought down in a phased manner to 50 per cent to reduce the input cost for producers in India and promote competition. The import duty on capital goods for general projects and machinery, which was 85 per cent prior to reforms, was brought down to 25 per cent in 1995 and unified for nearly four-fifths of machinery imports at 25 per cent in 1995. The number of customs duty rates were sharply reduced to 12 and a large number of end-use exemptions were eliminated. The excise duty regime has been greatly improved with a significant switch over from specific to ad-valorem duties to ensure built in revenue elasticity.

The ambit of MODVAT, entailing credit for taxes paid on inputs, was extended to cover capital goods, specified quality control, testing, pollution control and R&D equipment, petroleum products used in industry and spun yarn made from fibres. The number of ad-valorem excise duty rates were reduced to 10 and a large number of end-use exemptions eliminated.

These tax reforms have helped in restructuring the tax system by increasing the role of direct taxes and reducing that of customs duties. This will increase both the equity and efficiency of the tax system, as the former is regarded as more progressive and the latter as an efficiency-inducing tax. As a result of the reforms revenues from direct taxes are budgeted to rise from 2.1 per cent of GDP in 1990-91 to 3.0 per cent in 1995-96 (RE), while customs revenues declined from 3.9 per cent of GDP to 3.2 per cent (RE) over the same period. As a consequence, the share of direct taxes in the gross tax revenue of the Centre is expected to rise from around 19 per cent in

1990-91 to about 29 per cent in 1995-96 (RE), while that of customs revenue is expected to decline from 36 per cent to 32 per cent (RE) over the same period.

The success of the new approach is also shown by the fact that, despite the lowering of personal and corporate tax rates, the buoyancy of these taxes has increased. Average buoyancy of personal income taxes, as measured by the ratio of change in tax revenue to the change in the GDP at current prices, has risen from 1.1 during 1986-87 to 1990-91, to around 1.5 during 1991-92 to 1995-96 (RE). Similarly the buoyancy of corporate income tax revenues has risen from an average of 0.8 during 1986-87 to 1990- 91 to 1.7 in 1991-92 to 1995-96 (RE). Both are likely to be higher on 1995-96 (RE) basis. Despite the very large reduction in peak customs duty rates from over 300 per cent to 50 per cent, the revenue collection rate (ratio of revenue collected to value of imports), only fell from 47 per cent in 1990-91 to 29 per cent in 1995-96, for similar reasons.

The 1995-96 Budget estimated a net tax revenue loss to the centre of about Rs.1,600 crore based on conventional methods, which do not incorporate gains from simplification, rationalisation, improved tax compliance and administration. Available trends indicate that gains are likely to be much greater than these conventional loss estimates. For the first nine months of 1995-96 (April-December, 1995), collections from personal income tax and corporation tax at Rs. 21327 crore were 27.6 per cent higher than in the same period of 1994. Collections from excise and customs, at Rs. 53802 crore during April-December, 1995, show a growth of about 19 per cent.

Financial Developments

Reforms in the financial sector have included the phasing in of prudential norms for income recognition, classification of assets and provisioning for bad debts, revised formats for making balance sheet and profit and loss accounts reflect the actual financial health and a time schedule for attaining 8 per cent capital to risk weighted assets for the scheduled commercial banks. The Statutory Liquidity Ratio (SLR) and Cash Reserve Ratio (CRR) were brought down to reduce the pre-emption of bank credit by Government and government borrowing was undertaken at market interest rates. The effects of these reforms on the financial health and performance of banks is gradually emerging. There has been progress by public sector banks in moving to the target of 8 per cent capital to risk weighted assets ratio (CRAR) by March end, 1996. By end March, 1994, only four public sector banks had a CRAR over 8 per cent, four had between 6.7 per cent and 8 per cent and eight had a CRAR in the range of 4.3 per cent and 6.7 per cent. By end March, 1995 as many as 13 public sector banks reached CRAR of at least 8 per cent, while 10 banks had a CRAR of 4 per cent and above.

Only 4 banks have less than 4 per cent CRAR. In the private sector, all the banks had complied with 4 per cent norm by March, 1994 and propose to raise additional capital through public issue to attain 8 per cent CRAR by March, 1996. All new private sector banks start with 8 per cent CRAR.

The deregulation of bank interest rates undertaken in 1994-95 with the abolition of the minimum lending rate on bank loans above Rs. 2 lakh, was extended to the deposit side in 1995-96. From October 1, 1995 scheduled commercial banks became free to fix their interest rates on domestic term deposits of over two years. The stipulation of at least three slabs with a minimum interest rate differential of 0.25 per cent point imposed in April 1992 on term deposits, was also withdrawn. Banks already have the discretion to fix both maturities and interest rates on non-resident non-repatriable (NRNR) deposits. The entry of 9 new private sector banks during 1994-95 and 1995-96, and the potential future entry of more banks, is likely to spur competitiveness and cost consciousness, and greater attention to depositor interests.

The Board for Financial Supervision was set up in 1994-95 with statutory powers over financial institutions, banks and non-bank financial institutions. It is designed to provide guidance on the supervisory initiatives and interventions of RBI. Its Secretariat is provided by the newly set up Department of Supervision in RBI. In addition, there is also an Advisory Council to provide guidance. There are now five Debts Recovery

Tribunals functioning along with an Appellate Tribunal, for expediting the loan recovery process through adjudication. A major institutional step in 1995-96 has been the appointment of eight Ombudsmen under Banking Ombudsman Scheme, 1995 (Out of 15 to be appointed for the country as a whole), who will function to resolve customers grievances in a quick and inexpensive manner.

With the State Bank of India entering capital market to raise Rs. 3200 crore the share of the RBI in the capital of SBI has come down to 66 per cent from 99 per cent earlier. The Government made a capital contribution of Rs. 5700 crores in 1993-94, Rs. 5287 crores in 1994-95 and Rs. 852 crores in 1995-96 (BE) to public sector banks to enable them to attain capital adequacy target.

The entire range of reforms, aimed at promoting competition within a prudent regulatory regime, is beginning to bear fruit. The financial position of the scheduled commercial banks has improved in 1994-95. The number of public sector banks declaring operating profits went up from 19 in 1992-93 to 26 in 1994-95.

Only one reported an operating loss. The number of public sector banks making net profits rose to 19 in 1994-95 from 15 in 1992-93. The average ratio of non-performing assets to the total advances, for the public sector banks, came down to 20 per cent in 1994-95 from 26 per cent in 1992-93.

Among the all-India financial institutions the amendment of the IDBI Act, 1964 in March 1995, made possible Industrial Development Bank of India (IDBI) maiden capital issue in July 1995. A new development finance institution, namely, the North Eastern Development Finance Corporation Ltd., with an initial paid up equity base of Rs. 100 crore (and authorised capital of Rs. 500 crore), is set to commence operations soon.

In the field of rural finance the prudential norms relating to income recognition were introduced for Regional Rural Banks (RRBs). An Expert Group examined the major issues concerning managerial and financial restructuring of RRBs and the role which could be assigned to non-government organisations and self-group in improving the rural credit delivery system. Steps were taken to increase the flow of credit to the small scale industries (SSI) sector with a special programme to open 100 specialised SSI bank branches in 85 identified districts by March 1996. By December 1995, 56 branches had been set up. A number of special schemes/funds were announced in the budget speech of 1995-96, which aim at counteracting shortfalls in priority sector advances and augmenting the flow of funds to relatively neglected areas/sectors. These include:

(a) Rural Infrastructure Development Fund (RIDF) of Rs. 2,000 crore in the National Bank for the Agriculture and Rural Development (NABARD) to accelerate implementation of investment projects in agriculture irrigation and allied activities;

(b) a scheme for expanded provision of credit facilities to the Khadi and Village Industries Commission by a consortium of banks so as to increase production and employment in off-farm activities in rural areas and;

(c) a scheme for financing primary weavers'co- operative societies by the scheduled commercial banks to assist increased production of handloom cloth. The RIDF will be built with contributions by the scheduled commercial banks which have failed to achieve the target of priority sector advances. They will also be required to participate in the aforesaid schemes.

In the area of capital markets the abolition of the office of Controller of Capital Issues (CCI) in May 1992 and the setting up of Securities and Exchange Board of India (SEBI) with statutory powers and functions (February 1992) were the first decisive steps in the move from control to prudential regulation. Prudential regulation is as important as decontrol for the development of a healthy capital market, keeping in view investor interests.

The powers and functions of SEBI were strengthened in phases. SEBI has been empowered to regulate business in stock exchanges. Its ambit covers recognition of stock exchanges, their rules, articles, voting rights and nomination of public representatives, stock exchange listing and delivery contracts. The setting up of the National Stock Exchange (NSE) and computerisation of the Bombay Stock Exchange (BSE) will help improve the clearing and settlement mechanisms and substantially raise the levels of transparency.

SEBI has issued rules and procedures for registering and regulating the various market participants and intermediaries. These cover broker, bankers and registrars to an issue, merchant bankers, underwriters, portfolio managers, custodians, credit rating agencies, foreign institutional investors, venture capital funds, mutual funds and asset management companies. To enable SEBI to effectively carry out its functions of Stock Exchange regulation and investor protection, the Department of Company Affairs has delegated to SEBI powers to file complaints against violations of the Companies Act.

The notification covers issues pertaining to primary market such as listing of securities, refund of excess application money, delay in issues of shares and dispatch of dividend warrants. SEBI now has the authority to levy monetary penalties for a range of violations such as failure to redress investor grievances or observe rules and regulations by mutual funds, asset management companies, failure to disclose the aggregate of shareholding in a company, or to make public announcement for acquisition of share in the context of the takeover code.

Standards of disclosure and issue procedures have been tightened. Companies are now required to draw up their financial statements on a consistent basis with appropriate audit qualifications. They will be asked to indicate the sources of income from other than normal activities and to make the draft prospectus a public document. Finance companies are eligible to make an issue if they have operated for a minimum of two years, or are registered with RBI as a non-banking finance company or with SEBI as an intermediary.

The National Stock Exchange, which was established in 1993, has come of age, with daily average trading volume rising sharply in recent months. Screen based trading has also been instituted in the Bombay and Delhi Stock exchanges. Private mutual funds are now permitted and are allowed to apply for firm allotment in public issues. The carry forward system has been reformed.

The scrip-wise and broker-wise carry forward position shall be disclosed by the stock exchanges at the beginning of the carry forward session. Members doing financing of carry forward transactions will be subject to a cap of Rs. 10 crore. The depositories ordinance, re-issued in January 1996, will provide a legal framework for the establishment of depositories to record ownership details in book entry form. The dematerialisation of scrips that this makes possible will eliminate a number of hazards associated with paper based stock market trading, such as a high proportion of bad deliveries, high risk of loss, cumbersome procedures and long delays.

As a result of the past four years of reform, there has been a significant increase in market activity. Equity capital raised, mainly by the private corporate sector, has increased from Rs. 5562 crore in 1991-92 to Rs. 27621 crore in 1994-95. During April- December 1995, Rs. 14155 crore of capital has been raised. The market capitalisation of BSE almost doubled from Rs. 3,23,363 crore in 1991-92 to Rs. 6,44,478 crore at the end of December 1995.

The number of listed firms at the BSE has doubled from 2601 in 1991-92 to 5398 in December 1995. Besides UTI, there are now 9 public sector mutual funds and 16 private sector mutual funds in operation. During April-December 1994-95, Mutual Funds including UTI had raised Rs. 1,601 crore through 32 new schemes.

At the end of January 1996, 350 foreign institutional investors (FIIs) were registered with SEBI compared to only 10 in January 1993. They had invested a total of Rs. 14,129 crore in the securities market Indian companies were also permitted to access international capital markets through euro-equity shares and by the end of December 1995 Indian firms had raised US $ 5.18 billion through global depository receipts (GDRs) and foreign currency convertible bonds (FCCBs).

Thus the total inflow of foreign Portfolio capital into the Indian capital market since the launching of economic reforms amounts to $ 8.9 billion. This is further indication of improved international creditworthiness of India resulting from successful economic reforms.

External Sector Developments

The remarkable improvement in India's balance of payment witnessed in 1993-94 was consolidated further in 1994-95. Despite some widening of deficit in the current account, the overall balance of payment in 1994-95 remained very strong. The foreign currency assets of the Reserve Bank of India (RBI) rose from US $ 15.07 billion at the end of 1993-94 to a historical peak of US $ 20.81 billion at the end of 1994-95. Quick estimates of balance of payments for 1994-95 indicate strong improvements in exports and invisible receipts and in foreign investment flows.

The balance of payment position remained reasonably comfortable during 1995-96. For the third year in succession, export growth was robust, supported by a congenial domestic policy environment.

Import growth was also high, reflecting the continued good performance of the industrial sector. On the invisible account, net outflow under investment income rose significantly because of a rise in interest payments on foreign loans; but this was largely offset by the increase in inflows under non-factor services, especially tourism receipts. Private transfers in 1995-96 remained broadly at previous year's level.

As a result net inflows under invisibles account were only marginally lower than the previous year's level. As a result, net inflows under invisibles account were only marginally lower then the previous year. Reflecting these developments on the trade and invisibles account, the current account deficit widened to 1.6 per cent of GDP from 0.8 per cent of GDP in 1994-95. But the level of the deficit was reasonable and sustainable. On the capital account, foreign investment flows were the major component, as in the two previous years.

However, there was a considerable deceleration in portfolio investments mainly because of the subdued trend in GDR issues. Direct foreign investments, on the other hand, showed considerable improvement. The residual financing need was met by drawing down foreign exchange reserves. Foreign currency assets of the RBI declined by US $ 3.77 billion to a level of US $ 17.04 billion at the end of March 1996.

Export performance has been robust in recent years. Exports, according to DGCI&S data, recorded a growth rate of 18.4 per cent in 1994-95 and 20.9 per cent in 1995-96, in US dollar terms. The growth in imports, in US dollar terms, was also high at 22.9 per cent in 1994-95 and 26.9 per cent in 1995-96. The trade deficit, measured on the basis of DGCI&S data, amounted to US $ 4.54 billion compared to the deficit of US $ 2.32 billion in 1994-95.

Total foreign investment flows, including both direct and portfolio investment flows, which increased sharply to US $ 4.11 billion in 1993-94, rose further to US $ 4.90 billion in 1994-95. During 1995-96, total foreign investment amounted to US $ 4.20 billion, comprising US $ 2.11 billion of direct foreign investments and US $ 2.1 billion of portfolio investments.

The process of achieving current account convertibility was carried forward further in 1995-96. The RBI, in July 1995, announced further liberalisation in the release of foreign exchange for current invisible payments. The RBI permitted the authorised dealers, with effect from July 5, 1995 to provide exchange facilities to their customers without prior approval of the RBI, beyond the specified indicative limits for purposes such as, business travel, participation in overseas conference/seminars, studies abroad, medical treatments/check up, specialised apprenticeship etc., provide they are satisfied about the bonafides of the applications.

On the basis of recommendations of the Tax Reforms Committee, for improving the competitiveness of domestic industry and maintaining thrust towards simplification of procedures, the process of reducing peak tariff rate was continued in the Central Budget for 1995-96. The peak rate of customs duty, which had been reduced to 65 per cent in 1994-95 Budget from 85 per cent was further reduced to 50 per cent in the 1995-96 Budget. Substantial reduction in customs duty on critical raw materials for enhancing export competitiveness was also effected. The stability of the Indian rupee against the US dollar noticed since July 1993 at around Rs. 31.37 per US dollar continued through July, 1995. The rupee in relation the US witnessed a high degree of volatility during September and October 1995, and again in January through the first week of February 1996. The rate, however, stabilised following RBI's market intervention and announcement of certain measures aimed at augmenting the supply of foreign exchange and reducing the demand. The rupee-dollar rate at the end of March 1996 was Rs. 34.35 per US dollar.

Insurance Sector Developments

During the financial year 1994-95, the Life Insurance Corporation of India (LIC) achieved a growth rate of 32.03% securing total new business (sum assured) of Rs. 55468.82 crores under 108.88 lakhs policies. This compares with Rs. 42012.90 crores under 107.38 lakh policies during the previous year. New business under Group Insurance Scheme (including Group Gratuity was Rs. 50,651.85 crores covering 210.81 lakh lives.

The total rural new business procured by the Corporation during 1994-95 works out to be 39.1% of its total new business and the total number of policies issued in rural areas works out to be 45.1% of the number of policies issued during the period. The total business in force (individual Assurance) as on 31st March, 1995 was Rs. 2,54,572 crores under 655.29 lakh policies, compared with Rs. 2,08,619 crores under 608.73 lakh policies on 31st March 1994.

The Gross Premium income of the general insurance industry written direct in India during 1994-95 amounted to Rs. 4959 crores against Rs. 4449 crores in 1993-94. This amounts to a growth rate of 11.4% over the previous year. The net premium income of the general insurance industry during 1994-95 was Rs. 4102 crores compared with Rs. 3681 crores in 1993-94. It accounts for a growth of 11.4 per cent over the previous year. The gross profits of the general insurance industry was Rs. 503 crores in 1994-95. It accounted for a fall of 53.5% over the previous year. The net profit of the industry during 1994-

95 was Rs. 377 crores representing a fall of 43.71 % from the previous year. In pursuance of the recommendations of the Committee on Reforms in the Insurance Sector the Government has already set up an Insurance Regulatory Authority.

Social Sector Development

The Government has followed a three pronged strategy to help the weaker sections of the society; (i) overall, the programme of economic reforms is designed to promote rapid, broad based labour intensive economic growth; (ii) spending on anti-poverty programmes have been increased and new programmes have been launched and (iii) spending on social sectors such as Eduction and Health has been rapidly stepped up.

Central Plan outlay for social sectors and anti-poverty programmes have been stepped up substantially in the last three budgets.

The Government has increased outlay for education by 92 per cent from Rs. 952 crores in 1992-93 (BE) to Rs. 1825 crores in 1995-96 (BE), elementary education by 129 per cent from Rs. 284 crores in 1992-93 (BE) to Rs. 651 crores in 1995-96 (BE), health by 122 per cent from Rs. 302 (BE) crores in 1992-93 to Rs. 670 crores in 1995-96 (BE). The Central Plan Outlay for Rural Development which encompasses a major programme for poverty alleviation and employment generation was raised by 148 per cent from Rs.3100 crore in 1992-93 (BE) to Rs.7700 crores in 1995-96 (BE).

Five new anti-poverty programmes, namely, the National Social Assistance Programme (NSAP), the Mid Day Meal Programme, the Rural Group Life Insurance Scheme, the Indira Mahila Yojana and the Prime Minister's Integrated Urban Poverty Eradication Programme were launched in 1995-96. The Government has also accorded the highest priority to promoting sustainable Employment Intensive Growth in its economic reforms policies.

The incidence of poverty has also declined from 25.49 per cent in 1987-88 to 18.96 per cent in 1993-94. This significant decline in the poverty ratio has occured despite the major crisis of 1991-92.

Department of Expenditure

The Department of Expenditure comprises six main divisions, namely,

- Establishment Division,
- Plan Finance Division,
- Cost Accounts Branch,
- Organisation of Controller General of Accounts,
- Staff Inspection Unit and
- Finance Commission Division.

The Establishment Division is the nerve centre for the service conditions of the Central Government employees having financial content. It deals with pay scales, Pay Commission, etc. In addition, it is concerned with allowances such as Compensatory Allowances, House Rent Allowance, Dearness Allowance, Special Duty Allowance, Overtime Allowance etc.

It examines all proposals on travelling allowances rules, Central Government employees Group Insurance Scheme, 1980, General Financial Rules, Delegation of Financial Power Rules and other Financial Rules bearing financial content.

The following decisions/actions were taken during the year :

(i) The Pay Commission's interim report for grant of interim relief to Central Govt. employees and also for treating a portion of Dearness Allowance as Dearness Pay for the purpose of gratuity was considered. These recommendations were accepted by the Govt., involving an expenditure of Rs.1650 crores during 1995-96.

(ii) Ad-hoc bonus equal to 30 days' emoluments to the eligible Central Government employees was declared for the accounting year 1994-95.

(iii) During the year under report, Pay Research Unit brought out the 16th issue of the brochure on Pay & Allowances for the year 1993-94.

(iv) Consequent to the announcement made by the then Prime Minister in NDC in 1991 regarding reduction in staff by 10%, the Establishment Division initated action for reduction of staff and about 1.38 lakhs posts at different levels have been abolished by various Ministries/ Departments of the Government of India.

(v) To contain non-plan expenditure, various measures initiated during the last three years have continued in 1995-96 also.

(vi) For the year 1995-96, the latest estimates of Central Assistance to States for their Annual Plan amounted to Rs.16786.70 crores (including Rs.352 crores for Central Assistance for development of hill areas and Rs.176 crores for Border Area Development Programme). The Centre's share to the Calamity Relief Fund to the States amounted to Rs.880.18 crores during 1995-96. The States were also given Non-Plan Revenue Deficit Grant of Rs.4005.71 crores during the year.

(vii) During the year 1995, the Public Investment Board held 12 meetings and recommended for approval of 33 projects with a total capital cost of Rs.30,557.08 crores. The major areas of the new investments were Power, Coal and Petroleum & Natural Gas.

(viii) The Cost Accounts Branch of the Ministry of Finance (Department of Expenditure) completed 13 studies during the year.

(ix) The Controller General of Accounts brought out a Publication entitled "Accounts At a Glance - 93-94" featuring Government receipts and expenditure.

(x) As recommended by the 10th Finance Commission, the Government has since constituted an Inter-Ministerial Empowered Committee under the Charmanship of Additional Secretary (Expenditure) for monitoring the utilisation of public upgradation demands.

(xi) For controlling pollution, this Department has started fitting their staff cars with catalytic convertors or converting to Compressed Natural Gas (CNG). This Department has purchased 4 cars fitted with catalytic convertors. The CNG has been fitted in 3 cars. The

Ministry of Surface Transport has drawn up a programme for fitting CNG in all the other cars of this Deptt.

Department of Revenue

The Department of Revenue exercises control in respect of revenue matters relating to direct and indirect Union taxes through the two statutory Boards, namely the Central Board of Direct Taxes and the Central Board of Excise and Customs.

The Department is also entrusted with the administration and enforcement of controls and regulatory measures provided in the enactments concerning Central Sales-Tax, Stamp-Duties and other relevant fiscal statutes. Control over production and disposal of opium and its products is also vested in the Department.

Through the tax laws and their administration, the Department seeks to achieve three main objectives, namely to build up an atmosphere of mutual trust between the tax collector and the tax payer, to tackle the problems of tax-evasion and reduce tax arrears, and to give incentives by equitable legislation in furtherance of the socio-economic objectives of the Government.

During the Financial year 1995-96, the drive against smuggling, tax evasion etc., continued throughout the country in view of Government's firm resolve to continue to take strict action against socio-economic offenders.

The Central Economic Intelligence Bureau is the Central nodal authority for economic intelligence and is also charged with the responsibility of monitoring State Government actions under the COFEPOSA Act.

The COFEPOSA Act was administered vigorously to tackle the menace of smuggling and foreign exchange racketeering. During 1995-96, 324 detention orders were issued and 277 persons detained. The total number of persons under detention as on 31.3.96 was 328.

The Prevention of Illicit Trade in Narcotic Drugs and Psychotropic Substances Act provides for a maximum of 2 years preventive detention for drug traffickers. The PIT NDPS Cell is responsible for issuing detention orders and coordination on all matters with regard to preventive detention in narcotics cases. During the year 1995-96, 11 detention orders were issued by the Central Government and 11 persons were detained. Besides, 85 detention orders were issued by the State Governments and 74 persons were detained.

During the financial year 1995-96, a relentless drive against smuggling and tax evasion continued. During 1995-96, contraband goods worth Rs.600.27 crore (Prov.) were seized.

The Income Tax Department continued its drive against tax evaders during 1995-96, upto 31.3.96, 4612 searches were conducted leading to seizure of assets worth Rs. 458.14 cror. During the period April 1995 to March, 1996, 7,83,295 premises were surveyed leading to the addition of 13,16,764 new cases.

The collection of Union customs and excise duties in 1995-96, amounted to Rs. 35,509.83 (Prov.) crore and Rs.40,784.13 crore (Prov.) respectively as against the Budget estimates of Rs.29,500.00 crore and Rs.42,579.20 crore respectively.

The collection of Corporation Tax, Income-tax and interest tax upto 31st March, 1996 (financial year 1995-96) has shown a substantial increase over the collection upto 31st March, 1995 (financial year 1994-95) as will be clear from the figures given below:-

Rupees in crore

	Budget estimates 1995-96	Collection upto 31-3-96	Collection upto 31-3-95
Corporation Tax	15,500	16,485	13,611
Income Tax	13,500	15,463	12,162
Interest Tax	1,000	1,136	756
Total	**30,000**	**33,084**	**26,529**

3

Industrial Banking: History and Challenges

HISTORICAL OVERVIEW

The antiquated Indian banking system has its roots in the nineteenth century. The character and structure of the system has, however, changed substantially since 1969, when the major banks were nationalized. Prior to nationalization, banking was concentrated in urban areas. It was clear that a better banking system was needed to promote the economic goals of the new Indian state. Rural markets for industrial goods could not be developed so long as money lenders, charging usurious rates of interest, were the main source of rural credit. Moreover, the 'green revolution' depended on farmers finding substantial sources of credit to pay for fertilizers and hybrid seeds.

Since the mid-1970s, there has been a spectacular growth in the spatial distribution of bank branches and in the size of their deposits and advances. According to experts in banking this transformation has no parallel anywhere in the world (Anantharam Iyer, 1991). After nationalization, there was also a change in recruitment policy. For the first time, the doors of the banks were opened to everyone, irrespective of family status, caste, community, religion or gender. Recruitment was placed on a more systematic basis, with merit assessed by aptitude tests conducted by an external agency in a relatively impartial manner (Deekshit, 1991).

As the size of the banking sector increased, the industry became difficult to manage. Computer technology offered a possible solution. In India, a small number of industrial houses and a few educational, research and development institutions started using computers in the early 1960s. During the late 1960s and 1970s, service-oriented industries such as airlines, railways and insurance companies introduced computers to 'improve their functioning' and 'to provide better customer service' (Anantharam Iyer, 1991). Banks in India did not, however, introduce computers on a large scale because of the fear that these would result in retrenchment and unemployment (Goodman, 1991). For a long time Indian banks faced very little competition and operated in a protected economy. Thus no long-term policy or perspective for the banking sector was formulated: it was simply treated as part of the public sector. This is now changing. Well-computerized foreign banks are beginning to compete seriously with the nationalized banks. They aim at a profitable and wealthy part of the market and, in contrast to the nationalized banks, do not recognize any social responsibilities to small account holders or to a rural and semi-urban clientele.

TECHNOLOGICAL CHANGES, LEGISLATION AND BARGAINING

In India, the main agents affecting the introduction of new technology have been the unions, management and the workforce. The government has played a very indirect role in the process. In the early days of the massive introduction of computer technology into industry and services, union policies on new technology were basically defensive. They focused almost entirely on the immediate consequences of technological change on the workforce, especially the aspect of possible job losses.

However, these attitudes and the strategies of unions vis-à-vis computerization have begun to change, especially since the 1980s. Management in many places has been able to convince workers and unions that competition is becoming increasingly harsh, and computerization is not only inevitable for the health and survival of the unit but also beneficial to employees, because it may improve the competitiveness of the enterprise, enhance job security and improve employment conditions.

Many unions which have consistently opposed computerization have had to face their members who are keen on technological changes. As one EDP employee who is also a unionist put it, 'As a unionist I would oppose computerization, as an employee I would welcome it. That is my dilemma.'

Consequently, unions today are increasingly seeking to influence the process of technological changes so that new technology can be introduced in such a way as to benefit workers and minimise its adverse consequences. The last decade has seen several 'technology agreements' or 'computerization agreements', along with routine collective bargaining agreements which contain clauses related to technology.

Despite these agreements, most managers in India, including those in the public sector, have consistently regarded all aspects of technological changes as matters falling within the area of managerial prerogative. When consultation with unions has occurred, these have been far from fair since unions have lacked the requisite know-how and information.

The Reserve Bank of India (RBI) installed its first computer in 1968, and a larger one in 1979. But the United Commercial (UCO) Bank, the Standard Chartered Bank, Lloyds' Bank, Grindlays, and others had installed accounting and other machines before 1966. Operations such as payrolls had been computerized fairly early on. Some head offices began to use computers by the beginning of the 1980s. In September 1983. two of the major banking unions - the All India Bank Employees Association (AIBEA) and the National Confederation of Banking Employees (NCBE) signed an agreement with the Indian Banks Association (IBA), representing 58 bank managements. The unions wished to maintain surveillance of the process and to protect job prospects in the banking sector, but the final settlement was self-contradictory. On the one hand there were restrictions on computerization, with numerical limits on the numbers of mainframe computers, and even on the number of accounting machines which might be used in rural branches, but there was also a loop-hole which allowed the banks to use 'such number of mini-computers as are warranted by their needs and exigencies'.

The 1983 agreement provided an opening for individual banks to make their own computerization agreements, and many foreign banks immediately took advantage of this 'openness' to negotiate agreements giving them a free hand to introduce new technology, despite the careful restrictive approach of the AIBEA and NCBE.

In March 1987 the AIBEA and NCBE signed a new settlement with the IBA. The settlement was similar in its approach and concerns to the 1983 agreement. Although it allowed for an extension of new technology in both the operations computerized and the equipment used, the concern was largely still with ways of restricting and controlling the use of computers to protect existing staff and preserve the prospects for future staff.

The agreements also provided some additional allowances and protection for pregnant women. Taking advantage of the 'openness' clause in the 1983 and 1987 agreements, some of the AIBEA's own affiliates agreed to the installation of automatic teller machines and fax machines, which were beyond the purview of the industry level accord. There are signs that the AIBEA has been forced to reverse its earlier relatively liberal stance on computerization because of the campaign spearheaded in recent years by its arch rival, the Bank Employees' Federation of India (BEFI), which has been seeking recognition from the IBA.

However it would be misleading to look at the unions alone in explaining the slow rate of technological innovation. A highly-placed bank executive commented that the management of the banks lack perspective, because of the protection they had enjoyed, and were not really serious about computerization (Goodman, 1991).

There is also uncertainty among bank managers about the implications of computerization in terms of the hierarchy and their own positions. Employees of many Indian banks, including the State Bank of India and Bank of Baroda, said that management 'just dumped these machines here. They are hardly used, and some don't work.' A comprehensive policy seems completely absent. In contrast, the multinational banks have computerized almost totally, with the unions unable to have any say.

IMPACT OF COMPUTERIZATION ON THE WORKFORCE

Some of the general issues that have concerned unions and employees, especially women, in the wake of the introduction of new technology in the banking and finance sectors have been:

- Prospects of job losses and declining employment levels.
- Increase in workloads.
- Pressure for flexibility.
- Changes in job contents.
- Increase in insecurity in the workplace, and loss of union power.
- Increase in the proportion of 'non-bargainable' staff (i.e. those without an automatic right to unionize) as compared to the 'bargainable' staff.
- Changes in grading and pay.
- Changes in information and control.
- Changes in the autonomy of employees.
- Changes in health and safety conditions.

Job Losses

There have not been visible losses of employment in either the banking or insurance industries, due to the massive expansion and diversification in the two industries and to the high proportion of nationalized enterprises, in which workers are generally protected against job losses. Some of the foreign banks have undergone massive expansion in terms of the number of their branches and their areas of operation. In fact, in January 1992, 12 foreign banks sought permission to open 44 more branches in various major cities of India (Economic Times, 1992). There has however been a reduction in the rate of recruitment in the nationalized banks. According to a recent study covering three banks and two insurance companies, the growth of new jobs has dwindled. As the use of new technology expands, labour savings are likely to increase further in some operations (Chopra, 1991). The three developments that are likely to displace workers, and women in particular, are voice recognition, optical character recognition and artificial intelligence (Rajan, 1990). An employee at the Hong Kong bank observed that the entire category of typists had already been abolished.

II is possible to discern a tendency to reduce the proportion of 'bargainable' staff in both nationalized and foreign banks. The Banque Nationale de Paris reduced its bargainable staff from 200 employees in 1979 to just 135 in 1992, by not recruiting staff at the lowest levels and by asking about 35 employees to accept the so-called Voluntary Retirement Scheme (VRS) because computerization was expected to reduce the need for their labour.

Increase in Workloads

New technology could lessen the repetitive and heavy nature of certain operations. However, most employees in the insurance and banking industry, especially in the foreign banks, have experienced serious strain and heavy work-loads. According to an employee working in the cash department of the Citibank, Before computerization we used to do 30-40 cash entries per day; now we have to do more than 100. There is a greater pressure of work more work and more responsibility. The speed has increased enormously.

According to experienced unionists in ANZ Grindlays Bank, computerization, coupled with non-recruitment and non-replacement of retired staff, has led to a tremendous increase in workloads, 'after 20 years of employment, people are bound to be completely fagged out. Then the management will term them "unsuitable", "old" or "unfit"'.

The personnel officer of Grindlays, who disagrees with the union on everything else, admitted, 'Since the emphasis is entirely on productivity and efficiency, there has been intensification of work. Employees' efficiency levels have gone up ten-fold'. Personnel officers at the Life Insurance Corporation (LIC) confirmed this picture.

Pressure for Flexibility

Over the last decade and a half, management has consistently sought to have flexible manning levels. They have argued that they need operational flexibility in order to respond quickly to changes in the market, to introduce technological innovations, and to deal with fluctuations in the flow of work. This, they say, can be achieved by employing a core of secure, permanent, multiskilled, full-time employees and a 'periphery' of marginal, generally single-skilled workers who may be employed part-time or temporarily, and directly or indirectly, in a variety of 'new' ways (Huws et al., 1989) Computer technology demands functionally flexible multiskilled workers rather than specialists. The strategy of increasing flexibility in the employment system frequently targets women workers, who occupy the lower rungs of the job hierarchy. They are often forced to change work stations or leave the firm. Professionals and specialists, a majority of whom are men, benefit from the strategy.

Changes in Job Content

Changes in work methods caused by the introduction of computerization affect the content of work as well as the skills needed by employees. The direction of changes is, however, not uniform. Two divergent tendencies can be observed. In routine transactions, certain skills of a mechanical nature, which nevertheless require a measure of mental effort and concentration, are no longer required or are needed less.

The skills replacing them are equally mechanical but call for less mental effort. The level of skills required for the performance of routine transactions therefore actually falls, although the degree of attention and concentration required will be just as high or even higher. In contrast, in the area of customer services, computerization offers potential for an increase in both the necessary range and level of skills, for example, searching for, extracting and assimilating relevant information in response to a request. The realization of the potential is, however, contingent on the relevant organizational decisions being taken by management (Ozaki et al., 1992)

The impact of new technology on work content and the skills required of workers also depends on how rigidly jobs are defined and demarcated and on the skill levels of the existing workforce. Various studies seem to show that, in places where the tasks of workers have already been defined broadly and flexibly, with much overlapping, the reorganization of work after the introduction of new technology has been comparatively smooth and workers' resistance relatively minor. In places where the skill level of workers is high, technological change tends to strengthen the tendency towards the integration of planning and production tasks. Where skill levels are low there seems to be a trend towards polarization of skills. Computerization is also creating skills that are largely transferable from one enterprise to another, such as the skills of computer programmers (Ozaki et al., 1992).

Product innovations have generally led to an increase in the importance of formal skills. The informal skills, learned on the job, that characterized women's work are not seen as important. The professional and technical jobs increase in number and importance, and formal theoretical knowledge is becoming more important for employees in the banking sector (Tremblay, 1991). In India as elsewhere, categories such as junior clerks and tellers are becoming less important in the overall workforce as Automated Teller Machines (ATMs) multiply (Rajan, 1990).

An employee working at the bill discounting department in Citibank, Bombay, says:

> *Earlier, when a bill was brought to us, we made manual entries. The customer would present the bill. We had to scrutinise it, and then send it to the liability department for their approval. In the liability department, each client had one big card which showed her status. After approval, it was sent back to us for processing.*

That is:

1 calculate the interest using a calculating machine;

2 make debit/credit tickets;

3 balance the amount; and

4 send the tickets to the journal keeper, who would balance all the amounts.

Each department had a journal keeper. Now, we still have to scrutinise a bill. Then we key it into the programme - the bill programme. The computer shows the credit limit automatically. The ticket is then given to the officer, who takes it to the Credit Approval Committee. There are no manual interest calculations, no manual tickets, no journal-keeper.

There are positive aspects of computerization as weld. Although employees used to do the posting of debit and credit, they

did not necessarily know much about whether and why a particular debit or credit was passed. There is greater knowledge about these things now. There is also greater access to other types of work. Earlier I did not endorse documents. I do so now.

According to the personnel manager of the LIC, work had not been enriched or tasks enlarged, because jobs were set and functions well-defined. 'Computerization has made the jobs easier rather than interesting.' The personnel officer at the ANZ Grindlays Bank, in contrast, was adamant that employees' skills had increased ten-fold, but he was actually referring to their productivity or efficiency. He agreed however that many jobs have been 'realigned'.

For example, in bill discounting, work that was previously done by a team is now done individually by workers with their own machines. An employee at Grindlays comments, 'Earlier, there was greater interaction between employees. Team work was good work. We learnt more about the work. Now there is no time to look around, help or seek help from colleagues. You just sit there and bang at the keyboard'. The management of Grindlays argues that employees used to spend most of their time with books (e.g. tabulations) and now spend more time with customers. The unionists at Grindlays dismissed this claim, 'There have been no changes. Work has become more monotonous. The brain is getting more dull.'

Many employees expressed mixed feelings about computerization. While it relieved some work pressures and strains of particular types, it has made work dull. It increased efficiency, but decreased the feeling of team work and sharing. Work might be less arduous, but it also becomes less varied. Computerization is supposed to increase customer interaction, but many employees experienced a reduction, and all complained of an increased work tempo.

Increased Insecurity and Loss of Union Power

Deskilling contributes to a feeling of powerlessness vis-à-vis the employer. This feeling was expressed more definitely by employees working in foreign banks than by those employed either in the nationalized banks or the nationalized LIC, Four women employees in the Banque Nationale de Paris said that the closure of some branches and their awareness that they had not been given computer training at a time when nearly all the banking operations had been computerized had made them 'very scared.' All four were later made redundant.

At ANZ Grindlays, insecurity was said to have increased, with early retirements and no recruitment for the last four to five years, 'That itself creates insecurity. If there is a reduction, then it creates panic.'

Citibank employees reported feeling, on the one hand, that their workload was generally too heavy, and, on the other hand, that any temporary reductions made them fear that work had been contracted out. They said that contract workers had been employed for specific tasks, without informing the employees or the union.

This has become possible because of computerization. The feeling of insecurity has also increased because unions have been considerably weakened. The women who were forced to take the VRS (Voluntary Retirement Scheme) by the Banque Nationale de Paris say:

> There is virtually no union in the BNP. The union officials were bending backwards to sell the VRS to us. We didn't want to resign. We wanted to fight it out. But how can you do that without the firm backing of the union?

Even when a union is strong, women may not be protected against discrimination.

Increase in the Proportion of 'Non-bargainable' Staff

Control over the workforce provides the basis for controlling production processes, output levels, and scheduling. Over the years, this control has been loosened as unions have come to play a role in areas such as work intensity, output levels, health and safety, which were and still are considered to be 'management prerogatives'. One of the strategies available to wrest control back is to weaken unions, both numerically and in terms of the functions which the unionized workforce performs. This is one reason behind the dramatic and continuous increase in the non-bargainable category of workers, as compared to unionised workers. This casualization process has occurred in the banking and insurance industry as well as in manufacturing.

The number of workers in the bargainable categories is being reduced,5 for instance by using contract couriers in place of employing messengers. In 1973, 18.7 per cent of all workers in the banking industry were officers. By 1987 this had grown to 26.7 per cent. Over the same period, the percentage of clerical workers fell slightly, from 55.9 per cent to 52.4 per cent, and the percentage of workers in more subordinate positions fell quite significantly from 25.4 per cent to 20.9 per cent (Borkar, 1991).

In almost every industry in India, computer programmers are in the non-bargainable category. Computer programmers are usually in a position to anticipate changes and may use their knowledge to keep other workers and unions informed. Most new recruitment is done in the 'officer' category, though often these new employees do the same work as the bargainable employees.

In industries where the union has refused to cooperate with computerization, the management recruits 'officers' to do the work of data entry operators etc. The unionists are increasingly feeling that they have to bargain with the management about the content of work in the bargainable and non-bargainable categories, and be vigilant about any infringement.

Changes in Grading and Pay

There seems to have been no attempt to redefine a new grade structure in the banking and insurance industry after computerization was introduced. In the Banque Nationale de Paris a 'promotion agreement' was signed in 1987, under which all the clerical staff were promoted within three years to the status of Special Assistants, a supervisory category with an extra wage allowance. Everybody, including the lower grade staff, received the allowance, and there was a substantial increase in basic pay too. But there was no attempt at evolving a new grade structure, nor any training to equip employees to deal with the new type of work. All employees, including the women, have gained financially but there has not been any change in their job definition or real status.

All the banks have some allowance for EDP staff or computer operators. In the LIC the allowance was Rs 100. In the Hong Kong Bank only the most senior employees in the department got the allowance, although almost all the employees have to work on the terminals. The Union Bank of India employees who work on the computers get an allowance of Rs 350 per month. The Hong Kong Bank employees get an allowance of Rs 400. In the words of one computer operator in the Bank of Baroda, 'EDP staff are definitely graded highly in the Bank'.

Changes in Information and Control

Traditional craft workers often knew far more about their jobs than managers or supervisors, which gave them a lot of freedom as to how the work was done. But computers have enormously increased management's ability to collect and analyse information - about product performance, market trends, customers, sales, finance, and of course about employees. The tendency has been for management to learn more about how work is done, and to specify more tightly how jobs should be done - both in terms of method and speed. Every minute of your time is being recorded. How many words did you key in? How much time was required for posting debits and credits, for bill discounting? However, we cannot access information that is not in our jurisdiction. If one tries it, it is invalid; but the fact that you tried will be recorded in the computer. If one looks at it dispassionately, one would have an eerie feeling.

Employees felt that they were being watched and intimidated, increasing the sense of insecurity. Unions have not claimed a right to have access to information relevant for negotiating. Employees in ANZ Grindlays bank found such a demand difficult to even imagine. 'Management has total control over all information. Profits, costs etc. are under secret code. They have all the information about us though.'

Changes in Health and Safety Conditions

The introduction of new technology has also created a range of new hazards for the workers. The development of new materials, processes and substances, without adequate information being made available about their impact, may be creating problems which will not be perceived for many years. Increases in the scale and pace of production have contributed towards stress, especially where there is also inadequate support or training or an unfair distribution of workloads.

Some specific health and safety problems have been shown to arise from the introduction of computer-based equipment. Visual Display Units (VDUs) have been known to cause a number of health problems, especially if operated continuously for a long time. 'Video blues', eye problems, musculoskeletal problems, painful conditions such as tenosynovitis, varicose veins, ulcers, nausea, headaches, and skin diseases as well as reproductive problems such as miscarriages, stillbirths, birth defects, infertility, menstrual problems and low sperm counts have been very extensively documented (Labour Research Department, 1985). However, none of the bank employees had been given any health training. Most employees complained of eye strain, headaches, or a heavy feeling in the head, but they worked at the terminal from 9.30 a.m. to 4.30 p.m. with only breaks for lunch and tea in between. Three women in Citibank had had miscarriages, though none of them had any personal or familial history of miscarriages. Of the forty women interviewed only one had heard that working on the computers continuously could cause health problems. None of the training sessions had mentioned this problem. Though information on the health and safety aspects of working with computers is widely available, employees were ignorant of health hazards. This indicates their lack of access to information relevant to women, the unwillingness of management to share it, and the indifference of the union to issues of health and safety. This is a serious issue, especially because the number of women working on computers is increasing rapidly.

Women's Employment in Banking

Despite this increase, women are still concentrated at the clerical level, and the general picture is changing only very slowly. Women officers in banks are a recent phenomenon, which has become a little more significant since 1975 because of direct recruitment and promotions (Kanhere, 1991). Even in EDP activities, the share of women is low. A recent study of Indian banking notes that in one bank women constituted only 5 per cent of the EDP staff, about 12 per cent in another bank and 7 per cent in an insurance company. Women were not recruited as programmers (Chopra, 1991).

Computerization and Women in Foreign Banks

The effect of computerization on women bank employees, both clerical and officer grades, is of considerable significance as the process of computerization is soon to be intensified. A glimpse of the possible impact may be discerned from an analysis of foreign banks, in India. According to a unionist in Citibank,

> In 1970, out of a total workforce of 200, there were only ten women. Now, in 1992, 70 per cent of the workforce are women. This includes programmers as well as women officers. Management feels women are better on computers as they have routine clerical ambitions. Women really do more work and their frustration level is higher.

(Presumably, he means their endurance is higher.) A union official in Banque Nationale de Paris confirms this:

> Our managements' latest policy seems to be to recruit young girls and train them on computers. In our latest

recruitment in January and April 1992, ten new employees were recruited.

All ten were girls. Now we have women on all the customer counters. They are eager to learn, more sincere, obedient, less union-minded and also provide better customer service.

Table : Women employees in Indian nationalized banks, 1985 and 1990 (%)

Bank	Officers		Clerks	
	1985	1990	1985	1990
Allahabad Bank	3.5	3.66	9.7	11.03
Andhra Bank	9.1	9.54	19.2	21.88
Bank of Baroda	5.1	7.93	17.8	18.12
Bank of India	5.2	5.06	20.7	20.60
Bank of Maharashtra	6.3	6.75	29.9	31.62
Canara Bank	3.7	4.12	25.5	27.57
Central Bank of India	3.9	4.63	17.7	20.10
Corporation Bank	6.2	6.78	32.2	33.47
Dena Bank	1.8	2.02	17.9	18.9
Indian Bank	5.6	5.95	24.1	21.34
Indian Overseas Bank	5.9	5.56	17.9	18.43
New Bank of India	4.5	4.61	17.8	17.59
Oriental Bank of India	8.1	7.96	17.4	15.98
Punjab and Sind Bank	2.8	2.69	8.1	9.58
Punjab National Bank	4.1	4.45	16.0	16.54
Syndicate Bank	8.2	8.15	26.6	27.49
ICO Bank	4.1	3.00	11.6	11 90
Union Bank of India	5.9	6.27	18.8	22.15
United Bank of India	0.6	0.85	5.9	8.20
Vijaya Bank	11.8	12.23	20.3	21.22
State Bank of India	1.7	2.33	12.8	15.44
State Bank of Bikaner and Jaipur	1.6	1.89	7.8	7.66
State Bank of Hyderabad	3.1	3.88	13.7	16.78
State Bank of Indore	1.1	1.29	10.7	11.77
State Bank of Mysore	3.9	3.68	22.7	25.96
State Bank of Patiala	2.1	2.88	16.7	17.79
State Bank of Saurashtra	0.8	1.16	8.6	9.91
State Bank of Travancore	7.5	9.00	35.4	35.99
Total	3.9	4.9	17.3	18.77

Source: Documentation at the National Institute of Bank Management, Pune

A militant unionist at the Grindlays bank said that, in Bombay, the proportion of women employees had increased from 5 per cent in 1970 to about 50 per cent in 1992. Figures from Grindlays management showed that about 35 per cent of their workforce, nation-wide, were women. This is a higher proportion than in most of their nationalized counterparts (see Table). According to a union official at Grindlays: Earlier, the policy of multinational banks was not to recruit women employees. But over the last few years, they have changed. Management realised that women are more submissive, overworked, and have less time for union work. Besides, because of general socio-economic development, women do much better, especially in cities like Bombay.

The points which bank managements generally present in women's favour include:

- women employees are sincere and diligent and meticulously complete their work;
- they are time-conscious;
- they do not shirk responsibilities;
- they perform all types of jobs well;
- they are less involved in union activities;
- they are less often involved in frauds and corruption.

(Mankidy, 1986a)

An active woman unionist in the Hong Kong Bank confirmed the high recruitment rate of women, but explained it as due to the fact that women are better qualified and tend to put in greater effort. The better-qualified women apply for bank jobs, while similarly qualified men would tend to go in for jobs, such as engineering and computers, which employees regard as more challenging and which have better prospects in terms of job satisfaction and pay.

Another reason which was suggested is that women resign sooner than men. Of the twenty-seven girls recruited in the 1991 batch, three had left within the first year. The pay levels of new recruits are considerably less than for a senior person, so it is less expensive for the management to have a fresh supply of new recruits. The Hong Kong bank has about 500 employees in the head office, of whom more than 350 are women, including more than half of the officers.. However it is not clear whether this source of employment will persist. The RBI's National Clearing Cell in Madras has already extended its 'instant credit' facilities to Saturdays.6 Because of the increasing involvement with foreign share markets and banks and the time difference between countries, it may not be too long before the hours of these and other facilities are extended to Sundays and night shifts. This would have a significant impact on the recruitment, employment and promotion of women.

In Canada, where computerization has reached fairly advanced levels, banking jobs are coming to be more frequently occupied by men (Tremblay, 1991). Amin Rajan, in his study of the finance sector at an international level (1990) observes that, 'In the short term technology has created job opportunities for women. In the longer term, however, this process is likely to disadvantage women.'

THE QUALITY OF WOMEN'S WORK

The banking and insurance sectors today offer more prospects for jobs for women - both qualitatively and quantitatively. However there are some common problems faced by women managers, officers and clerical groups in banking and insurance, in the course of their careers. These include the burden of the dual role, sexual harassment in the workplace, the refusal of men to accept women as colleagues or seniors, the need to work twice as well as men to gain recognition, and the lack of solidarity among women.

According to a study by Kamala Srinivasan (1991) 50 per cent of women complained that extra work is always shunted to women. They also complained about sexual harassment from colleagues, managers, or customers. Women also felt dissatisfied that they were not sent out for training. Some obstacles arise from women's specific difficulties in demanding promotion - because promotions are linked with transfers; or they have difficulties in working late; or because women shy away from responsibility, having a low opinion of their own abilities and a negative attitude to accepting recognition (Mankidy, 1986a).

Some women employees feel that these constraints are intensified by being forced to adopt the behaviour of the 'successful manager or officer' which has been established by men. They argue that women could find their own strategies which would achieve the same result (Mankidy, 1988).

One way of improving prospects for women could be to restructure the work, for example with flexible working hours, part-time job assignments, split location positions performed partly at home, and job-sharing (Mankidy, 1988). Some of these suggestions have already been tried out elsewhere, for example in Japan, where the results for women have not been entirely positive. None the less, examination of this experience could be a basis for working out alternatives which do not disadvantage women (International Labour Office, 1989).

Women's Needs and Aspirations with Regard to Employment and Training

Technological change usually involves changes in job content, making many traditional skills obsolete and creating a demand for new types of skills. Training and retraining ensure not only that the enterprise obtains the optimal benefits from new technologies, it is also an effective way of protecting the employment of workers affected by technological change and other structural changes.

Workers, and the trade union movement, are divided about training. Some unions, such as the BNP (Banque Nationale de Paris) union, seem to have relinquished not only any initiative, but also responsibility for both the employees who are being forced to quit and those who are allowed to stay. Despite the 1986 agreement giving the union a right to participate in determining and formulating the training, there has been no move from the office-bearers of the union, all men, to take the initiative.

One union officer said that they 'had not realised the importance of this clause at the time. And now it is too late.' Women employees at the BNP were almost desperate to be given retraining. They were too young - about 39 to 42 years of age - to retire. They saw no other way to retain their employment. They were also keen to learn new skills.

The union in Citibank, on the other hand, participated actively in the computerization process as well as the training process. But even in Citibank there seems to be no long-term view as to the type of jobs and skills which will be required in the future. The younger recruits have been given a one-week training course in computer languages, which they did not use in the year following the course.

They were then given a very brief, functional on-the-job type course. As one senior woman employee now working in the Bill Discounting department says: 'We were given a half-day "familiarity with the word-processor" course, and printed sheets telling us what to press for which function.'

The Citibank women employees felt they knew too little, apart from their own little work area, and they wanted to know more so that they would not be adversely affected when it came to promotions. The attitude of women at the Hong Kong bank was similar.

The ANZ Grindlays Bank Employees' Union had a very different perspective, 'We have completely opposed computerisation. There are no skills involved in operating computers. It only deadens your mind. We cannot participate in such a process. We believe in struggle.' In the Indian banks, the younger women and those between 31) and 45 years old seemed keen on their jobs as careers, whereas many in the 30-45 age group had many more responsibilities at home - although some of the latter felt that learning about computers at work would also help them to assist their children in their studies, since computers have been introduced in many schools. Many women felt that learning to use computers, and being in the EDP department, would protect them against transfers to remote areas, as EDP departments are located only in the metropolitan cities.

Most of the older women, especially those above 50, felt they would not be able to cope with any new retraining. They would undertake it if it was necessary for the job. However, a small minority of women above 50 years of age also seemed keen to take up a new challenge. As one woman put it,

As women, we are used to challenges, at home, at work, in combining the two roles, and in relationships with in-laws, neighbours, community, children, colleagues, and bosses. As we grow older, these challenges become routine matters. When you no longer have in-laws, when children are well settled elsewhere, when neighbourhood relationships are settled and repetitive, what do we do? We are used to challenges. New skills are merely one such challenge. Why not take it up?

Another woman disagreed, but from a very different point of view.

I'm not sure that computer skills are any skill at all. What are we doing? The generalised use of computers is only a means of deskilling and flattening us all. Very soon using computers will be like using our pencils. Then all of us will be declared unskilled and redundant again. We need to do something else.

In the Banque Nationale de Paris, thirty-seven people had to leave under the Voluntary Retirement Scheme, including ten women. At the same time they recruited ten young women to work on the computers at the customer counter. A 39 year old woman who was forced to take the VRS explains the strategy thus:

> *For over two years, we were given very little work and we were shunted about from one department to another, one floor to another. We were treated like badli (casual) workers and were made to feel redundant and easily disposable. We pleaded to the management that we be given training on the computers. But they declined. We have a seniority of over twenty years, our pay levels are quite high, thanks to our earlier struggles. We are very confident and know our management inside out. Why should they want us any more?*

Another woman activist working in the BNP says, they would have to spend money giving us training. Now they've killed so many birds with one stone. One, the new girls are already trained. Two, the girls start at a much lower rate, about half our wage levels. Three, they are new, more enthusiastic to please the management. Four, the management has succeeded in creating an atmosphere of terror and uncertainty. These young girls are bound to be affected by this atmosphere and work with heads bent. Five, they have no experience with this management and are not affected by the union movement. The management has succeeded in throwing out all the active members of the union. Those active workers that remain are likely to be promoted to the management category.

On the issue of computerization and training, there seems to be fairly divergent views among bank managements too. By and large, the nationalized Indian banks seem to feel that 'it is better to retrain a banker in computer skills than train a computer specialist in banking'. To this end, the Indian Banks' Association has developed training packages for various types of personnel. The National Institute of Bank Management has a very wide range of training programmes for top management, and every bank has its own programmes for their staff. The foreign banks again seem to operate differently. In contrast to the BNP management, the Grindlays bank has not introduced an early retirement scheme, and has retrained its existing personnel. However according to the Personnel Department at the ANZ Grindlays, it is likely that the bank will insist that new recruits have some knowledge of computers.

One woman employee who had attended a training course arranged by the management at a professional computer training institute, said, The whole management approach to training is like their approach to our work - extraction. In both it is the superiors or the experts laying the ground rules, without any input or participation expected from us. Participation is only a hindrance, a point of delay, precious time wasted. I had a feeling of being steam-rollered rather than of having learnt something.

Another suggested: Workshops should be organized in such a way that women are collectively given the space to handle PCs, and with manuals explaining what needs to be done. One can have experts in at crucial times like an introductory familiarizing talk, and when we feel we need someone to guide us, but not experts breathing down our necks like supervisors on an assembly line.

In fact, the women felt that such training sessions would also achieve a great deal from the point of view of the management. The crux of the problems created by technological changes appears to be that the entire strategy is still technology-centred. Behind the technology-centred approach is a mechanized world-view in which computers, a machine carrying out the brain work of the human, are superior to people. In one of the training sessions we were told how computers may be used to level the hierarchies and authorities that exist in the workplace. But in practice a new hierarchy has been created, alongside the earlier one. You can do only this, and can have access to only this, while the authorities have a greater range of activities and access to greater areas of information.

Despite their criticism of the training programmes organized by the management, the women employees are extremely keen on learning new things and new skills. In fact, the new generation of bank and insurance employees, including women, are very serious about their work and career-conscious. Reports of workshops with women clerks, officers and managers have indicated both the problems women face and their commitment to face these challenges for a better career. A senior unionist who has been active in the bank unions notes a shift,

The attitude of the employees is changing. They no longer look at the unions as an expression of their aspirations, but as an agency which will deliver the goods. They are with the union because they mistrust the management. Their real interest however is their career.

The unions too have begun to organize workshops for women employees. These workshops discuss the problems women employees face in their multiple roles, how women deal with these, and what their experiences are. Similar workshops are organized by the National Institute of Bank Management (NIBM), for women managers. Women clerical staff, officers and managers have reacted to these positively. One woman working in the EDP Department at the insurance corporation observes'

We feel the thirst for more knowledge and better career prospects. Stagnation somehow scares us. Training programmes and institutions which acknowledge this, and our dilemmas and situation, are well received. But there are fewer of those than we need. In some of the courses in the National Institute of Bank Management, women managers are encouraged to talk about their ideas and suggestions as well as their experiences as women in banking. Many other unions and management training institutes are organizing similar courses. Women feel that this needs to be done more systematically and more often, so that a greater range of issues and diverse sections of women employees might be covered.

WOMEN EMPLOYEES ORGANIZING

The interests of women employees have been expressed in different ways. In the early 1980s the Women's Wing of the All India Conference of Bank Officers' Organizations (AICOBOO), open to women officers only, was formed. However the issues that concern them relate to all women employees. According to one of the spokeswomen of the Women's Wing, There is a pressing need for women to form strong pressure groups to see that the right to education and employment do not remain merely on paper. The problems of working women can be dealt with more effectively through collective action.

The discrimination experienced by women working in banks is mainly in terms of the lack of infrastructural facilities, the transfer policy, and assumptions that women would not be interested in training or in promotions. The Women's Wing of the AICOBOO has been taking up these issues systematically. One outcome of their work has been the charter of demands they submitted to their union confederation. These included:

- Infrastructural facilities such as crèches and day care centres.
- Provision of hostels for working women, accommodation for divorced, separated and widowed women with children.

- Special leave with a lien on service, for up to say five years, to meet certain contingencies specific to women, extending this facility to men also whenever required.
- Provision for a woman with a child less than three years old to work for fewer hours and receive proportionate pay.
- Family pension and voluntary retirement for men and women after twenty years of service.
- Provision for flexi-hours and part-time employment in suitable cases.
- Although maternity leave (12 weeks in all) is regarded as fairly satisfactory, additional provisions required are medical benefits, hospitalization, leave for the purpose of child care, paternity leave for at least ten days, further leave also for those who have to look after an infant in special circumstances.
- Discrimination exists in our laws with regard to women . . . especially with regard to taxation, which needs to be looked into. (Mankidy, 1989)

The specific demands put forward by the Women's Wing include a uniform transfer policy in all banks for women officers, and a cell to deal with women's issues in every bank's personnel department. They are currently trying to formulate demands relating to training programmes and time off for women to do union work.

Similarly the All India Bank Employees Association (AIBEA) has initiated a women's wing of the union to take up issues specially affecting women. The Reserve Bank of India has a Women's Forum for the same purpose. The unions in the LIC have begun to organize women-only meetings and workshops.

The Insurance Employees Association decided in 1991 to organize women employees more effectively, as the number of women employees was increasing day by day, with over 75 per cent of the new recruits being women. The association has demanded crèche facilities, special leave and better working conditions for women, and the removal of hidden discrimination.

The demands put forward by the Punjab National Bank Employees' Union include:

- Inter-region transfers of women on a priority basis.
- Arranging pre-promotion training programmes women who want to take tests relating to promotions.
- Displacement on promotion to be avoided.
- Protection for pregnant women who work on computers.
- Women should be given temporary transfers on request during pregnancy, etc.

The unions and the management have begun to acknowledge the separate needs of women employees and the specificity of the issues they face. Yet women employees' concerns and aspirations have not been adequately addressed by either. The training programmes organized by management do not include the vast majority of women employees. A 1986 study by the IBA showed that only 20 per cent of staff received some training in any one year (Madhukar, 1986). Officers of the NIBM reported that the situation had not changed since then.

The sessions organized by the unions are at a mass level and do not allow for the much-needed interaction and sharing of experiences. These too are organized fairly erratically. One senior woman employee notes,

Both types of programmes - union and management- seem one-sided rather than multidimensional. In the union workshops and meetings, we are addressed as union members; in the management training programmes we are bank employees. But all of us are much more than that. We are employees, we are women, we are home-makers, we are thinking and feeling human beings, we are ambitious and much more. Training programmes need to keep this perspective in mind. Women feel the need for different types of inputs too.

In the wake of liberalization and globalization and the changes in Indian banking, they want to know what is happening in the banking and finance sectors in other countries in terms of women's employment and organizing, what the experiences of women in those countries have been and what strategies they have used.

Many women employees, including women officers, also feel that they would like to know and interact with women in other sectors too. As a young insurance officer said, 'What is happening to women nationally is of concern to us and is going to affect us.'

Such interconnections between the women's wings of the banking and insurance unions and the women's movement in the country and outside have begun to be explored recently, and a few women employees at all levels have begun participating in women's movement conferences.

However, there is as yet no reciprocal interest from the women's movement in the concerns of employees in banking and finance. Developments in this area would also strengthen the links between the various forums and organizations that represent the interests of women bank and insurance employees.

This would also necessarily include a wider forum for national and international solidarity for the exchange of information, strategies and forms of organization.

CONCLUSION

The last decade has seen a systematic rise in the employment of women in the banking and finance sector. The result of a multiplicity of factors, including: profound social changes taking place in India regarding women's education and employment; the changing policies of management, especially after the nationalization and reorganization of the LIC and of major banks; the policies of the Indian government; international changes in banking and finance and, not least, the technological changes being effected in the industry. Computerization has had positive and negative implications for the workforce. It has affected employment levels and workloads and brought increasing pressure for flexibility.

It has changed the content of work, and brought reduced job security and a shift towards more non-bargainable employees, which affects the nature and stability of the union. There have been changes in grading and pay, and in the means by which the workforce and information are controlled. The autonomy of employees and their conditions of work, and health and safety, have been affected also.

These all have a specific impact on women employees, who are being recruited in large numbers in the banking and finance sector, mainly in the clerical category. Women employees are increasingly looking at their work in terms of career prospects and are keen on learning new skills and advancing in their careers, despite severe limitations. They are organizing themselves into unions and separate women's caucuses within and outside unions.

While the rate of recruitment has slackened in India since the mid-1980s, there has not yet been a reversal, as has happened in some western countries. Women employees feel the need to broaden their vision by relating to each other and sharing information about national and international trends.

This is an important basis for both interaction with the national women's movement and for international solidarity and sharing of experiences and working on future strategies.

This is especially relevant in the context of the introduction and extension of new technology in workplaces, as new technology has made the globe a much smaller place in terms of the spread of technologies and management strategies.

Women employees need a constant process of discussion and strategy formulation if they are not merely to respond to these changes, but to become more proactive, to make suggestions and changes to suit their short and long-term interests.

4

Raising Industrial Finance from Banks

When a company is growing rapidly, for example when contemplating investment in capital equipment or an acquisition, its current financial resources may be inadequate. Few growing companies are able to finance their expansion plans from cash flow alone. They will therefore need to consider raising finance from other external sources. In addition, managers who are looking to buy-in to a business ("management buy-in" or "MBI") or buy-out (management buy-out" or "MBO") a business from its owners, may not have the resources to acquire the company. They will need to raise finance to achieve their objectives. There are a number of potential sources of finance to meet the needs of a growing business or to finance an MBI or MBO:

- Existing shareholders and directors funds
- Family and friends
- Business angels
- Clearing banks (overdrafts, short or medium term loans)
- Factoring and invoice discounting
- Hire purchase and leasing
- Merchant banks (medium to longer term loans)
- Venture capital

A key consideration in choosing the source of new business finance is to strike a balance between equity and debt to ensure the funding structure suits the business. The main differences between borrowed money (debt) and equity are that bankers request interest payments and capital repayments, and the borrowed money is usually secured on business assets or the personal assets of shareholders and/or directors. A bank also has the power to place a business into administration or bankruptcy if it defaults on debt interest or repayments or its prospects decline. In contrast, equity investors take the risk of failure like other shareholders, whilst they will benefit through participation in increasing levels of profits and on the eventual sale of their stake. However in most circumstances venture capitalists will also require more complex investments (such as preference shares or loan stock) in additional to their equity stake.

The overall objective in raising finance for a company is to avoid exposing the business to excessive high borrowings, but without unnecessarily diluting the share capital. This will ensure that the financial risk of the company is kept at an optimal level.

Business Plan

Once a need to raise finance has been identified it is then necessary to prepare a business plan. If management intend to turn around a business or start a new phase of growth, a business plan is an important tool to articulate their ideas while convincing investors and other people to support it. The business plan should be updated regularly to assist in forward planning. There are many potential contents of a business plan. The European Venture Capital Association suggest the following:

- Profiles of company founders directors and other key managers;
- Statistics relating to sales and markets;
- Names of potential customers and anticipated demand;
- Names of, information about and assessment of competitors;
- Financial information required to support specific projects (for example, major capital investment or new product development);

- Research and development information;
- Production process and sources of supply;
- Information on requirements for factory and plant;
- Magazine and newspaper articles about the business and industry;
- Regulations and laws that could affect the business product and process protection (patents, copyrights, trademarks).

The challenge for management in preparing a business plan is to communicate their ideas clearly and succinctly. The very process of researching and writing the business plan should help clarify ideas and identify gaps in management information about their business, competitors and the market.

TYPES OF FINANCE-INTRODUCTION

A brief description of the key features of the main sources of business finance is provided below.

Venture Capital

Venture capital is a general term to describe a range of ordinary and preference shares where the investing institution acquires a share in the business. Venture capital is intended for higher risks such as start up situations and development capital for more mature investments. Replacement capital brings in an institution in place of one of the original shareholders of a business who wishes to realise their personal equity before the other shareholders.

There are over 100 different venture capital funds in the UK and some have geographical or industry preferences. There are also certain large industrial companies which have funds available to invest in growing businesses and this 'corporate venturing' is an additional source of equity finance.

Grants and Soft Loans

Government, local authorities, local development agencies and the European Union are the major sources of grants and soft loans. Grants are normally made to facilitate the purchase of assets and either the generation of jobs or the training of employees. Soft loans are normally subsidised by a third party so that the terms of interest and security levels are less than the market rate.

There are over 350 initiatives from the Department of Trade and Industry alone so it is a matter of identifying which sources will be appropriate in each case.

Invoice Discounting and Invoice Factoring

Finance can be raised against debts due from customers via invoice discounting or invoice factoring, thus improving cash flow. Debtors are used as the prime security for the lender and the borrower may obtain up to about 80 per cent of approved debts. In addition, a number of these sources of finance will now lend against stock and other assets and may be more suitable then bank lending. Invoice discounting is normally confidential (the customer is not aware that their payments are essentially insured) whereas factoring extends the simple discounting principle by also dealing with the administration of the sales ledger and debtor collection.

Hire Purchase and Leasing

Hire purchase agreements and leasing provide finance for the acquisition of specific assets such as cars, equipment and machinery involving a deposit and repayments over, typically, three to ten years. Technically, ownership of the asset remains with the lessor whereas title to the goods is eventually transferred to the hirer in a hire purchase agreement.

Loans

Medium term loans (up to seven years) and long term loans (including commercial mortgages) are provided for specific purposes such as acquiring an asset, business or shares. The loan is normally secured on the asset or assets and the interest rate may be variable or fixed. The Small Firms Loan Guarantee Scheme can provide up to £250,000 of borrowing supported by a government guarantee where all other sources of finance have been exhausted.

Mezzanine Debt

This is a loan finance where there is little or no security left after the senior debt has been secured. To reflect the higher risk of mezzanine funds, the lender will charge a rate of interest of perhaps four to eight per cent over bank base rate, may take an option to acquire some equity and may require repayment over a shorter term.

Bank Overdraft

An overdraft is an agreed sum by which a customer can overdraw their current account. It is normally secured on current assets, repayable on demand and used for short term working capital fluctuations. The interest cost is normally variable and linked to bank base rate.

Completing the Finance-raising

Raising finance is often a complex process. Business management need to assess several alternatives and then negotiate terms which are acceptable to the finance provider. The main negotiating points are often as follows:

- Whether equity investors take a seat on the board
- Votes ascribed to equity investors
- Level of warranties and indemnities provided by the directors
- Financier's fees and costs
- Who bears costs of due diligence.

During the finance-raising process, accountants are often called to review the financial aspects of the plan. Their report may be formal or informal, an overview or an extensive review of the company's management information system, forecasting methods and their accuracy, review of latest management accounts including working capital, pension funding and employee contracts etc. This due diligence process is used to highlight any fundamental problems that may exist.

CAPITAL MARKET AND THE TRADE CYCLE

Our analysis of the nature of working capital, and of the demand for short-term funds, brought us to a number of conclusions. The original purpose of our investigation was to make it easier for us to make up our minds about the controversy "business credit versus stock exchange credit." We shall defer the application of our conclusions to this problem until the next chapter. For the present we shall deal with certain by-products of our analysis. These by-products are, in my opinion, relevant to several problems, but especially to the theory of the money market and of the trade cycle.

The supply of money capital on the money market is drawn from a number of different sources. One of There are them is transfer credit which may take various forms ere and may originate in various ways: it may come from fer credit, the short-term postponement of consumption, from long-term savings which are waiting for a suitable investment, from long-term savings whose owners are anxious to keep them in a form such that they can be withdrawn at any moment, from industrial capital which has been withdrawn from one line of production and is awaiting investment in another, from corporation profits which have not yet been distributed as dividends, from depreciation allowances which have not yet been reinvested, from the savings which became the proceeds of notations of bonds or shares awaiting gradual investment, &c. On the other side —created the banks provide a considerable amount of credit,— credit, that is purchasing power which has been created out of nothing, which means that nobody has given up the use of that buying power which is accruing to the borrower.

This type of credit is furnished in just the same forms as transfer credit, through discounting bills, call loans, various forms of advances, overdrafts, security purchases and so on. There is a third source of credit which is intermediate between these two sources, and which we discussed in the last —and credit chapter. This is credit which is granted out of liquid cash balanced surplus casn reserves, either with or without the agency which has the of the banks. So far as concerns the character of this the first but type of credit, its place in the monetary circulation the effects of and inflationary effects, it could be counted as the second *m* type "circulation credit" or created credit, but it has the peculiarity of bearing a deceptive resemblance to transfer credit, with the result not only that it is almost impossible to distinguish in practice but also that it has been fused together with short-term transfer credit in monetary theory.

It is this type of credit which gives rise to the much discussed seasonal easing and tightening of the money market, and has given the latter the stamp of being the unstable part of the credit market. George Halm, in his discussion of the problem of interest rates on the money market and the capital market, did not concern himself with created credit or with credit granted out of surplus cash balances, and, as he himself admits, this deprived him of the possibility of explaining "the important but difficult problems connected with the seasonal movement of interest rates on the money market." What it also did, and this he failed to see, was to cause him to overlook the influences exerted by the money market on the course of the trade cycle; and all that he perceived therefore were the repercussions of the trade cycle on the money market.

The seasonal and monthly movements on the money market are directly attributable to the practice of Credit from surplus cash lending surplus cash balances, i.e., to the utilization balances may of liquid funds. Transfer credit may in general be ^thl^and looked upon as a stable element in the supply of money seasonal capital. Credit which is newly created by the banks for accommodating commercial borrowers may be the money regarded for the most part as merely supplementing the loans made out of surplus cash balances: it will usually come into play either at periods when these balances are not available (due to seasonal requirements, end-of-the-month and quarterly payments, &c.) or when they have already been exhausted (due to the cyclical movement).

Thus the unstable factor on the money market, both on the supply side and on the demand side, is the surplus funds of firms. At those times of the year when commodity stocks are low, the cash balances of firms in a strong capital position flow onto the money market. Since at these times the demand for working capital on the part of firms in a weaker capital position is low, there is no immediate outlet for the increased supply of short-term credit. For reasons that have been explained above, the elasticity of demand for short-term credit, unlike that The elasticity for long-term credit, is small, and interest rates on short-term the money market consequently fall sharply. Since funds is there is practically no really "temporary" outlet for money capital that is only available for a short time, it is clear that there are no "short-term investments" available for all the cash balances that are offered on the loan market.

One outlet for the large supply would be in the other interconnected credit market, viz., the capital market, the market for long-term credit. The method of con-verting "short money'-into "long money" which involves least risk for the person wishing to make the transfer, is as a rule provided by the security market. One might suppose that the low call rate would induce bears to "cover" their short sales, and that it would induce bulls to buy for the rise. Professional speculators are, however, more cautious than this. They know that the lowering of the call rate is only seasonal, and that this seasonal movement is a fact of common The monthly knowledge. It is therefore easy to see why the seasonal and seasonal oscil ations of fluctuations m interest rates on the money market do market rates not cause seasonal fluctuations in security prices. For, are rot taken "if a seasonal variation in stock prices did exist, secuifties6 general knowledge of its existence would put an end markets. to it." Thus the conversion of the seasonal supply of short-term money into investment money through the stock exchange loans will not take place on a large scale before the boom is under way. And the direct utilization of seasonal surpluses of cash for making temporary investments in securities is not attractive before the boom comes, owing to the cost of buying and selling. For these reasons the capital market, where the elasticity of demand for money capital is high, will not reflect (and absorb), the fluctuations in interest rates on the money market.

If the entrepreneur were unable to find a borrower for his short-term surpluses of cash, and therefore had to resign himself to keeping the funds in his till or on his banking account, there would be no withdrawal of funds from the money market and no increased demand for short-money at certain periods when inventories are high, when the harvest is being moved and so on. If, however, some event or change in psychology in conjunction with the low interest rates on the money market induce entrepreneurs to borrow some more short-term funds, the next date when heavy payments become due or the next time when stocks are being moved, will cause a tightening of the money market. Because the tendency towards tightness at these dates is eased by the banks through the creation Bank loans of additional credits, entrepreneurs do not feel any tightness of anxiety about providing for these heavy payments, the money market on and this has led to the lending and borrowing of critical "liquid" funds on the money market. We might also say then that it is the creation of credit by the banks which is at the root of the fluctuations, because if the entrepreneurs were not confident of obtaining help from the banks in case of need, they would not lend their cash balances to the money market for fear of becoming illiquid.

Thus, while temporary surpluses of cash are the element in the supply which is the direct source of the monthly and seasonal fluctuations in interest rates on the money market, a necessary condition of these movements is the existing banking system. The apparent effect of the creation of credit by the banks is admittedly to mitigate the fluctuations on the money —they mitimarket, because bank credit fills the gap when the fluctuations entrepreneurs withdraw their funds. Without the of the rates,— elasticity of bank credit, which is regarded as being so beneficial in this case, the fluctuations would at first be wider: in fact the tightness of the money market at the critical payments dates would become really "critical." But bad experiences would soon lead entrepreneurs, for the sake of assuring their own liquidity, to refrain from lending out their temporary —but thereby surpluses of cash, and so the direct cause of fluctuations infrom the on the money market would disappear. It is apparent, temporary therefore, that the invisible effect of the elasticity of balances bank credit is exactly the opposite of the visible effect: which cause the mitigating the fluctuations and easing the difficulties fluctuations. arising out of them means enabling the fluctuations or their causes to arise.

The classification of credits granted, out of surplus cash balances as a third type of credit, intermediate between transfer credit on the one side and credit created by the banks on the other, has a number of advantages. Lending out of temporary surpluses of cash balances is in principle possible without the agency of the banks. As most people have become accustomed to think of credit creation as being due solely to the banks, credit granted out of surplus cash balances is treated as transfer credit, despite the fact that nobody refrains from buying, as this purchasing power is being transferred, and that this credit has just the same iDnationary effects as credit created by the banks. The fact that there can be inflationary credits which are not bank credit at all, may have an important bearing on the development of the theory of credit.

A not inconsiderable number of students of the theory of banking, especially those who are connected with practical banking, still persist in arguing that the banks have no power to "create" inflationary credit, and deny even more emphatically that this bank credit has the place in the complex of causes of the trade cycle which is assigned to it in monetary theories of the trade cycle. Perhaps this opposition (to what is only a causal explanation but is often taken as an accusation of personal guilt) will decrease once it is realized that credit which is not granted by the banks at all may also have inflationary effects.

The way in which surpluses of circulating capital can be interchanged between firms, even without the agency of the banks, has been described already in the previous chapter. No long argument is needed to prove that the possibilities of transferring these temporary surpluses of cash between firms are multiplied by the operations of banks acting as intermediaries. What is meant here is not the fact that the substitution of time deposits for circulating media may create increased lending facilities (although this works in the same direction), but the circumstance that the concentration of the supply of temporary surpluses of funds allows them to be utilized more fully. This applies particularly to those countries where the use of cheques is still so undeveloped that the possibilities of credit creation by the commercial banks are very small. The "inflationary" interchange of cash balances between firms remains, from the point of view of the banks, apparently a purely transfer operation, and can, of course, not be treated as the creation of new money.

It is not possible in practice to identify a loan Neither the granted by a bank according to its origin. The Tank can borrower can never know the source of the purchasing know power which he has been lent, and neither can the loan bank. It was originally believed that a bank could at Activates' least distinguish savings deposits from current or creates accounts, and could accordingly lend the funds 8 obtained by the former (time deposits) as transfer credit, and might be conscious of creating new credit on the basis of the funds obtained by the latter (demand deposits). Quite apart from the fact that at circulating media. The credits which are not newlycreated by the banks, but only transferred through them, are not however all "pure" transfer-credit: this term properly applies only to funds deriving from new savings or newly disinvested capital, whereas the deposits of type represent what we have called temporary surplus cash balances. Thus, although the credits granted from these deposit funds are not created by the banks, but only transferred by them, they are nevertheless inflationary in their effect.

The position may be summarized by the following classification: A monetary system which was intended to avoid any inflationary or deflationary move would have to ward off anything which involved any change in the supply of money—including demand deposits—or any diminution in the demand to hold money on the part of individuals and firms. The already existing volume of credit outstanding, which can no longer exert any kinetic effect on interest rates, would have to be maintained. (This view was put into practice almost a hundred years ago in Peel's Bank Act with its fixed balances, brings us to the conclusion that there are funds which do not differ in the least outwardly from credit deriving from the transfer of already existing purchasing power, but which nevertheless, if they are put to some "productive use," exert the same effect as credit newly created by the banks. Whether this additional supply of credit is utilized through the capital market or through the money market, whether the lenders follow strict rules about liquidity or not, whether they provide loans for stock exchange speculation or for the working capital of industry, a movement away from equilibrium in the economic system is made possible. Even the introduction of "certificates of origin" for deposits—which an ingenious But, alas, we believer in control might suggest—would not enable Identify the the banks to keep track of the true nature of their nature of deposits. deposits.

It may seem a little surprising if we attempt to connect the same phenomena as were invoked in explanation of monthly and seasonal fluctuations on The monthly the money market with the theory of *cyclical* fluctua-an seasonal tions. Nevertheless I think that it is not unreason-market fluctuations able to assume some such connexion. I am tar trom piay believing that it is possible to discover the "germ of " the trade cycle" in this phenomenon, but I do think trade cycle, that it is possible to show that credit granted out of surplus cash balances is closely connected with the beginning of the upswing.

The "double utilization" of money capital which is made possible by lending from surplus cash balances, and the extension of roundabout methods of production to which such lending gives rise, would be doomed to a very short existence in the absence of other support: it could not survive the next date when heavy payments became due. What is a surplus balance at certain times is not at all "surplus" at other times, and if they have been put to some "productive use" in the meantime they are now *simultaneously* indispensable to both the lender and the borrower, or some third person to whom the funds may have passed. Whoever is forced to dispense with them has to go out of production, because he is no longer able to obtain the means of production. His exit from production paves the way towards re-establishing a state of equilibrium in the production structure.

Disturbances of this kind are, however, still not *cyclical* movements. The movement away from the (theoretical) equilibrium in the upward direction lasts, as experience shows, for several years, and the movement back from the crisis through the depression to something near a new (theoretical) equilibrium again lasts several years.

The movement which has just been described lasted no longer than a season—or even a month—because the tendency towards an extension of production was brought to a swift end by the advent of the next payments date. But what happens if the payments at this date are facilitated, i.e., if the economic system is spared "unnecessary" difficulties, by short-term lending from the banks?

The extra heavy demand for money lasts only a short time, and then the harmless credits, having performed their task, will flow back to the banks. There has been fairly general agreement in financial circles, and among students of banking policy, that the economic system ought to be helped over these payments dates, and no small part of the efforts towards working out a scientific monetary policy in the last one hundred and fifty years has been directed towards overcoming or easing the periodic stringency at certain dates when heavy payments fall due. Even the worst enemies of inflationism favoured such a policy.

When the funds, which were temporarily "superfluous" and were therefore invested, are needed at the payments dates, the utilization of funds "twice over" is bound to be frustrated. If, however, new credit is created by the banks so as to help the economic system over the critical days, then the use of funds twice over in production can be continued. All that is necessary to enable the "upward" movement of the economic system towards disproportionality in production to continue for a longer period of time, is for the banking system to give assistance at certain times of strain.

The payments dates might to a certain —which help extent be taken as indicators of the liquidity of the system or as a test of the adequate adjustment of tests on the capital supply and production structure. This test loses its meaning of course if bank credit provides the producers for the duration of the "inspection" with the necessary amounts of money capital.

Since the maintenance of the expanded volume of The money production requires not merely the continued use of industrial the amount of credit once furnished, but thel repeated expansion, x which in turn administration of further doses (see the analysis given makes in Chapter XI), the continuation of the upswing will Unison require increasing loans from surplus cash balances the money and will involve increasing stringency at the payments dates and increasing intervention from the side of bank credit to overcome it. It is clear, therefore, that the fluctuations in interest rates on the money market will soon become more marked than they had been previously. What Halm took to be the mere *influence* of the trade cycle on the money market is, as I see it, the *reaction* of the cycle on the money market, after the latter has furnished the "motive power" to the cyclical movement. The further the use of money market credit has progressed or the more intensively credit is being used in production, the heavier and more urgent will be the demand for credit on the money market at the critical payments dates. Thus Halm is right in saying that "The real shortage of capital at the top of the boom is a shortage of shortterm capital disposition."

The mere intervention of bank lending at end-ofthe-month, quarterly, and other payments dates will of course not be sufficient to develop the upswing into a full-fledged boom. At a certain stage of the upswing it will be necessary for there to be a more vigorous and continuous expansion of bank credit in addition The start of to the loans from surplus cash balances and the occacan beSWmg sional intervention of the banks at the payments dates. fina teed But lending out of surplus cash balances is sufficient through loans surplus to give the initial motive power for business recovery. balances seems to me a not unimportant fact that the startwithout bank.. credit ing point of the upswing is to be found not in an expansion. expansion of credit newly "produced" by the banks but in a "natural growth" of credit.

A theory of the trade cycle which does not explain the continual recurrence of cycles as well as the course of the individual cycle cannot be entirely satisfactory. If we ascribe a role in trade-cycle causation to loans and disbursements out of surplus cash balances we must also try to analyse their role in causing the cycle to recur. The turning point in the cycle comes, as we know, not because there is an actual contraction of credit at that point, but when merely a brake is placed on the further expansion of credit. The volume of circulation media which was augmented by the expansion of bank credit need not fall back, in the depression, to the previous level; equilibrium might be established just as well at the higher level of the volume of circulating media with a potentially higher price level. This is what usually happens in the case where the credit inflation derives from increased gold production: a new equilibrium position is eventually found with a larger quantity of money than before.

According to many theories of the trade cycle it is necessary for there to be a new inflationary move—a new inflation by the central bank or a new gold-inflation—before a new cycle can begin. The same would be true of cycles which are started off by loans from surplus cash balances where these loans are not of a periodic or seasonal character but are based on a sudden change in the technique of payments. If as a result of a change in the habits of If dishoardpayment (e.g., improvements in collections, and place only expansion of the clearing system) or in the division of functions in the business structure (e.g., an increase in vertical integration in an industry), the demand to hold cash balances declines, the cash surpluses will not be merely temporary surpluses but permanent ones. Such a rise in the "efficiency of money" or increase in the velocity of circulation does undoubtedly —it can contain the germ of a trade cycle, but the habit of holding reduced cash balances or the increased velocity not its of circulation will most likely become permanent parameters of the economic system.

None of these "causes" of the trade cycle explains the periodic recurrence of the cycle (at least so far as endogenous factors are concerned) but it is a different matter with temporary surplus balances. These cash balances are superfluous at certain times and not superfluous at others. A rise in the velocity of circulation of money due to the lending out of these The tempor-

balances need not be permanent. After the crisis the firms are likely to hold again disltoarded at those balances which they need at certain moments in the start of the upswing, their own businesses and which are "superfluous" again when during other intervals. Whereas in the case of many the crisis is other factors in the trade cycle, the impetus which contributed to the upswing disappears with the conclusion of one cycle, this does not happen in the case of fluctuations in surplus cash holdings.

Assuming that the loans and disbursements out of surplus balances together with bank credit served to finance the over-investment, then, when the depression comes and the undertakings which cannot be maintained are compelled to close down, the surplus cash balances will be set free again. As the process of liquidation progresses, the funds which were previously invested "twice" come back, and the general urge to sell out stocks and to defer all postponable purchases in the expectation of a further fall in prices makes it impossible to find a productive outlet for these free cash balances. It is easy to see then why it is that in times of depression, during the "liquidation of the crisis" interest rates on the money market hover just above the zero level.

It takes some time before the economic system gets the crisis and depression "out of its limbs." It is only after a certain lapse of time that the crippling feeling of uncertainty begins to wear off, and the risk estimates by potential lenders and borrowers gradually fall. When finally confidence has returned and the —they are spirit of enterprise has reawakened, the firms which then free to nave accumulated large balances of cash during the other upturn, period of liquidation find that these liquid funds are superfluous and that there are outlets for them. As soon as the "surplus cash reserves" have found "productive employment" the economic system is moving into the upward phase of the cycle.

The introduction of surplus balance credit into the analysis of the trade cycle supplements modern monetary theory in two respects, namely, in (1) that the start of the upswing can be explained without reference to an expansion of bank credit, and (2) that the upswing can be explained on the basis of an expansion of bank credit of a much smaller magnitude than was previously assumed.

Both these circumstances go far to meet the favourite objections of those who still reject that theory of the trade cycle which stresses the expansion in the volume of money. Mises emphasis on the interest rate policy of the banks as the primary cause Monetary of the cycle was attacked by both bankers and V Y theorists. Many people found it difficult to accept a inflation psychological factor on the side of bankers and mone-an increased tary authorities as a satisfactory explanation of the periodic recurrence of cycles.

Hayek was able, without abandoning the main lines of the theory of credit cycles, to show that the money rate of interest may be below the equilibrium rate not because of positive action on the part of the banks but because there is a rise in the natural rate of interest unaccompanied by any rise in the money rate.

So, for example, technical progress, which creates increased investment opportunities and thus the natural rate of interest, may lead to increased borrowing from the banks. In this case of bank credit is not the result of active inflationism, as Mises considered it, but of passive inflationism. By a change m data m the economic system but without any action on the part of the banks, a money rate of interest which was previously in harmony with the equilibrium rate may become a rate that is conducive towards expansion.

However, Hayek's theory still treats the financing of the upswing as being exclusively due to an expansion of credit by the banks. The exposition given here on the other hand ascribes an even more passive attitude to the banks in the cycle; in fact, part of the funds used to finance the boom are seen as coming from quite another source of supply, viz., temporary surplus cash balances. Here the passive inflationism of the banks is at the beginning confined to giving assistance, if necessary, by increased lending at the critical payments dates, and does not assume the leadmg role until a more advanced stage of the cycle, of credit by the banks need enter in only at a later phase and to a smaller extent than was formerly supposed.

INDUSTRIAL INVESTMENT AND THE QUALITY OF CREDIT

We have still to give an answer to the question whether credit is liable to exert different effects, according to the purpose for which it is granted. It was necessary to clarify first the problems connected Are the with the distinction between circulating and fixed edit capital. Now that we have progressed thus far, we dependent on may venture to comment on the effects of loans which are differentiated according to the kind of use to which they are put.

The answer is simpler in the case of transfer credit than in the case of inflationary credit. In the case of genuine savings it has been customary in the literature to inquire whether there is congruence between the duration for which the credit is granted and the duration for which the investment is made. We have already observed (§ 84) that from the point of view New shortof the economic system as a whole, short-term credits can rarely be regarded as short-term investments. The long-term investments division oi Junctions m the productive process may for the cause what is from a collective point of view a longterm investment to take on the appearance of a shortterm investment from the private point of view. If the demand for short-term credit predominates on the market, then the spread between the interest rates will tend to cause the available credit supply to take the corresponding form. If the demand for long-term credit predominates, then an increasing proportion of the available supply of capital will go through the stock exchange. The raising of capital through the issue of stocks makes the individual firm independent of the length of time for which the individual capitalist or speculator wants to invest his funds.

There has consequently been a tendency for industrial capital requirements to be financed to an ever-increasing extent on the securities exchanges, and the amount of industrial credit which has been obtained via the stock exchange is far greater than all other forms of credit.

At certain times (prior to the nineteen thirties) the securities exchange was the *only* channel through which credit flowed into industrial production. Towards the end of depression periods capitalists and financiers held back from all long-term commitments, and at the same time entrepreneurs, after their bad experiences of the crisis, fought shy of borrowing at short term for investment purposes. Thus there was for some time almost no supply of long-term funds to industry and almost no demand for funds on the money market. The link was often re-established via the securities market. The belief that funds invested through the securities exchange can be withdrawn in liquid form had the effect of causing the superfluity of funds on offer on the money market eventually to find its way onto the securities exchange, in the first instance, of course, onto the bond market. At this point loans to customers who wanted to make security purchases, and security purchases on their own account, were the only outlets which the banks had for the vast funds which they commanded. It was not considered permissible to make *direct* long-term loans to industry out of these funds, and there was no demand for short-term loans by industry. The only investment outlets which remained open to the banks, therefore, were security loans and security purchases, in other words, *indirect* long-term credits to industry. (In recent years, of course, their place has been taken by the financing of public works and other public loan expenditures.) Frequently credit, perhaps after a couple of transfer operations, will take whatever form is dictated by the demand. It is therefore rather idle to try to distinguish the effects of the credit according to the form and use originally intended.

The length of time for which the funds are invested is likewise dictated by the demand, and as will be shown below, the term for Term, form, which the credit is designed by those who originally creditfare not supply it, is not what is finally decisive. Therefore a determined rise, followed later by a decline, in the amount of win of the short-term transfer credit—no less than a credit-*len&ev*creation cycle—is capable of giving rise to marked disturbances. Even the most careful selection of borrowers cannot prevent this.

If one wished to distinguish the effects of a new credit according to the use to which it is put, one would have first to assume that without this credit the borrower concerned would not have succeeded in obtaining funds. This assumption is important because, if it is not fulfilled, the effect of the credit is entirely independent of the direct and concrete use to which it is put. For if this use would have been If the covered in the absence of the granting of this particular credit, the real beneficiary of the increase in obtained supply is a borrower who was previously excluded from the market but is now able to obtain funds and who he who is the actual beneremams *in concreto* unknown. It is important fioiary of the to assume also that the impetus comes from an increase new credit-in the supply of credit and not from an increase in the demand. (This assumption, however, detracts considerably from the practical importance of the question.)

In accordance with these assumptions we may suppose that an entrepreneur receives a loan for productive activity (or for an expansion of productive activity) which he was unable to carry out previously for lack of the necessary money capital. Now that he is equipped with the money capital, the entrepreneur will be able to attract the means of production (original factors as well as intermediate products) to his enterprise. A theory which started out from the assumption of full employment would have to say that the means of production which are demanded with the new money capital were previously destined to go to other producers. If the new money capital is the result of the creation of credit, the diversion of the means of production to the new productive activity will take place by way of the bidding up of prices on the market. Professor Strigl concluded from this—I The marginal think justifiably within the narrow confines of the assumptions stated above—that the credit can only find an investor in employment in those lines of production where the because of increase in prices of the means of production plays a the relative smaller role in cost calculations than the fall in weight of interest interest charges. This would not be the case where changes. Circulating capital" because, where working capital (materials that are used up in the process) is concerned, an increase in its price will be a weightier consideration than the reduction in interest charges.

The reverse is true in the case of fixed capital, and it would therefore be profitable to use the additional credit only for investment in fixed capital.

The answer to the question under consideration is in large part contained in the assumptions. It has been assumed that the demand is given and that the supply of money capital increases. The result must therefore be the satisfaction of a demand that was previously unsatisfied. If this investment opportunity which can now be exploited with the aid of the newly created credit was previously excluded by the competition of other ways of using money capital this must obviously have been due to the interest factor. Investment opportunities which cannot be taken up because credit is "too dear" must be of the kind where the interest factor plays a relatively large role : this is only the case with long-term investments. An investment which is made possible only by the creation of new credit can therefore only be an investment in fixed capital.

Generations of practical bankers, and authors of books about banking, have preached that bank credit Bank credit should not be used for investment in fixed capital. ^ 3 Even if the length of the period for which working working capital is invested is greater in the economic system °api a ' as a whole than in the single undertaking, it will still —which be possible to liquidate working capital with less culty and at smaller loss than fixed capital. The liquidatedd "inflationary effects" should therefore be milder and capital, less harmful if a credit expansion serves to finance working capital than if it is used to finance fixed capital. But is it possible to prevent the credit from being invested in fixed capital? The foregoing exposition, based on the assumption of a given demand for Is t h e demand for credit, leads one to answer this question in the negative. But is the "given" demand for working capital really perfectly inelastic? inelastic?

Technically, an increase in working capital might take place without any increase in fixed capital if production could be extended within the limits allowed by the existing fixed capital equipment. The volume of production, at any time, is determined by marginal cost and marginal revenue. The marginal costs, i.e., the increase in total costs due to an increase in production, consist for the most part in wages and raw material costs. The interest on the investment in wages and materials is of relatively minor importance and the effect of a decrease in the interest rate on marginal costs is microscopically small. This is explained by the fact "that we have there a fraction of a fraction of a fraction. The volume of working capital is only a ratio of the total annual prime costs, a ratio which depends on the rate of turnover; naturally, the *interest* on the working capital is only a percentage of that; and finally, a decrease in the rate of interest is only a fraction of the latter. "3 The marginal cost curve will hardly fall noticeably in response to a reduction in the interest rate, and it is scarcely worth talking about a fall in the interest rate leading to an extension of production within the existing fixed capital equipment.

The increase in the supply of money capital can, however, raise the demand for certain products and may thus lead to an extension of production through the rise in the marginal revenue curve. There are here three possibilities:

If the increase in the supply of credit is inflationary in origin money incomes will rise and this will lead to an increase in the demand for consumption credit. The money incomes rise not as the direct creates result of the increase in the credit *supply* but as the increased result of the *utilization* of the credit, and, moreover, only subsequent as the result of the utilization of inflationary credit. But here we are concerned with the form of the investprimary use of the credit, to finance either working or fixed capital of producers. The possibility that the utilization of the credit may lead to a secondary demand for consumers' goods, and that this may lead to a tertiary derived demand for working capital, is another matter.

The second possibility is the fundamental idea behind Hawtrey's theory of the trade cycle. It has often been objected to this, that the demand of traders for stocks is influenced by interest costs only to a minute extent. There is a good deal of truth in this objection : it is not at all likely that the interest-rate-sensitivity of the traders demand for stocks will be persuades anything like as important as the interest-rate-sensitivity of the producers' demand for fixed capital. The third possibility brings us back to our thesis that the increase in the supply of credit will as a rule cause more credit to be used to finance fixed capital, mentin The utilization of additional credit for extending pro-equipment duction *without* simultaneous or previous investments in fixed capital is hardly likely to take place.

The misdirection of investment would, it is true, not have such far-reaching effects if the money capital were used to produce "liquid" goods instead of being used to construct fixed capital equipment. This is so, not so much on account of the "period of turnover of the capital" or the slower or quicker rate of amortization, as on account of the greater or lesser variety in related to the purposes for which the concrete capital goods can used. The loss of value is usually in inverse prospe iificity of portion to the number of uses to which the goods can equipment since fixed capital goods mostly consist of the type of capital that is least capable of being used for a purpose other than that for which it was originally intended, they are the ones that are most likely to be subject to capital losses.

Considerations such as these, however, are neither of theoretical nor of practical importance, for, as we —investment have seen, the desire to find exclusively "mobile" m workfng investments for the additional credit cannot be fuleaptai can be filled. Circulating capital will be increased as the thn ugh joint result of the credit expansion only to the extent that capital equipment that is first constructed joinc with with the aid of the inflationary credits needs raw complementary goods to go with it, and denved from the increase in demand for consumers' goods, which results in due course from the increase in money incomes, gives rise to a derived demand for working capital.

Our conclusions may seem to conflict with the facts of experience, and practical bankers in particular will defend themselves energetically against the insinuation that they grant their customers short-term credits for long-term investment. Conservative bankers are convinced that they finance only goods in process and give only advances on goods sold. But they forget that by giving the producers these funds for investing in "working capital" they put those producers in the position of being able to use their own capital in a different way than formerly. The granting of the bank credit to the producer frees the funds which were previously tied up in the running of his business, and he can now undertake the investments he plans with his "own funds."

The concrete visible use to which The banker.. cannot know the new credit is put is not, therefore, m any way the indirect identical with the investment which the credit has Jses,of the, funds which *de facto* made it possible to realize. he lends;— The investment which the credit expansion makes possible need not even take place in the firm of the actual borrower. Bankers could otherwise adopt the simple expedient of refusing any kind of loans and advances to entrepreneurs who undertake investment in fixed capital. In fact, however, the bank credit which the entrepreneur borrows for himself in the real first instance may be re-lent by him to somebody else may be in in the form of a trade credit, and thus make it possible other firms for the firm which directly or indirectly takes over the products of the first entrepreneur to embark on investment. Or the bank credit may place the entrepreneur in the position of buying more on a cash basis and less on trade credit, and so enable the firms which directly or indirectly supply him with materials to undertake investments.

Lastly, the bank credit may release some other credit and so, by easing the general credit market, make it possible for investment to be undertaken at some undeterminable point in the careful economic system. The great care which a banker takes selection of in choosing between would-be borrowers will, of nm course, react beneficially on the quality of the bank's the bank investments, but it will not prevent additional credit butnoTthe from leading to the immobilization of capital some-economy from imwhere m the economy. mobilization.

If it is the inherent tendency of new credits (whether they be transfer credits or credits newly created by the banks) to find their way into investments in fixed capital, and if it is, therefore, of no credit avail to attempt to direct the credits into certain can not avert outlets by lending in a particular *form* and under its use for particular *conditions*, then the mistrust of stock exchange credits with respect to their "quality" is groundless. We are no longer talking of the charge against stock exchange speculation that it may take the newly granted credits away from industry.

For, in so far as one were concerned merely with the problem of how to prevent short-term credit from being used for fixed capital investment, the stock exchange would have to be praised and blessed *if* it actually did withhold the new funds from industrial investment. What we have to consider here is whether the "misuse" of the credits in production will not be made worse if the short-term funds are first transferred by stock exchange witchcraft into long-term funds. "The harm which is caused by too much lending to the stock exchange lies in fact not so much in the possibility that there may be a shrinkage in the amount of lending to industrial borrowers says Reisch on this point, "as in the fact that in this case credits will be put at the disposal of the stock exchange which are by their economic character totally unsuited to the purchase of securities."

Commenting on this it has to be said that credits which are by their nature unsuited to security purchases are just as unsuited to any other kind of industrial credit. For if every additional credit may have the effect of a long-term credit, it is obviously immaterial in what garb this credit is dressed. This gives a final negation to the —the banks question raised at an earlier juncture as to whether the exchange danger that investments will be misdirected is greater credits are when the credit is granted to the stock exchange than no worse than when the same amount of credit is granted directly to equal amounts industry. direct credit

Aside from the fact that the effect of the credit is to industrynot decided by its outward form (discount, security loan, overdraft) nor by the way in which it finds its way into production (through loans to producers or traders or through purchases of securities, &c.) nor by the concrete purpose for which it is used directly (trade credit, working capital or fixed capital), the banks have no means of damming up the flow of newly created credit to the stock exchange. So long as the expansion of credit continues, the newly created credit will flow onto the stock exchange even though the authorities send a policeman after every credit. When rates on call loans rise considerably above the discount rate, the banks attempt to rediscount their holdings of bills in order to be able to use their funds on the stock exchange.

If the banks, under the pressure of the official credit policy, do not dare to expand their lending at call, but there is nevertheless a tendency for the credit expansion to continue to the benefit of "legitimate productive activity", then ordinary Besides, the business men will create commercial bills and will dlrfctIoans divert the "direct credits to industry" to the stock mate exchange. For nobody will prevent industry— attracted by the high rates on call money—from kept from being passed placing its liquid funds, oi which it will have an on to a boomabundance in consequence of the "legitimate industrial credits" at the disposal of the stock exchange and from financing new issues with them at the same time. In periods of boom—periods of credit inflation— practically every credit becomes a stock exchange credit. The campaign against stock exchange credit will be brought to a successful conclusion only when a check is placed on credit expansion. And the check on credit expansion by the banks will not necessarily in all circumstances stop the increase in stock exchange credits immediately. Thus, for example, the restrictive credit policy of the American monetary authorities in 1928 achieved small success because the expansion was stimulated further by the reduction in the liquidity preferences of the economic system.

The notion that it is possible to pursue an "effective" credit expansion and at the same time to avoid a stock exchange boom is absurd. Discrimination in lending is bound to fail so long as the discrimination does not Qualitative imply restriction. This is, of course, possible and is effectiver practicable: the demand for direct business loans and only if it discounts might rise more slowly than the demand for quantitative security loans, so that a discrimination against security restriction. loans would act as a check on credit expansion in general. So far, however, as credits are created, they will tend, even when they flow straight into industry without first going through the stock exchange, to increase the demand for productive goods and in consequence to raise the value of plants producing means Effective" of production. This is bound to be reflected in an increase in the values of titles to these undertakings. stock exchange boom always march market will be presented no matter where the together. increased credits are initially placed. It is thus a mistaken judgment to regard security loans as the villain of the piece and to look upon discounts as being devoid of all evil. For both, either visibly or invisibly, tend to follow the path that offers the greatest attractions. It is not the form the credit takes nor the exact place where it enters the system that makes it dangerous: it is, instead, its amount.

THE STOCK MARKET, EASY CREDIT, BEARER CREDIT

Now that we have established that stock exchange loans are no more dangerous in their effect than other kinds of loans granted in the same volume, we must consider whether the volume of lending may not be influenced by the stock exchange, and whether this influence is not such as to tend to increase the total volume of credit.

The question we are asking here is the reverse of the one which we asked at the beginning. Our original question was whether lending to the stock exchange caused *too little* credit to go to industry. The question we are asking now is whether lending to the stock exchange may not cause *too much* lending, or whether "excessive speculation on the stock exchange... does not *eo if so* produce an inflation.

Whether or not there is any sense or justification in talking about the "causes" of an inflation depends not only on the definition of the concept of inflation but also on the prevailing institutions. If inflation is defined as an increase in the effective circulation of money, it has a certain sense, and is methodologically legitimate, to refer for example to a certain improvement in the technique of payments as the "cause" of an inflation. Whether, however} it is also justifiable to talk about objective causes of an increase in the volume of money depends on the prevailing institutions. Under the institution of the gold standard there may in fact be a cause of a gold inflation in the sense of a causal nexus which is explicable in economic terms. Under the gold standard the discovery of new There may be rich gold mines, or a technical improvement in gold in mining, would have to be regarded as causes of an the case of an inflation.

The increase in the volume of money would be the "necessary consequence" of the changes in the inflation—conditions of gold production. Under the type of monetary system, however, where the volume of the circulation is controlled by a central monetary authority there is nothing according to which the fact of an increase in the volume of money can be deter but none mined by reference to any proposition of economic theory. In this case an inflation is not the automatic trolled" or regular effect of objectively given facts, but is the inflation, result of a certain policy. There may be more or less obvious motives behind the policy; the policy may be easily rationalized; it may be explicable on ideological, psychological or teleological grounds; but an inflationary policy of this kind cannot be said to be governed by any causal necessity of the type discussed in economic theory.

If in any particular monetary system the issue of money takes place through lending by a bank which has a monopoly and is controlled by the state, then it is within the power of the administrators of credit policy either to grant credit or not to grant it. Their decision is not guided by the principle of maximizing the profits of the issuing bank, and is not therefore determinate in the sense of economic theory. The fact that at any particular moment requests for more credits or for larger credits may be made to the bank is under these circumstances no "cause" for granting these requests.

It would be different under a system of free banking where the issue of money was independent of political aims. If the reserves of a multiplicity of competingbanks were dependent on nothing else but gold production and gold movements—and could not be increased or decreased by central bank policy—

the situation would be such that an inflation would be explainable as the economic consequence of certain circumstances (such as gold production, liquidity preferences, demand for credit). When, however, the supply of credit is managed by a central authority, an inflation is not the result of economic behaviour such as the behaviour of the buyer, the producer, the trader or the saver, but the result of "intervention" just like any measure of tariff policy, labour policy or tax policy.

The prevailing monetary systems in England and the United States are a compromise between political and economic determinants of the volume of credit. Many present-day students of monetary theory are inclined to exaggerate one or the other of these two aspects. Those advocates of an active trade-cycle policy who hold the official credit policy of the monetary authorities responsible for all fluctuations in investment and business activity exaggerate one aspect. Those members of the Keynes school, who regard an increase in investment opportunities as involving a simultaneous increase in money incomes, exaggerate the other aspect: they regard fluctuations in the demand for credit as the dominating "cause" of inflation and deflation. As I see it, the truth does not even lie exactly midway between these two views. I believe that inflation might be attributed more to political factors and deflation more to economic factors. The monetary authorities can do very little to avoid deflation; on the other hand they can avoid inflation by withdrawing appropriate quantities of reserves from the banks, so that the latter will not grant credit to the full extent to which it is sought under given conditions, or will grant credit only under more strict conditions.

Requests for credit come to the banks from many Whether or different sources. Since the granting of credit (apart crease in the from personal loans) is influenced by the security that demand for credit and an the borrower has to offer, and since particular types increase in of cover or collateral (bills of exchange, shipping documents, warehouse receipts, securities) have proved lead to more to be specially suitable for bank credit, it has often loans been supposed that the possibilities of granting credit were strictly limited by the available quantity of these kinds of "security." In particular it was supposed for a long time that there was a strict dependence of the total volume of bills and requests for their discount on the volume of trade. It has frequently been pointed out that this is a mere superstition.

The number of bills coming forward for discount is largely dependent on the credit policy of the banks. An increase in the demand for loans against bills can in principle just as well lead to a tightening of the discount market as to the granting of the loans. It all depends on the policy of the banks, or on their reserve —depends position as determined by the policy of the central bank. Just as the desire to get bills discounted cannot be treated as the "cause" of the granting of the discount credit, neither can the request for loans against longterm securities be regarded as the cause of the granting of these loans. If the banks look upon securities with certain market values as sufficient cover for a loan of a certain figure, this does not mean to say that they are bound to give credit to everybody who can offer this kind of collateral. It may be argued against really be made effective in deterring the banks from expanding credit, they would undoubtedly represent a considerable step forward. But it is hardly to be expected that they would be effective so long as the precondition of credit expansion, an easy money policy on the part of the reserve banks (or large excess reserves resulting from a previous easy money policy of the monetary authorities) prevails.

In the United States the monetary authorities have felt themselves obliged to impose relatively narrow limits to lending against securities. According to the provisions of the Securities Exchange Act of 1934 the Federal Reserve Board can issue rules and regulations concerning the amount of credit that may be granted against securities. The fixing of invariable margin requirements which are based on the current market prices for securities does however create the undesirable "pyramiding" effect described above no matter whether the margin requirements are high or low. In order to avoid this effect the Federal Reserve Board in 1934 issued the following regulation: "A. loan on a security must not be greater than whichever is the higher of: (1) 55 per cent, of the current market price of the security, or (2) 100 per cent, of the lowest market price of the security since July 1, 1933, but not more than 75 per cent, of the current market price."5 For some time this regulation created an "anti-pyramiding zone"; soon, however, the prices of securities rose so high that only the first of the two rules was applied and the second one was therefore later revoked.

The conclusions reached on the basis of an investigation by the Twentieth Century Fund, New York, contain the proposal that a maximum loan value of a share of stock should be fixed at some multiple of the net earnings of that stock over the five years preceding the loan. A rule of this kind would mean that the loan value would change little and only once a year. Increases in the market prices of shares would, therefore, not permit increased amounts of lending. Another rather arbitrary method of dealing with the problem is to lower the percentage up to which credit can be obtained on the basis of a given market value of securities when the market values rise, and to raise it when the market values fall. The Federal —now they Reserve Board seems to have decided in favour of this puiated to method: in January, 1936, when stock prices were changes security on the increase, margin requirements were raised, and valuation. in October, 1937, when stock prices had collapsed, margin requirements were lowered. The lowering of the requirements came much too late, however, and the Board was severely criticized for that reason. "If this method of control is to be used, it should be... flexibly and promply applied."

The idea behind all these measures against an expansion of lending against securities is presumably that they will prevent the stock exchange boom from having "inflationary effects." So far as the credit expansion in general is really restricted through such measures, they are appropriate to their purpose, and in many situations are fully justified. If, however, Such they merely serve to divert the stock exchange credits into other forms of credit creation, they accomplish far as they nothing. This has been demonstrated in the previous rea v c are expansion.

If increases in security prices give the banks the opportunity to increase the volume of their lending against securities, it may look as though the stock exchange were the cause, and the expansion of credit the effect. If there exists a latent capacity and willingness on the part of the banks to extend more credit^ then such a conclusion is admissible. To put the same thing in technical terms: When the supply of bank credit is perfectly elastic the demand determines the volume of credit granted. It is then a disputable point as to whether it is more sensible to say: "The increase in the demand for credit by speculators leads to the inflation" or "the perfect elasticity of the credit supply leads to the inflation." Since the perfect, or practically perfect, elasticity of the credit supply is the result of political measures, I think there is little justification in the accusation that the blame for the credit inflation lies with stock exchange speculation.

An idea connected with the problem of the influence of security transactions on the volume of credit is the supposed "duplication of credit" resulting from the system of financing capital requirements through security issues. According to this idea not only are the actual firms able to obtain credit: the owners of the titles (securities) to the property of those firms are able to obtain credit as well by using the securities as collateral for loans. Thus the capital value of the firm presumably serves twice as a basis for credit.

It is certainly true that the security form of financing business has made it easier to borrow. But it is quite untrue to say that this has made possible a doubling of the basis of credit. When the owner of capital placed his money capital at the disposal of a firm, this was acknowledged in the form of shares or in the form of bonds. If for any reason he now desires to withdraw the whole or part of his money capital, he will look for another person who possesses free money capital to take over his title. This may take place either through the definitive or conditional purchase of the securities, or through a loan against those securities.

Fundamentally the same process comes into play The company in both cases: the place of the first capitalist is taken by a second capitalist who provides the money capital issuing securities; invested in the undertaking. It the owner of securities borrows on them, this does not mean that the investor company which issued them *and* the owner who borrows against the on them have raised capital: all that it means is that this capital raised by the company has been provided atitution, not partly by the owner of the securities and partly by of funds. the person who gave the latter a loan against those securities.

It would, however, also be possible for a firm to obtain additional credits (*e.g.*, bank loans) besides the capital procured through the issue of securities, and for the shareholder at the same time to borrow on his shares. Does this not involve a duplication of credit borrow made possible by the method of raising capital through additional the issue of securities ? It is easy to see that this is not so once we realize that much the same thing can take place without the security form of finance. A partnership, N & Co., may secure a loan and at the same time Mr. N may be able to obtain a loan for his personal needs on the strength of his position as chief partner of N & Co. The condition for granting a personal loan of this kind will probably be that the lender considers Mr. N (perhaps on the basis of references and other information) as a credit-worthy person on account of the considerable volume of personal funds which he has invested in his firm. If, on the other hand, the firm is deep in debt, the partners will have a lower credit rating. The same applies, again, to the firm which, has raised its capital by an issue of securities. If the corporation has, in addition, borrowed so much that the relationship of its borrowings to its share capital is considered to be unfavourable charges squeeze the dividends, then the shares of this company will fall in value and will give diminished possibilities of borrowing against them.

As the level of indebtedness of the company is expressed in the price of the shares, and this price is accordingly only a reflection of the net worth of the company, the "credit rating" of the shares reduces itself to the portion of the capital which the company really "owns," and does not make possible any duplication of credit. The fact that the capital of the undertaking is raised in the form of securities merely makes it easier to transfer ownership of the capital invested in it, and so enables the individual owners to liquidate their capital more easily and more completely. In other words, the security method of financing enterprises makes it easier for investors to use the titles to the capital as collateral for loans or to replace their own funds readily by the capital of other investors. In times of growing optimism, however, investors may be able to get more money capital loaned on their securities than the corporations have received wke n they issued them. This is the kernel of truth in the idea of the "duplication of credit" under the system of security capitalism.

We have already discussed the allegation that stock exchange speculation produces the temptation for the banks to expand credit and thus to cause an inflationary *easiness* of credit. *No* less deserving of attention is the opposite claim that stock exchange speculation causes credit, particularly industrial credit, to become *dearer*. This latter argument is not Stock entirely disposed of by our investigation into the possibility of capital absorption. For it is quite conceivable that the stock exchange may not tie up higher capital either temporarily or permanently, and that, interest rates, nevertheless, it may raise the price of credit *(i.e.,* the not "absorb" interest rate) by bidding for it on the market. credit. It seems to me that it is precisely this point which has awakened so much practical interest in the whole of this group of problems.

The borrower who had to pay a higher rate of interest at times of a booming stock market felt that his interests were harmed by the competition of the stock exchange.9 Practical business men were thus originally concerned only with the tendency towards a rise in the cost of credit. This was then connected up with the absorption of capital. Our study of this possibility has, however, given rather negative results, for we came to the conclusion that a tying up of "genuine" (i.e., non-inflationary) money capital on the stock exchange was extremely unlikely. We are thus brought back to the single point as to whether stock exchange speculation is the cause of higher interest rates.

The mere trading of securities, the exchange of ownership of already existing securities, is, according to George Halm, quite irrelevant from the point of view of the cost of credit. "The purchases and sales which take place on the market for credit titles... cannot exert any influence at all on the pricing of capital disposition. Of course, the conditions of demand and supply of the particular categories of credit titles may change. But the supply and demand conditions for capital disposition do not change in the least." According to this view the rate of interest is one of the factors determining the price of securities, but the interest rate is not in turn dependent on the level of security prices. The value of securities is calculated as the capital value of the expected return, and is thus the result of so-called capitalization, which combines the two factors—the return and the capitalization rate. If the expected return and the capitalization rate are given, then, allowing for a risk and uncertainty premium, the price of the security is also determined. If the yield prospects or the capitalization rate change, then the security prices will also change. But the latter are to be regarded as the dependent variable in this relationship.

The foregoing description is, however, a very much simplified one which leaves many factors out of account. In the first place we have been talking about *the* capitalization rate, whereas in fact there are a number of different interest rates. Furthermore, we referred to *the* expected yield, while in fact there may be sharp divergencies between the yield estimates of different individuals in the market. Lastly, the rate of interest and the yield prospects were regarded as data with respect to which no changes were to be expected in the near future. The introduction of these complications of reality make many qualifications necessary.

According to Halm the capitalization rate on the securities market is the result of two components—the "static long-term rate of interest" and the "money market rate." This is perfectly correct, although, the definition and measurement of the "static long-term interest rate" remain unsolved problems. Strangely enough, however, it is the effect of the "money market rate" on security prices that has been cast into doubt. An investigation of Richard N. Owens and Others have Charles O. Hardy has sought to show that the money the effect of market rate had no influence on security prices.

The mterest on final conclusions derived from 111 pages of text and price,— an ample appendix are that the theory of the influence of the money market rate on security values is false, because the costs of buying and selling securities usually "eat up" any gain from the difference between the interest rates; that interest plays no role relative to the profits derived from changes in security pricesground that and that the speculator does not require any capital the cost whatsoever for his transactions. These are not very exceed tohfe serious objections. Certainly the expenses are a con-gain from sideration and the height of commissions and sales Spreads,— taxes represents an important friction. The important thing is, however, the size of the difference (between the money market rate of interest and the yield on securities) and the expected duration of the rate level —and that on the money market. Admittedly the interest charge charges are does not play a very large role in connexion with the trivial as against profits derived from changes m security prices. It is from securityimportant, however, not to confuse security prices changeswith *changes* in security prices. It is a fact that a One should speculator who expects a considerable rise in security between prices will hardly be deterred by a high interest rate, security The existence of an influence from the side of expected prices and expected price *changes* on the interest rate is, however, not price changes incompatible with the existence of the influence of the interest rate on security prices.

The influence of the money market rate on the securities market cannot be seriously contested. Not only the rise of security prices during periods when the money market rate remains for a long time below the "static long-term rate," but also the sharp break in the speculation curve when the increased money market rates finally lead to a higher capitalization rate, are far too striking phenomena to be covered up in statistical series.

Exactly what is meant when it is said that the interest rate influences security prices, but that security prices do not influence the interest rate so long as no changes take place in the supply of, or demand for, money capital, can best be explained by the aid of an example. An illustra-Let us assume that the dividend prospects of the given— companies A, B, C, and D are estimated at 8, 6, 5, and 4 dollars respectively. In order to simplify the mere arithmetic of our example we may assume that these dividends are regarded as permanent—as perpetual annuities—and we shall also abstract from considerations of risk and uncertainty. If it is possible to obtain loans at 4 per cent., and no change is expected in this respect either, then under the given assumptions the securities market will set values of 200, 5 With respect to the third objection we may say that, even if speculation as a whole requires no money capital, the securities of the individual speculator represent capital investment; and if the prices rise he possesses "more capital," and will, if he does not expect any further change in the prices, compare the potential yield of the funds obtainable from realizing the securities with the expected yield of the security holdings.

150, 125, and 100 dollars on securities A, B, C, and D respectively. Now suppose that the yield prospects of the D shares rise from 4 to 5 dollars. If this is generally known and is expected with certainty, then the value of the D shares will rise from 100 to 125 dollars, no matter whether there is any actual turnover of security titles or not. The interest rate of 4 —which per cent, will not be affected. If the improvement in better prothe yield prospects is known only to a few speculators, raise prices then it will pay these people to borrow money to buy of existing shares at any price between 100 and 125 dollars,

But even this demand for funds will not raise raising the interest rate or will only do so for a few rateB. hours, since as soon as the purchase of the securities is effected, a supply of credit will be forthcoming from the side of the seller. On a well-organized market the seller may lend to the buyer—and the increase in the price of the shares will come about without any increase in the interest rate.

The matter is different if the D company, in view of the increased profitability of its business, wishes to expand its production. If the acquisition of the necessary capital is to take the form of an issue of shares, the new shares will perhaps be issued at a price of 120 dollars. Here—where there has been a rise in the price of the shares from 100 to 120 If, however, dollars—the credit market will be altered by an effective demand for new credit, and if the supply of credit industry, is unchanged (and if it is not perfectly elastic) the raising of capital by the company will lead to a rise in the interest rate. This rise then appears to have been induced by the securities market, but it has in fact been caused by the demand from industry.

It is this peculiar misunderstanding which has led to the attempt to construct an antithesis between industrial credit and the securities market. In actual fact it is the securities market on which industry raises the bulk of its capital requirements. Only a relatively small part of the capital requirements of industry is obtained by direct borrowing from the banks; it is called "industrial credit" by the latter: evidently the reason is that it is only in these cases that the name of the industrial undertaking appears on the bank's books. In the case of advances where the account is held in the name of the industrial firm, in the case of discount credit where the firm's name is written on the bill, and in the case of documentary credit where the name is written on the documents, the banks assume that they are lending to industry, whereas in the case of loans against securities, brokers' loans, loans at short notice, and call loans the other parties to the contract often seem to be speculators in securities. In fact, however, the securities exchange is the chief market for industrial credits. "For industry as a whole industrial credit which is in the form of shares and bonds is the most important part of the credit which is really decisive for industrial development."

Once we have recognized that the investment titles of industry are traded on the stock exchange, we are bound to see a speculative upswing of security prices as a cheapening of industrial credit. "Viewed from the standpoint of industry... the stock exchange boom implies a decline in the real rate of return' on securities and acts, therefore, only as an improvement in the facilities for obtaining capital." The argument that the passage of capital over the stock exchange is "costless" is a view which has been put forward in particular by Cassel. Against this argument Reisch has attempted to prove that the stock exchange leads to an increase in the cost of obtaining capital. The *purchaser* of shares, Eeisch argued,8 is willing to concede a high interest rate in the hope of making profits on changes in security prices; it is therefore improbable that the seller of the shares will place his proceeds at the disposal of industry at a *low* interest rate. Evidently the seller of the shares is here looked upon as lending money to industry; in reality, however, industry itself is a seller of shares.

The more the buyer pays for the shares, the more cheaply does industry obtain the capital it requires. As Reisch speaks, at a later stage in his exposition, of industrial over-investment as the result of the stock exchange movement, he implicitly recognizes the reduction in the cost of obtaining-capital. For the lowering of the cost of obtaining capital which is reflected in the high prices at which new issues can be placed, or at which old holdings of securities can be realized, makes it possible to undertake extensive new investment.

The boom on the stock exchange undoubtedly Most writers involves a cheapening of industrial credit. The industrial cheapening which took place in the United States in credit during the twenties the years 1927-29 was, in my opinion, unnatural in wasexceedthe sense that it was the result of an inflationary and that this expansion of credit. Against this view, Lmdley M. was due to Eraser holds that "the stock market boom... was in inflation essence a natural reaction to the general economic conditions."1 The supply of voluntary savings was so great, according to Fraser, that, with the —rather than inelastic industrial demand for capital, it could only to increased genuine invested through a sharp rise in security prices, saving a cheapening of credit. Hence Eraser criticized the view "that speculation was making money too cheap for producers and entrepreneurs. No doubt that is a sounder view than either the doctrine that a stock market boom has no practical effect on industry at all, or—still more—the popular belief that it tends to *deprive* 'legitimate business' of the credit to which it is entitled."

Eraser thus agrees with me that the stock exchange boom brings cheaper credit to industry; he insists merely that industrial credit in the United States towards the end of the twenties was not unhealthily cheap. There can, of course, be no proof of either view; the figures of bank deposits and their velocity of circulation do, however, I think, speak against Fraser's view.

Anybody who speculates on the rise in the price of a security is prepared to pay a higher interest rate for direct credit than he actually obtains in the form of dividends on his security. This difference partly explains the cheapening of the security form of industrial credit. When industry receives the new (cheap) capital and/or when the seller of shares withdraws from the stock market with his profits, call money rates rise. The rise in call money rates3 also brings in its train, however, a rise in discount rates and rates for other kinds of bank credit, and anybody who requires credit in this form has to submit to a rise in its price.

It might be argued that industry will react more markedly to a change in the costs of carrying working capital (financed by discounts or bank advances) than to movements in the costs of long-term credit, especially as existing industries do not usually have to take account of fluctuations in the rate of interest on the capital market.

Their requirements of long-term capital are usually covered once for all, and a fall in the capitalization rate and a rise in the price of their shares is of less interest to them than their current payments in respect of short-term loans. Thus industries which have no intention of raising more long-long-term term capital complain about credit becoming dearer, and it is such complaints that have led to the mistaken with assumption that industry has to compete with the exchange for credit whereas what really happe nstso ciks credit, that long-term credit competes with short-term credit. So far as industry, which complains of the high rate of interest charged by the banks, has covered its permanent working-capital requirements by short-term loans, it is provided, by the situation of which it complains, with an excellent opportunity for financing its capital requirements in a more solid way and converting the "dear" bank credit into cheap long-term credit by increasing its capital stock. So far as periodic temporary capital requirements are concerned, it is questionable whether industry is seriously vulnerable in respect to the rise in short-term rates. Where the capital requirements of a firm fluctuate, the deplored movement of interest rates changes the "capital optimum," making it profitable to raise more capital at long-term. The complaints of industry There is another problem which is both narrower and wider than the question of the effect of stock exchange loans on the interest rate. This is the question of the effect of stock exchange loans on the Stock lending capacity of the banks.

It has sometimes been credits may presumed that stock exchange loans decreased the lending capacity of the banks both absolutely and capacity of relatively. So far as concerns loans to brokers from another sources than the banks, this view of the diminished lending capacity of the banks is the reverse of the truth. The loans "on account of others," which could be made by the banks in the U.S. prior to 1933, reduced the direct loans and the demand deposits of the banks and thus increased their excess reserves.

To be sure the banks had to be careful since they knew that they must be prepared to step in and extend credit to brokers on their own account in case the "other" lenders should demand repayment of their loans. In this sense the loans to brokers by "others" released Loans by less bank credit than would otherwise have been the release credit. As regards the direct loans by the banks to brokers, these reduced the remaining lending capacity of the banks no more and no less than any other form of credit. Benjamin M. Anderson observed, quite rightly, that: "An increase in commercial bank loans of whatever kind, whether stock market loans, commercial loans, real estate mortgage loans, or loans of any other kind, tends to reduce the ability of the banks to make other loans, and tends to raise rates of interest to other borrowers. The point is that when a bank makes a loan, it must either pay out cash from its reserves, reducing its ratio of reserves to deposits, or else increase its deposits, which again reduces the ratio of reserves to deposits, though at a less rapid rate." So far as I know, it was never denied that loans to brokers diminished the capacity of the banks to grant *other* loans. It would, however, be wrong to infer that lending to the stock exchange deprives industry of credit, for with few exceptions stock exchange credit *is* really industrial credit. Strangely enough, B. M. Anderson was numbered among the adherents of the hypothesis of capital absorption by the stock exchange.8 What Anderson really said when he made the above remark was, however, nothing more than that a loan which has already been granted (e.g., to industry in the form of stock exchange credit) does, of course, decrease the banks' capacity to grant further loans.

Does the stock exchange cause credit to be dearer? This question, we have seen, has little point. The securities exchange is a part of the credit market; it is the market for credit which is long-term in character but can be easily realized. Is it possible that the existence of a market can increase the price of the thing that is traded on that market ? It is easy to see that every increase in the supply of credit on this part of the market means a *cheapening* of the particular kind of credit that is traded on it, and it is equally clear that if the total supply of credit remains unchanged the credit dealt with on the other parts of the market must become dearer. Direct credit thus usually tends to become dearer as a result of the competition of the security form of credit when the former

1. The appearance of an increased demand for long-term may be due term capital which tends to raise the rate on the capital to—market. Such a demand for capital finds expression in a new security issue or in the unloading of unsold increased demand for holdings of previous issues. The increase in the rate long-term of interest on the capital market appears in the form of a decline in security prices.
2. The witholding of the capital supply from long term investments (following a crisis) which raises the rate in the capital market and lowers the rate on the investiments:—
3. The appearance of an increased supply of short or an term capital which causes the money market rate to fall

short-term funds. In all these cases, sooner or later, a movement towards equilibrium will set in, tending to wipe out the difference. The increase in the price of direct bank credit through an increased volume of funds going to the stock exchange is in every case an essential element in this equilibrating movement. Is it possible that loans to the stock exchange may cause the price of direct bank credit to rise above the rate of interest on the capital market? This is least likely to happen when the gap between the (originally lower) money market rate and the (originally higher) The capital market rate was exclusively due to the first two market funds of the three principal causes. For as soon as the yield securities margin is removed the demands of the "stock markets may exchange" on the money market will cease. The balancing closing together of the money market rate and real factor. yields will have removed the cause of the tendency for bank credit to become dearer.

If the first-mentioned causes are accompanied by the third-mentioned cause, then the case is different. If the gap between the interest rates is partly caused by an abundance of funds on the money market, thi& usually inflationary supply of credit may eventually lead to a cumulative movement which may in its later stages drive the money market rate up above the capital market rate. The funds which are offered on the money market may originally have come from current new savings or current depreciation funds and may have been withheld from the capital market because of lack of confidence (cause No. 2). As soon, however, as these funds begin to flow over into the capital market, the inflationary sources of the supply of funds to the money market (hitherto idle cash balances and newly created bank credit) will start If the money flowing very freely.

The elasticity of this supply market funds spring from allows the cumulative upswing to attain such a speed goes not being an equalization process cumulative which would come to an end with the decline in the — capital market rate (i.e., with the increase in security prices) and the rise in the money market rate: instead of this it develops into a boom with excessive financial and real investment. The capital market rate (i.e., real yields) is pressed down by the feverish expectations of further rises in security prices, and the money market rate is driven up by the demands for credit for with the the excessive extension of production. True, it is the stock exchange on which the producers' demand for the long-term credit manifests itself; but to blame the loans to the stock exchange for the fact that credit becomes dearer is to refuse to go below the surface of things. If we reason closely, the explanation of the fact that bank credit can become so much dearer has to go back to the fact that bank credit has originally been too easy. Stock exchange credit does not here play the role of the ultimate cause.

CONCLUSIONS

An evaluation of the results of our investigations may be facilitated by an abstract in catalogue form. The critic of this book should, however, not be tempted by such a handy digest to save time by skipping the first sixteen chapters and to form his opinion An abstract On the basis of the abstract. It is only intended to list of issues provide the reader who has struggled his way through which contains the shortest possible (and hence inexact) formulation of those of our theses which deviate from accepted doctrine or constitute controversial issues. Moreover, we include only those theses which are relevant to the general attitude toward the problems of the stock market, credit and capital formation; that is to say, we include only theses which may have practicalpolitical significance rather than theses which constitute "intermediate products" of theoretical analysis, whatever may be their significance as instruments for arriving at definite findings. An investment of money capital which securities but also those from sales of old securities may go into real investment.

4. Money capital may go into real investment, into consumption, into hoards (and cancellation of money), or into a chain of interpersonal transfers.
5. No additional money capital is needed for a rise in security prices.

6. Higher security prices, sometimes a symptom of an increased supply of investible funds, call forth issues of new securities and sales of old securities by industrial producers.
7. Abundant funds, especially those of inflationary origin, may not find ready outlets in real investment.
8. Extensive and lasting stock speculation by the general public thrives only on abundant credit.
9. Losses by stock-market speculators constitute no real capital losses to society.
10. An increase in stock-exchange turnover need not involve an increase in the demand for money on the part of stock-exchange members or of traders holding current accounts with stock-exchange members; the clearing mechanism may obviate any increase in payments.
11. Clearing balances need not be higher in times of high or rising stock prices or turnover than in times of low or falling stock prices or turnover. Clearing balances rise because of an uneven distribution of selling and buying among different brokers.
12. An increase in clearing balances can be settled without an increase in brokers' bank balances through a faster turnover of existing volumes of bank balances and bank loans.
13. Customers' brokerage deposits function in boom times as a peculiar type of "money" for the speculating public.
14. If speculators who sell ask for cheques from their brokers, and send cheques for their new purchases, bank deposits are tied up. However, widespread trading by the general public, involving long chains of cheque transactions, develops only in times of credit inflation.
15. A continual rise of stock prices cannot be explained by improved conditions of production or by increased voluntary savings, but only by an inflationary credit supply.
16. The volume of brokers' loans tells us nothing about the amount of funds that have flowed onto the stock

exchange. Brokers' loans are increased through an excess of customers' withdrawals over new deposits of funds.

17. Rising stock prices may lead to an increase in brokers' loans through induced withdrawals of profits and proceeds.
18. Brokers' loans rise also when sellers withdraw funds in order to loan them to brokers. The sum total of brokers' loans may be a multiple of the funds actually involved.
19. If the seller lends, via the broker, to the buyer, brokers' loans rise without requiring any funds or any bank credits. Brokers' loans can be rapidly liquidated if call-money lenders buy securities from margin debtors.
20. Brokers' loans which constitute credits by the seller to the buyer represent no funds which anybody might have used for anything else; neither the seller nor the borrower has liquid funds.
21. Bearish sellers may keep a liquid position not only by holding idle the balances received from bullish buyers but also by holding call-money claims. Large brokers' loans do not reflect idle funds.
22. Capital gains are not money income to society and do not constitute investible funds.
23. Any decrease in the effective supply of money capital is likely to cause disturbances in the production process.
24. An inflated rate of investment can probably be maintained only with a steady or increasing rate of credit expansion. A set-back is likely to occur when credit expansion stops.
25. A "crash-proof" distribution of expanded credit is rather improbable. Both producers' credit and consumers' credit may create disproportionalities and lead to major disturbances. A price-stabilizing credit expansion may unstabilize the production structure.
26. Credit inflation is "healthy" if it compensates for deflation through current net hoarding, or for an increase in the number of holders of cash balances or in the number of "stopping-stations" in the money flow.

27. The use of credit for financing working capital does not assure "self-liquidation" or liquidation free of disturbance. For the economy as a whole circulating capital mostly constitutes long-term investment and, if the volume of production is to be maintained, even permanent investment.
28. Seasonal fluctuations in the producers' capital demands are not manifestations of fluctuating capital requirements of the economy. The fluctuations came into being when temporarily liquid surplus cash balances were put to use.
29. Surplus cash balances in times of seasonally low inventories need not reflect seasonal unemployment of productive resources. The transition to a system of loaning out these temporary surplus funds may have inflationary effects.
30. Business surplus balances due to reduced production, and consumers' surplus balances due to postponed consumption, if loaned out, represent genuine "transfer credit/' whereas surplus balances due to regular pulsations in the money flow, if loaned out, act like "created credit."
31. Credit loaned out of surplus cash balances may make for monthly and seasonal easing and tightening of the money market.
32. The start of a general business upswing can be financed out of surplus cash balances without an expansion of bank credit. The temporary surplus cash balances, dishoarded at the beginning of the upswing, are set free again when the crisis is liquidated; they are then disposable for another upturn.
33. New short-term credits usually involve longterm investments for the economy as a whole. The banker cannot know the indirect uses of the funds which he lends. Careful selection of borrowers may protect the banker from losses but not the economy from immobilization.

34. The effect of a certain amount of bank loans may be the same whether they are given as stockexchange credits or as direct commercial credits to industry. Qualitative credit control is effective only if it involves quantitative control.
35. If bank reserves are controlled by the monetary authorities, credit inflation should not be attributed to the stock-exchange boom. However, margin regulations may be an effective means of checking the expansion.
36. The stock exchange is the foremost market for industrial capital funds. Higher security prices mean cheaper capital for industry. It is not the stock market which competes with industry for funds, but rather industrial long-term credit which competes with industrial short-term credit.
37. The flow of money-market funds to securities markets may close the gap between long-term and short-term rates. If the funds spring from inflationary sources, a cumulative movement may emerge which can drive money-market rates above long-term rates.

The theses stated above were not, I repeat, selected because I considered them the representative results of my analysis. My object was to stress here those issues which a practical banker or politician Are the findmight find interesting. Practical men are often theoretical sceptical of theoretical analysis. "That may be all analysis right in theory, but is it true in practice? ", is one of their queries. And when they are assured that theory tries to explain things of the real world, another doubt arises concerning the value of the results of analysis: "That may all be so, but what does it teach us? How does it help us?"

The practical man is inclined to regard scientific findings as valuable only if they are an aid to the formulation of definite plans of conduct, definite policies. It is usually forgotten that the findings of analysis cannot be instrumental in designing policies before the ends and goals, in the order of their relative sign of importance, are decided upon. It is utterly useless, policies for example, to try to devise a policy of controlling stock-exchange credit before it is clear whether it aims of policy is considered more important to avoid cyclical fluctuations in industry or to strive toward full industrial employment, or to save the public from losses through I believe that the upswing breeds a host of disproportionalities in the production and price structure, which turn out to be untenable and result in a depression.

To hold this view is not equivalent to upholding the postulate that an upswing ought to be avoided at all costs. Such a postulate would appear to be sensible only if there were another way of improving depressed economic conditions. Since such an alternative would Expansion most likely include cost reductions as a remedy for necessarily maladjustment, it has been termed the ''deflationary ^ ^ route" toward re-employment. If one believes that economic route to be impassable for institutional or political con ltlons# reasons, or to be too stony and strenuous and unduly painful, one may take the position that the "inflationary route" is preferable in spite of its ups and downs. (Professor Ropke once contrasted the "sadistic trade "Sadistic" cycle theory" with the "frivolous trade cycle theory the former recommending painful cost reductions with-trade cycle out considering the solution through public loan expenditures, the latter recommending generous public spending without considering the solution through cost adjustments.) Those who believe, on the one hand, that distortions Those who in the production set-up are likely to result from credit expansion, and on the other hand, that cost reductions and efficacy would be both politically feasible and economically reductions effective, would clearly oppose any inflationary policies. They would resist credit expansion whether any form, it were demanded for the sake of stabilizing prices in a progressive economy, or for the sake of furthering production in a stagnating economy, or for the sake of pushing consumption or stimulating investment, or creating employment. Indeed, they would have to go further than the staunchest anti-inflationists, and suppress those merely momentary expansions of bank credit on days of massed payments, because these bank loans might support an expansion of loans out of existing surplus cash balances.

It is hardly possible to devise, even in pure theory, a system which completely excludes all and every expansion of credit. The claims that a system of free banking would, in the long run, be less conducive to credit creation than a central reserve system, do not seem to be acceptable. The claims that a system of absolutely fixed, or rigidly managed, volumes of note and cheque deposit circulation would abolish all inflationary possibilities, are not tenable either^ they are, to say the least, exaggerated. If, therefore, such radical reforms as the introduction of the 100% plan cannot guarantee full success in this respect we shall have to content ourselves with the discrete exercise of the existing powers of monetary management.

Perfect monetary control would require perfect foresight. Short of this, monetary management needs at least the capacity of quickly recognizing what has been going on. In this regard, close observation of stock-exchange transactions, of stock prices and of stock-exchange credits is, I believe, of major importance, and can furnish significant clues for intelligent monetary management. In point of fact, the central banking authorities in various countries have been studying these records intently, especially since the middle of the twenties, and, relying on certain partly erroneous interpretations of their data, they were at times led to take more or less drastic action against stock-exchange credits. These actions and official charges and attacks against the stock exchange have evoked reactions on the side of "defenders" of the stock market. In these quarters, supported by recognized authorities in the field, it was held that it was none of the central banks' business to watch, or, much less, to try to control, the stock exchange or stock-exchange credits.

Many of the arguments against the intervention of the monetary authorities and against the "official' theories were correct. Yet, the suspicious attitude false reasonof the central authorities towards the excessive volume of stock-exchange credit was certainly justified. The official view that the stock exchange with its demand for credit was a dangerous competitor of trade and industry was, of course, untenable. And the official view that stock-exchange credit should be restricted but that, at the same time, credit in other forms should be allowed to expand, was wide open to criticism. But so much is certain that the volume of stock-exchange credits must not be ignored; it is important both *per se* and as a part of the total —but the volume of bank loans. The volume of loans in conjunction with stock-market movements may be a valuable guide of credit policy.

The days when gold movements could be held to be the one and only guide of monetary management Guides of are definitely gone. Other indices have been accepted, or proposed, as "assistant guides" or even as chief not equally.... sensitive to guides. Their sensitiveness with respect to movements "inflation." beyond the "zero point of inflation" varies with changing circumstances—unless one defines the zero point of inflation in terms of one of the indices (such as a certain price level or level of employment). If net inflation is defined as an expansion of the volume of money (and money substitutes) in excess of spontaneous net hoarding, and of requirements arising from an increased coefficient of money transactions (e.g., more stopping-stations in the money flow), then it is impossible to rely on any simple index that might work as an "inflatiometer."

Gold move-Gold movements have never been a good guide in that respect. Whenever expansion took place at a fairly even pace in all of the various gold standard countries, there would be no international gold move-—foreign ments to indicate that expansion. The foreign exchange rates-exchange market, though more sensitive than the gold flow, would likewise fail to record "parallel inflations'' —am commodity price credit may rise without any funds flowing to or from the stock exchange, if sellers lend to buyers. On the other hand, borrowed bank funds may pass through the stock exchange and onto industry without any rise in the volume of stock-exchange credits, if the buyers have obtained loans from others than brokers. For these reasons the volume of *all* bank credits would aid bank credits have to be watched together with the movement ol as well as security prices and, moreover, together with the volume of security issues. The volume of security issues, however, may rise merely through notations by investment trusts and holding companies without any new funds going to industry. On the other hand, borrowed funds may go into industry, via the stock market, without any new security issues, if industrial firms sell securities which they have previously carried among their assets. Thus, we see that none of the indices mentioned—security prices, stock-exchange credits, total bank credit, security issues—is fully reliable as evidence for or against the presence of inflation. Yet, if all of these indices show an upward (or downward) movement, the presumption is very strong that inflation (or deflation) in the sense denned is taking place, even if the level of commodity prices does not show the least upward (or downward) tendency.

To regard stock-market data as an important guide of credit control is one thing; it is quite another thing to regard the stock market as an appropriate working point for credit control. One may accept The stock the barometer-function of stock-market activity and yet prefer general discount policy, open-market policy sidereda and other measures affecting the excess reserves of commercial banks as the best means of credit control. On the other hand, one may belittle the stock market as a guide and yet accept discrimination against stock-exchange credit, margin regulations, and control of flotations as efficient means of credit control. In other words, one may believe that the stock market is both a good "compass" and a good "steering wheel" of monetary control; or one may believe the one without believing the other.

5

Financing the Corporate Sector

Corporate finance is an area of finance dealing with the financial decisions corporations make and the tools and analysis used to make these decisions. The primary goal of corporate finance is to maximize corporate value while reducing the firm's financial risks. Although it is in principle different from managerial finance which studies the financial decisions of all firms, rather than corporations alone, the main concepts in the study of corporate finance are applicable to the financial problems of all kinds of firms.

The discipline can be divided into long-term and short-term decisions and techniques. Capital investment decisions are long-term choices about which projects receive investment, whether to finance that investment with equity or debt, and when or whether to pay dividends to shareholders. On the other hand, the short term decisions can be grouped under the heading "Working capital management". This subject deals with the short-term balance of current assets and current liabilities; the focus here is on managing cash, inventories, and short-term borrowing and lending (such as the terms on credit extended to customers). The terms Corporate finance and Corporate financier are also associated with investment banking. The typical role of an investment banker is to evaluate investment projects for a bank to make investment decisions.

CAPITAL INVESTMENT DECISIONS

Capital investment decisions are long-term corporate finance decisions relating to fixed assets and capital structure.

Decisions are based on several inter-related criteria. Corporate management seeks to maximize the value of the firm by investing in projects which yield a positive net present value when valued using an appropriate discount rate. These projects must also be financed appropriately. If no such opportunities exist, maximizing shareholder value dictates that management return excess cash to shareholders. Capital investment decisions thus comprise an investment decision, a financing decision, and a dividend decision.

THE INVESTMENT DECISION

Management must allocate limited resources between competing opportunities ("projects") in a process known as capital budgeting. Making this capital allocation decision requires estimating the value of each opportunity or project: a function of the size, timing and predictability of future cash flows.

Project Valuation

In general, each project's value will be estimated using a discounted cash flow (DCF) valuation, and the opportunity with the highest value, as measured by the resultant net present value (NPV) will be selected (see Fisher separation theorem; John Burr Williams: Theory). This requires estimating the size and timing of all of the incremental cash flows resulting from the project. These future cash flows are then discounted to determine their *present value* (see Time value of money). These present values are then summed, and this sum net of the initial investment outlay is the NPV.

The NPV is greatly influenced by the discount rate. Thus selecting the proper discount rate—the project "hurdle rate"—is critical to making the right decision. The hurdle rate is the minimum acceptable return on an investment—i.e. the project appropriate discount rate. The hurdle rate should reflect the riskiness of the investment, typically measured by volatility of cash flows, and must take into account the financing mix. Managers use models such as the CAPM or the APT to estimate a discount rate appropriate for a particular project, and use the weighted average cost of capital (*WACC*) to reflect the financing mix selected. (A common error in choosing a discount rate for a project is to apply a WACC that applies to the entire firm. Such an approach may not be appropriate where the risk of a particular project differs markedly from that of the firm's existing portfolio of assets.)

In conjunction with NPV, there are several other measures used as (secondary) selection criteria in corporate finance. These are visible from the DCF and include payback period, IRR, Modified IRR, equivalent annuity, capital efficiency, and ROI; see list of valuation topics.

Valuing Flexibility

In many cases, for example R&D projects, a project may open (or close) paths of action to the company, but this reality will not typically be captured in a strict NPV approach. Management will therefore (sometimes) employ tools which place an explicit value on these options. So, whereas in a DCF valuation the most likely or average or scenario specific cash flows are discounted, here the "flexibile and staged nature" of the investment is modelled, and hence "all" potential payoffs are considered. The difference between the two valuations is the "option value" inherent in the project. The two most common tools are Decision Tree Analysis (DTA) and Real options analysis:

- The DTA approach attempts to capture flexibility by incorporating *likely events* and consequent *management decisions* into the valuation. In the decision tree, each management decision in response to an "event" generates a "branch" or "path" which the company could follow. (For example, management will only proceed with stage 2 of the project given that stage 1 was successful; stage 3, in turn, depends on stage 2. In a DCF model, on the other hand, there is no "branching"-each scenario must be modelled separately.) The highest value path (probability weighted) is regarded as representative of project value
- The real options approach is used when the value of a project is *contingent* on the *value* of some other asset

or underlying variable. (For example, the viability of a mining project is contingent on the price of gold; if the price is too low, management will abandon the mining rights, if sufficiently high, management will develop the ore body. Again, a DCF valuation would capture only one of these outcomes.) Here, using financial option theory as a framework, the decision to be taken is identified as corresponding to either a call option or a put option-valuation is then via the Binomial model or, less often for this purpose, via Black Scholes; see Contingent claim valuation. The "true" value of the project is then the NPV of the "most likely" scenario plus the option value.

Quantifying Uncertainty

Given the uncertainty inherent in project forecasting and valuation, analysts will wish to assess the *sensitivity* of project NPV to the various inputs (i.e. assumptions) to the DCF model. In a typical sensitivity analysis the analyst will vary one key factor, while *ceteris paribus* holding constant all other inputs. The sensitivity of NPV to a change in that factor is then observed (calculated as " NPV / " factor). For example, the analyst will set annual revenue growth rates at 5% for "Worst Case", 10% for "Likely Case" and 25% for "Best Case"-and produce three corresponding NPVs.

Using a related technique, analysts may also run scenario based forecasts so as to observe the value of the project under various outcomes. Under this technique, a scenario comprises a particular outcome for economy-wide, "global" factors (exchange rates, commodity prices) *as well as* for company-specific factors (revenue growth rates, unit costs). Here, extending the example above, key inputs in addition to growth are also adjusted, and NPV is calculated for the various scenarios. Analysts then plot these results to produce a "value-surface" (or even a "value-space"), where NPV is a function of several variables.

Another application of this methodology is to determine an "unbiased NPV", where management determines a (subjective) probability for each scenario-the NPV for the project is then the probability-weighted average of the various scenarios. Note that for scenario based analysis, the various combinations of inputs must be *internally consistent*, whereas for the sensitivity approach these need not be so.

A further advancement is to construct stochastic or probabilistic financial models-as opposed to the traditional static and deterministic models as above. For this purpose, the most common method is to use Monte Carlo simulation to analyze the project's NPV (introduced to finance by David B. Hertz in 1964). Here, the cash flow components that are (heavily) impacted by uncertainty are simulated, mathematically reflecting their "random characteristics". The simulation produces several *thousand* trials (in contrast to the scenario approach above) and outputs a histogram of project NPV. The average NPV of the potential investment-as well as its volatility and other sensitivities-is then observed. (Typically, an add-in such as Crystal Ball is used to run simulations in spreadsheet based DCF models.)

Here, continuing the above example, instead of assigning three discrete values to revenue growth, the analyst would assign an appropriate probability distribution (commonly triangular or beta). This distribution-and that of the other sources of uncertainty-would then be "sampled" repeatedly so as to generate the several thousand realistic (but random) scenarios, and the output is a realistic, representative set of valuations. The resultant statistics (average NPV and standard deviation of NPV) will be a more accurate mirror of the project's "randomness" than the variance observed under the traditional scenario based approach.

The Financing Decision

Achieving the goals of corporate finance requires that any corporate investment be financed appropriately. As above, since both hurdle rate and cash flows (and hence the riskiness of the firm) will be affected, the financing mix can impact the valuation. Management must therefore identify the "optimal mix" of financing—the capital structure that results in maximum value.

(See Balance sheet, WACC, Fisher separation theorem; but, see also the Modigliani-Miller theorem.)

The sources of financing will, generically, comprise some combination of debt and equity. Financing a project through debt results in a liability that must be serviced—and hence there are cash flow implications regardless of the project's success. Equity financing is less risky in the sense of cash flow commitments, but results in a dilution of ownership and earnings. The *cost of equity* is also typically higher than the *cost of debt* (see CAPM and WACC), and so equity financing may result in an increased hurdle rate which may offset any reduction in cash flow risk.

Management must also attempt to match the financing mix to the asset being financed as closely as possible, in terms of both timing and cash flows. One of the main theories of how firms make their financing decisions is the Pecking Order Theory, which suggests that firms avoid external financing while they have internal financing available and avoid new equity financing while they can engage in new debt financing at reasonably low interest rates.

Another major theory is the Trade-Off Theory in which firms are assumed to trade-off the Tax Benefits of debt with the Bankruptcy Costs of debt when making their decisions. An emerging area in finance theory is Right-financing whereby investment banks and corporations can enhance investment return and company value over time by determining the right investment objectives, policy framework, institutional structure, source of financing (debt or equity) and expenditure framework within a given economy and under given market conditions. One last theory about this decision is the Market timing hypothesis which states that firms look for the cheaper type of financing regardless of their current levels of internal resources, debt and equity.

The Dividend Decision

The dividend is calculated mainly on the basis of the company's unappropriated profit and its business prospects for the coming year. If there are no NPV positive opportunities, i.e. where returns exceed the hurdle rate, then management must return excess cash to investors. These *free cash flows* comprise cash remaining after all business expenses have been met. This is the general case, however there are exceptions. For example, investors in a "Growth stock", expect that the company will, almost by definition, retain earnings so as to fund growth internally. In other cases, even though an opportunity is currently NPV negative, management may consider "investment flexibility" potential payoffs and decide to retain cash flows; see above and Real options.

Management must also decide on the form of the distribution, generally as cash dividends or via a share buyback. There are various considerations: where shareholders pay tax on dividends, companies may elect to retain earnings, or to perform a stock buyback, in both cases increasing the value of shares outstanding; some companies will pay "dividends" from stock rather than in cash. (See Corporate action.) Today it is generally accepted that dividend policy is value neutral (see Modigliani-Miller theorem).

WORKING CAPITAL MANAGEMENT

Decisions relating to working capital and short term financing are referred to as *working capital management*. These involve managing the relationship between a firm's short-term assets and its short-term liabilities. The goal of Working capital management is to ensure that the firm is able to continue its operations and that it has sufficient cash flow to satisfy both maturing short-term debt and upcoming operational expenses.

Decision Criteria

Working capital is the amount of capital which is readily available to an organization. That is, working capital is the difference between resources in cash or readily convertible into cash (Current Assets) and cash requirements (Current Liabilities). So the decisions relating to working capital are always current decisions, i.e., short term decisions.

The short term decisions of the firm are similar to those of long term in terms of risk and return, but they differ in many other ways like time factor, discounting consideration, liquidity etc. So these decisions are not taken on the same basis as long term decisions. These decisions have different criteria like cash flow and profitability.

- The most important criterion for making short term decisions is cash flows. And the best measure of cash flow is net operating cycle or cash conversion cycle. It represents the time difference between cash payment for raw materials and cash collection for sales. Another aspect of cash conversion cycle is gross operating cycle which is same as net operating cycle except the fact that it does not take into account the creditors deferral period. Cash conversion cycle indicates the firm's ability to convert its resources into cash. Because this number effectively corresponds to the time that the firm's cash is tied up in operations and unavailable for other activities, management generally aims at a low net count.
- In this context, the most useful measure of profitability is Return on capital (ROC). The result is shown as a percentage, determined by dividing relevant income for the 12 months by capital employed; Return on equity (ROE) shows this result for the firm's shareholders. Firm value is enhanced when, and if, the return on capital, which results from working capital management, exceeds the cost of capital, which results from capital investment decisions as above. ROC measures are therefore useful as a management tool, in that they link short-term policy with long-term decision making. See Economic value added (EVA).

Management of Working Capital

Guided by the above criteria, management will use a combination of policies and techniques for the management of working capital. These policies aim at managing the *current assets* (generally cash and cash equivalents, inventories and debtors) and the short term financing, such that cash flows and returns are acceptable.

- Cash management. Identify the cash balance which allows for the business to meet day to day expenses, but reduces cash holding costs.
- Inventory management. Identify the level of inventory which allows for uninterrupted production but reduces the investment in raw materials-and minimizes reordering costs-and hence increases cash flow; see Supply chain management; Just In Time (JIT); Economic order quantity (EOQ); Economic production quantity (EPQ).
- Debtors management. Identify the appropriate credit policy, i.e. credit terms which will attract customers, such that any impact on cash flows and the cash conversion cycle will be offset by increased revenue and hence Return on Capital (or *vice versa*); see Discounts and allowances.
- Short term financing. Identify the appropriate source of financing, given the cash conversion cycle: the inventory is ideally financed by credit granted by the supplier; however, it may be necessary to utilize a bank loan (or overdraft), or to "convert debtors to cash" through "factoring".

Financial Risk Management

Risk management is the process of measuring risk and then developing and implementing strategies to manage that risk. Financial risk management focuses on risks that can be managed ("hedged") using traded financial instruments (typically changes in commodity prices, interest rates, foreign exchange rates and stock prices).

Financial risk management will also play an important role in cash management. This area is related to corporate finance in two ways. Firstly, firm exposure to business risk is a direct result of previous Investment and Financing decisions. Secondly, both disciplines share the goal of creating, or enhancing, firm value. All large corporations have risk management teams, and small firms practice informal, if not formal, risk management.

Derivatives are the instruments most commonly used in Financial risk management. Because unique derivative contracts tend to be costly to create and monitor, the most cost-effective financial risk management methods usually involve derivatives that trade on well-established financial markets. These standard derivative instruments include options, futures contracts, forward contracts, and swaps.

See: Financial engineering; Financial risk; Default (finance); Credit risk; Interest rate risk; Liquidity risk; Market risk; Operational risk; Volatility risk; Settlement risk.

RELATIONSHIP WITH OTHER AREAS IN FINANCE

Investment Banking

Use of the term "corporate finance" varies considerably across the world. In the United States it is used, as above, to describe activities, decisions and techniques that deal with many aspects of a company's finances and capital. In the United Kingdom and Commonwealth countries, the terms "corporate finance" and "corporate financier" tend to be associated with investment banking-i.e. with transactions in which capital is raised for the corporation.

Personal and Public Finance

Corporate finance utilizes tools from almost all areas of finance. Some of the tools developed by and for corporations have broad application to entities other than corporations, for example, to partnerships, sole proprietorships, not-for-profit organizations, governments, mutual funds, and personal wealth management. But in other cases their application is very limited outside of the corporate finance arena. Because corporations deal in quantities of money much greater than individuals, the analysis has developed into a discipline of its own. It can be differentiated from personal finance and public finance.

CORPORATE FINANCE INDIA

This site provides comprehensive information on Corporate Finance India. It also focuses on types of services offered by Corporate Financing Community in India.

The economic renaissance in the 1990s brought by liberation of Indian economy had a stupendous effect on the financial health of India. The Indian financial market which was previously insulated from foreign investors were thrown open for foreign investments. And with modern economic policies (at par with western countries) in operation large quantum of foreign direct investments/FDI started to flow into the Indian market. The rise in business activities and its subsequent rise in financial activities led to the need of proper and accurate financing for corporates in India. Corporate Finance India provides businessman, investors and entrepreneurs with finance and advice for proper and risk free investments with an eye for maximum returns. Corporate Finance India community relies on ready-to-use data, projections and informations on India's economy. The projections/future-movements of the financial market are based on information and data collected from daily activities of the finance market. Corporate Financiers in India advices their clients after taking into consideration financial environment of the market along with important decisions taken by the Government which, compliments the financial health of the country. Corporate Finance India focuses on the provision of corporate advice and funding for Indian companies who wish to take advantage of the liquidity of the Indian financial markets. Corporate Finance India provides the following services to the Indian Corporate Markets.

- Corporate Finance.
- Debt and equity funding.
- Start up and Growth capital.
- Pre-IPO finance.
- Real Estate Sales and Acquisition.
- Company Sales and Acquisitions.

Corporate Finance India focus has been on entrepreneurial clients, whether individuals or businesses, and on providing funding and investment in entrepreneurial businesses. Corporate Finance India offers a complete solution to its clients objectives through market research. Corporate Finance India companies has an extensive network of investors and funding institutions and group of corporate associates. The Corporate Finance India community offers professional, personalized service and expertise both responsively and pro-actively.

INTERNATIONAL BUSINESS IN INDIA

The current scenario for 'International Business in India' is more than heartening. With stupendous growth of more than 7% annually, improvement and stabilization of relations with neighboring countries and record setting rise of its stock indexes, India continues to grab international attention. It is destination of opportunity with its high-potential workforce and burgeoning middle class and as an increasingly dynamic competitor.

India being a multi-cultural, multi-lingual and multi-religion state, it is not advisable to formulate a uniform business strategy. The eastern part of the country is known as the 'land of the intellectuals' and is regarded as the cultural hub of the country. The southern part is known for its technology acumen and western part is the commercial-capital of the country. The north is where the political power sits and operates the country. ' International Business Opportunity in India ' exists in ares like-

- Information Technology and Electronics Hardware.
- Telecommunication.
- Pharmaceuticals and Biotechnology.
- R&D.
- Banking, Financial Institutions and Insurance & Pensions.
- Capital Market.
- Chemicals and Hydrocarbons.
- Infrastructure.
- Agriculture and Food Processing.
- Retailing.
- Logistics.
- Manufacturing.
- Power and Non-conventional Energy.

Sectors like Health, Education, Housing, Resource Conservation & Management Group, Water Resources, Environment, Rural Development, Small and Medium Enterprises (SME) and Urban Development are untapped and offers huge scope. With highest numbers of technical, medical, business management graduates and highest numbers of Phd.s coupled with an energetic English speaking mass India offers 'services' with 50-70% less cost from their western counterparts.

For 'International Business in India' b odies like CII, FICCI and different Chambers of Commerce provides a variety of business facilitation services by-

- Closely working with Government and business promotion organizations in India and the respective partner countries.
- Also hosts high-level Government dignitaries and help build close working relationships between Governments and business organizations.
- It also exchanges business delegations, joint task forces and identify bilateral business co-operation potential and make suitable policy recommendations to Governments.

With opportunities galore for ' International Business in India' the trend is mind boggling. ' India International Business' community along with Indian Domestic Business community is steadily emerging as the Knowledge Capital of the world. The World Bank and different rating organizations have forecast that at 7-8% of Economic growth, she will be worlds second largest economy by 2050.

Indian Businesses

Indian Businesses are slowly shifting their base from agriculture to major industrialization. Numerous types of Businesses in India are coming up. As India is developing the Iron & Steel Businesses in India, IT Businesses in India, Indian Businesses in Travel & Tourism, Indian Businesses in Business Process Outsourcing, Food Business market in India, Soft Drinks Businesses in India and various other types of businesses are coming to the forefront and taking the center stage.

The marketplace for Indian Businesses is quite varied including industries in the field of Agriculture & Forestry, Automobiles, Business Services, Chemicals, Computers, Construction, Education, Electrical, Electronics, Engineering/ Machinery, Entertainment, Import & Export, Fashion & Advertising, Food Processing, Government of India Websites, Immigration, India Neighborhood, Intelligence, International, IT/ITes, Minerals & Metals, Packaging & Paper, Real Estate in India, Regional Portals, Travel & Tourism and many others. The scope of doing business in India has grown in its magnitude.

Some of the major companies in the IT sector are Wipro, Tata Consultancy Services, Infosys Technologies, HCL Ltd, Satyam Computer Services, Cognizant Technology Solutions, Patni Computers, BFL MphasiS, Polaris, i-flex, IBM, Hewlett-Packard and Accenture. In general the major Indian Businesses are the Tatas, Birlas, Ambanis and many more.

The Government has played a major role in the transformation of the Indian Business scenario in India. The major changes initiated by the Government for the betterment of the Indian Businesses are in the form of macroeconomic reforms, tax reforms, finance reforms and freeing of capital markets, reforms in the regulation of business firms, revitalization of the Indian private sector, removal of exchange controls and convertibility, trade reforms, and foreign direct investment. The Foreign companies are showing massive interest in the Indian Businesses. The number of Businesses in India have increased at an impressive rate. More and more foreign companies are having their branches in India. They are either holding hands with the Indian Businesses by entering into a partnership with them or they are building up their own offices in India. The future of Indian Businesses looks bright and assuring.

INTRODUCTION TO CORPORATE FINANCE

In July 1999, Carleton "Carly" Fiorina assumed the position of CEO of Hewlett-Packard (HP). Investors were pleased with her view of HP's future: She promised 15 percent annual growth in sales and earnings, quite a goal for a company with five consecutive years of declining revenue. Ms. Fiorina also changed the way HP was run. Rather than continuing to operate as separate product groups, which essentially meant the company operated as dozens of minicompanies, Ms. Fiorina reorganized the company into just two divisions.

In 2002, HP announced that it would merge with Compaq Computers. However, in one of the more acrimonious corporate battles in recent history, a group led by Walter Hewlett, son of one of HP's cofounders, fought against the merger. Ms. Fiorina ultimately prevailed, and the merger took place. With Compaq in the fold, the company began a two-pronged strategy. It would compete with Dell in the lower-cost, more commodity-like personal computer segment and with IBM in the more specialized, high-end computing market.

Unfortunately for HP's shareholders, Ms. Fiorina's strategy did not work out as planned, and in February 2005, under pressure from HP's board of directors, Ms. Fiorina resigned her position as CEO. Evidently, investors also felt a change in direction was a good idea; HP's stock price jumped almost seven percent the day the resignation was announced.

Understanding Ms. Fiorina's rise from corporate executive to chief executive officer, and finally, ex-employee, takes us into issues involving the corporate form of organization, corporate goals, and corporate control, all of which we discuss in this chapter.

WHAT IS CORPORATE FINANCE?

Suppose you decide to start a firm to make tennis balls. To do this, you hire managers to buy raw materials, and you assemble a workforce that will produce and sell finished tennis balls. In the language of finance, you make an investment in assets such as inventory, machinery, land, and labor. The amount of cash you invest in assets must be matched by an equal amount of cash raised by financing. When you begin to sell tennis balls, your firm will generate cash. This is the basis of value creation. The purpose of the firm is to create value for you, the owner. The value is reflected in the framework of the simple balance sheet model of the firm.

The Balance Sheet Model of the Firm

Suppose we take a financial snapshot of the firm and its activities at a single point in time.

The assets of the firm are on the left-hand side of the balance sheet. These assets can be thought of as current and fixed. *Fixed assets* are those that will last a long time, such as buildings. Some fixed assets are tangible, such as machinery and equipment. Other fixed assets are intangible, such as patents and trademarks. The other category of assets, *current assets,* comprises those that have short lives, such as inventory. The tennis balls that your firm has made, but has not yet sold, are part of its inventory. Unless you have overproduced, they will leave the firm shortly.

Before a company can invest in an asset, it must obtain financing, which means that it must raise the money to pay for the investment. The forms of financing are represented on the right-hand side of the balance sheet. A firm will issue (sell) pieces of paper called *debt* (loan agreements) or *equity shares* (stock certificates).

Just as assets are classified as long-lived or short-lived, so too are liabilities. A short-term debt is called a *current liability.* Short-term debt represents loans and other obligations that must be repaid within one year. Long-term debt is debt that does not have to be repaid within one year. Shareholders' equity represents the difference between the value of the assets and the debt of the firm. In this sense, it is a residual claim on the firm's assets.

From the balance sheet model of the firm, it is easy to see why finance can be thought of as the study of the following three questions:

1. In what long-lived assets should the firm invest? This question concerns the left-hand side of the balance sheet. Of course, the types and proportions of assets the firm needs tend to be set by the nature of the business. We use the term capital budgeting to describe the process of making and managing expenditures on long-lived assets.

2. How can the firm raise cash for required capital expenditures? This question concerns the right-hand side of the balance sheet. The answer to this involves the firm's capital structure, which represents the proportions of the firm's financing from current and long-term debt and equity.
3. How should short-term operating cash flows be managed? This question concerns the upper portion of the balance sheet. There is often a mismatch between the timing of cash inflows and cash outflows during operating activities. Furthermore, the amount and timing of operating cash flows are not known with certainty. The financial managers must attempt to manage the gaps in cash flow. From a balance sheet perspective, short-term management of cash flow is associated with a firm's net working capital. Net working capital is defined as current assets minus current liabilities. From a financial perspective, the short-term cash flow problem comes from the mismatching of cash inflows and outflows. It is the subject of short-term finance.

Capital Structure

Financing arrangements determine how the value of the firm is sliced up. The persons or institutions that buy debt from (i.e., loan money to) the firm are called *creditors*.1 The holders of equity shares are called *shareholders*.

Sometimes it is useful to think of the firm as a pie. Initially, the size of the pie will depend on how well the firm has made its investment decisions. After a firm has made its investment decisions, it determines the value of its assets (e.g., its buildings, land, and inventories).

The firm can then determine its capital structure. The firm might initially have raised the cash to invest in its assets by issuing more debt than equity; now it can consider changing that mix by issuing more equity and using the proceeds to buy back (pay off) some of its debt. Financing decisions like this can be made independently of the original investment decisions.

The decisions to issue debt and equity affect how the pie is sliced.

The pie we are thinking of is depicted in Figure 1.2. The size of the pie is the value of the firm in the financial markets. We can write the value of the firm, *V*, as *V* _ *B* _ *S* where *B* is the value of the debt and *S* is the value of the equity. The pie diagrams consider two ways of slicing the pie: 50 percent debt and 50 percent equity, and 25 percent debt and 75 percent equity. The way the pie is sliced could affect its value. If so, the goal of the financial manager will be to choose the ratio of debt to equity that makes the value of the pie—that is, the value of the firm, *V*—as large as it can be Current liabilities.

Shareholders' Equity

The Financial Manager

In large firms, the finance activity is usually associated with a top officer of the firm, such as the vice president and chief financial officer, and some lesser officers. Figure 1.3 depicts a general organizational structure emphasizing the finance activity within the firm. Reporting to the chief financial officer are the treasurer and the controller. The treasurer is responsible for handling cash flows, managing capital expenditure decisions, and making financial plans. The controller handles the accounting function, which includes taxes, cost and financial accounting, and information systems.

We think the most important job of a financial manager is to create value from the firm's capital budgeting, financing, and net working capital activities. How do financial managers create value? The answer is that the firm should:

1. Try to buy assets that generate more cash than they cost.
2. Sell bonds and stocks and other financial instruments that raise more cash than they cost.

Thus, the firm must create more cash flow than it uses. The cash flows paid to bondholders and stockholders of the firm should be greater than the cash flows put into the firm by the bondholders and stockholders. To see how this is done, we can trace the cash flows from the firm to the financial markets and back again.

The interplay of the firm's activities with the financial markets is illustrated in Figure 1.4. The arrows in Figure 1.4 trace cash flow from the firm to the financial markets and back again. Suppose we begin with the firm's financing activities. To raise money, the firm sells debt and equity shares to investors in the financial markets. This results in cash flows from the financial markets to the firm (*A*). This cash is invested in the investment activities (assets) of the firm (*B*) by the firm's management. The cash generated by the firm (*C*) is paid to shareholders and bondholders (*F*). The shareholders receive cash in the form of dividends; the bondholders who lent funds to the firm receive interest and, when the initial loan is repaid, principal. Not all of the firm's cash is paid out. Some is retained (*E*), and some is paid to the government as taxes (*D*).

Over time, if the cash paid to shareholders and bondholders (*F*) is greater than the cash raised in the financial markets (*A*), value will be created.

IDENTIFICATION OF CASH FLOWS

Unfortunately, it is not all that easy to observe cash flows directly. Much of the information we obtain is in the form of accounting statements, and much of the work of financial analysis is to extract cash flow information from accounting statements. The following example illustrates how this is done.

TIMING OF CASH FLOWS

The value of an investment made by a firm depends on the timing of cash flows. One of the most important principles of finance is that individuals prefer to receive cash flows earlier rather than later. One dollar received today is worth more than one dollar received next year.

The Midland Company refines and trades gold. At the end of the year, it sold 2,500 ounces of gold for $1 million. The company had acquired the gold for $900,000 at the beginning of the year. The company paid cash for the gold when it was purchased. Unfortunately, it has yet to collect from the customer to whom the gold was sold. The following is a standard accounting of Midland's financial circumstances at year-end:

By generally accepted accounting principles (GAAP), the sale is recorded even though the customer has yet to pay. It is assumed that the customer will pay soon. From the accounting perspective, Midland seems to be profitable. However, the perspective of corporate finance is different. It focuses on cash flows:

The perspective of corporate finance is interested in whether cash flows are being created by the gold trading operations of Midland. Value creation depends on cash flows. For Midland, value creation depends on whether and when it actually receives $1 million. The Midland Company is attempting to choose between two proposals for new products. Both proposals will provide additional cash flows over a four-year period and will initially cost $10,000. The cash flows from the proposals are as follows:

RISK OF CASH FLOWS

The firm must consider risk. The amount and timing of cash flows are not usually known with certainty. Most investors have an aversion to risk.

At first it appears that new product *A* would be best. However, the cash flows from proposal *B* come earlier than those of *A*. Without more information, we cannot decide which set of cash flows would create the most value to the bondholders and shareholders. It depends on whether the value of getting cash from *B* up front outweighs the extra total cash from *A*. Bond and stock prices reflect this preference for earlier cash, and we will see how to use them to decide between *A* and *B*.

The Midland Company is considering expanding operations overseas. It is evaluating Europe and Japan as possible sites. Europe is considered to be relatively safe, whereas operating in Japan is seen as very risky. In both cases, the company would close down operations after one year. After doing a complete financial analysis, Midland has come up with the following cash flows of the alternative plans for expansion under three equally likely scenarios—pessimistic, most likely, and optimistic:

If we ignore the pessimistic scenario, perhaps Japan is the best alternative. When we take the pessimistic scenario into account, the choice is unclear. Japan appears to be riskier, but it also offers a higher expected level of cash flow. What is risk and how can it be defined? We must try to answer this important question. Corporate finance cannot avoid coping with risky alternatives, and much of our book is devoted to developing methods for evaluating risky opportunities.

THE CORPORATE FIRM

The firm is a way of organizing the economic activity of many individuals. A basic problem of the firm is how to raise cash. The corporate form of business, that is, organizing the firm as a corporation, is the standard method for solving problems encountered in raising large amounts of cash. However, businesses can take other forms. In this section we consider the three basic legal forms of organizing firms, and we see how firms go about the task of raising large amounts of money under each form.

The Sole Proprietorship

A sole proprietorship is a business owned by one person. Suppose you decide to start a business to produce mousetraps. Going into business is simple: You announce to all who will listen, "Today, I am going to build a better mousetrap."

Most large cities require that you obtain a business license. Afterward, you can begin to hire as many people as you need and borrow whatever money you need. At year-end all the profits and the losses will be yours. Here are some factors that are important in considering a sole proprietorship:

1. The sole proprietorship is the cheapest business to form. No formal charter is required, and few government regulations must be satisfied for most industries.
2. A sole proprietorship pays no corporate income taxes. All profits of the business are taxed as individual income.

3. The sole proprietorship has unlimited liability for business debts and obligations. No distinction is made between personal and business assets.
4. The life of the sole proprietorship is limited by the life of the sole proprietor.
5. Because the only money invested in the firm is the proprietor's, the equity money that can be raised by the sole proprietor is limited to the proprietor's personal wealth.

The Partnership

Any two or more persons can get together and form a partnership. Partnerships fall into two categories: (1) general partnerships and (2) limited partnerships. In a *general partnership,* all partners agree to provide some fraction of the work and cash and to share the profits and losses. Each partner is liable for all of the debts of the partnership. A partnership agreement specifies the nature of the arrangement. The partnership agreement may be an oral agreement or a formal document setting forth the understanding.

Limited partnerships permit the liability of some of the partners to be limited to the amount of cash each has contributed to the partnership. Limited partnerships usually require that (1) at least one partner be a general partner and (2) the limited partners do not participate in managing the business. Here are some things that are important when considering a partnership:

1. Partnerships are usually inexpensive and easy to form. Written documents are required in complicated arrangements, including general and limited partnerships. Business licenses and filing fees may be necessary.
2. General partners have unlimited liability for all debts. The liability of limited partners is usually limited to the contribution each has made to the partnership. If one general partner is unable to meet his or her commitment, the shortfall must be made up by the other general partners.

3. The general partnership is terminated when a general partner dies or withdraws (but this is not so for a limited partner). It is difficult for a partnership to transfer ownership without dissolving. Usually, all general partners must agree. However, limited partners may sell their interest in a business.
4. It is difficult for a partnership to raise large amounts of cash. Equity contributions are usually limited to a partner's ability and desire to contribute to the partnership. Many companies, such as Apple Computer, start life as a proprietorship or partnership, but at some point they choose to convert to corporate form.
5. Income from a partnership is taxed as personal income to the partners.
6. Management control resides with the general partners. Usually a majority vote is required on important matters, such as the amount of profit to be retained in the business.

It is very difficult for large business organizations to exist as sole proprietorships or partnerships. The main advantage to a sole proprietorship or partnership is the cost of getting started. Afterward, the disadvantages, which may become severe, are:

(1) unlimited liability,

(2) limited life of the enterprise, and

(3) difficulty of transferring ownership. These three disadvantages lead to

(4) difficulty raising cash.

The Corporation

Of the many forms of business enterprises, the corporation is by far the most important. It is a distinct legal entity. As such, a corporation can have a name and enjoy many of the legal powers of natural persons. For example, corporations can acquire and exchange property. Corporations can enter into contracts and may sue and be sued. For jurisdictional purposes, the corporation is a citizen of its state of incorporation (it cannot vote, however). Starting a corporation is more complicated than starting a proprietorship or partnership. The incorporators must prepare articles of incorporation and a set of bylaws. The articles of incorporation must include the following:

1. Name of the corporation.
2. Intended life of the corporation (it may be forever).
3. Business purpose.
4. Number of shares of stock that the corporation is authorized to issue, with a statement of limitations and rights of different classes of shares.
5. Nature of the rights granted to shareholders.
6. Number of members of the initial board of directors.

The bylaws are the rules to be used by the corporation to regulate its own existence, and they concern its shareholders, directors, and officers. Bylaws range from the briefest possible statement of rules for the corporation's management to hundreds of pages of text. In its simplest form, the corporation comprises three sets of distinct interests: the shareholders (the owners), the directors, and the corporation officers (the top management).

Traditionally, the shareholders control the corporation's direction, policies, and activities. The shareholders elect a board of directors, who in turn select top management. Members of top management serve as corporate officers and manage the operations of the corporation in the best interest of the shareholders. In closely held corporations with few shareholders, there may be a large overlap among the shareholders, the directors, and the top management. However, in larger corporations, the shareholders, directors, and the top management are likely to be distinct groups.

The potential separation of ownership from management gives the corporation several advantages over proprietorships and partnerships:

1. Because ownership in a corporation is represented by shares of stock, ownership can be readily transferred to new owners. Because the corporation exists

independently of those who own its shares, there is no limit to the transferability of shares as there is in partnerships.

2. The corporation has unlimited life. Because the corporation is separate from its owners, the death or withdrawal of an owner does not affect its legal existence. The corporation can continue on after the original owners have withdrawn.
3. The shareholders' liability is limited to the amount invested in the ownership shares. For example, if a shareholder purchased $1,000 in shares of a corporation, the potential loss would be $1,000. In a partnership, a general partner with a $1,000 contribution could lose the $1,000 plus any other indebtedness of the partnership.

Limited liability, ease of ownership transfer, and perpetual succession are the major advantages of the corporation form of business organization. These give the corporation an enhanced ability to raise cash.

There is, however, one great disadvantage to incorporation. The federal government taxes corporate income (the states do as well). This tax is in addition to the personal income tax that shareholders pay on dividend income they receive. This is double taxation for shareholders when compared to taxation on proprietorships and partnerships.

Today, all 50 states have enacted laws allowing for the creation of a relatively new form of business organization, the limited liability company (LLC). The goal of this entity is to operate and be taxed like a partnership but retain limited liability for owners, so an LLC is essentially a hybrid of partnership and corporation. Although states have differing definitions for LLCs, the more important scorekeeper is the Internal Revenue Service (IRS). The IRS will consider an LLC a corporation, thereby subjecting it to double taxation, unless it meets certain specific criteria. In essence, an LLC cannot be too corporationlike, or it will be treated as one by the IRS. LLCs have become common. For example, Goldman, Sachs and Co., one of Wall Street's last remaining partnerships, decided to convert from a private partnership to an LLC (it later "went public," becoming a publicly held corporation). Large accounting firms and law firms by the score have converted to LLCs.

A Corporation by Another Name...

The corporate form of organization has many variations around the world. The exact laws and regulations differ from country to country, of course, but the essential features of public ownership and limited liability remain. These firms are often called *joint stock companies, public limited companies,* or *limited liability companies,* depending on the specific nature of the firm and the country of origin.

The names of a few well-known international corporations, their country of origin, and a translation of the abbreviation that follows the company name.

CORPORATION PARTNERSHIP

Liquidity and Shares can be exchanged without Units are subject to substantial marketability termination of the corporation. restrictions on transferability. There Common stock can be listed on is usually no established trading stock exchange. market for partnership units.

Voting rights Usually each share of common stock Some voting rights by limited entitles the holder to one vote per partners. However, general partner share on matters requiring a vote has exclusive control and and on the election of the directors. management of operations. Directors determine top management.

Taxation Corporations have double taxation: Partnerships are not taxable. Partners Corporate income is taxable, and pay personal taxes on partnership dividends to shareholders are also profits.

Reinvestment and Corporations have broad latitude on Partnerships are generally prohibited dividend payout dividend payout decisions. from reinvesting partnership profits.

All profits are distributed to partners.

Liability Shareholders are not personally liable Limited partners are not liable for for obligations of the corporation. obligations of partnerships.

General partners may have unlimited liability.

Continuity of existence Corporations may have a perpetual life. Partnerships have limited life.

THE GOAL OF FINANCIAL MANAGEMENT

Assuming that we restrict ourselves to for-profit businesses, the goal of financial management is to make money or add value for the owners. This goal is a little vague, of course, so we examine some different ways of formulating it in order to come up with a more precise definition. Such a definition is important because it leads to an objective basis for making and evaluating financial decisions.

Possible Goals

If we were to consider possible financial goals, we might come up with some ideas like the following:

- Survive.
- Avoid financial distress and bankruptcy.
- Beat the competition.
- Maximize sales or market share.
- Minimize costs.
- Maximize profits.
- Maintain steady earnings growth.

These are only a few of the goals we could list. Furthermore, each of these possibilities presents problems as a goal for the financial manager.

For example, it's easy to increase market share or unit sales; all we have to do is lower our prices or relax our credit terms. Similarly, we can always cut costs simply by doing away with things such as research and development. We can avoid bankruptcy by never borrowing any money or never taking any risks, and so on. It's not clear that any of these actions are in the stockholders' best interests.

Profit maximization would probably be the most commonly cited goal, but even this is not a very precise objective. Do we mean profits this year? If so, then we should note that actions such as deferring maintenance, letting inventories run down, and taking other short-run cost-cutting measures will tend to increase profits now, but these activities aren't necessarily desirable.

The goal of maximizing profits may refer to some sort of "long-run" or "average" profits, but it's still unclear exactly what this means. First, do we mean something like accounting net income or earnings per share? As we will see in more detail in the next chapter, these accounting numbers may have little to do with what is good or bad for the firm. Second, what do we mean by the long run? As a famous economist once remarked, in the long run, we're all dead! More to the point, this goal doesn't tell us what the appropriate trade-off is between current and future profits.

The goals we've listed here are all different, but they do tend to fall into two classes. The first of these relates to profitability. The goals involving sales, market share, and cost control all relate, at least potentially, to different ways of earning or increasing profits. The goals in the second group, involving bankruptcy avoidance, stability, and safety, relate in some way to controlling risk. Unfortunately, these two types of goals are somewhat contradictory. The pursuit of profit normally involves some element of risk, so it isn't really possible to maximize both safety and profit. What we need, therefore, is a goal that encompasses both factors.

The Goal of Financial Management

The financial manager in a corporation makes decisions for the stockholders of the firm. Given this, instead of listing possible goals for the financial manager, we really need to answer a more fundamental question: From the stockholders' point of view, what is a good financial management decision? If we assume that stockholders buy stock because they seek to gain financially, then the answer is obvious: Good decisions increase the value of the stock, and poor decisions decrease the value of the stock. Given our observations, it follows that the financial manager acts in the shareholders' best interests by making decisions that increase the value of the stock. The appropriate goal for the financial manager can thus be stated quite easily: The goal of financial management is to maximize the current value per share of the existing stock.

The goal of maximizing the value of the stock avoids the problems associated with the different goals we listed earlier. There is no ambiguity in the criterion, and there is no short-run versus long-run issue. We explicitly mean that our goal is to maximize the *current* stock value.

If this goal seems a little strong or one-dimensional to you, keep in mind that the stockholders in a firm are residual owners. By this we mean that they are only entitled to what is left after employees, suppliers, and creditors (and everyone else with a legitimate claims) are paid their due. If any of these groups go unpaid, the stockholders get nothing. So, if the stockholders are winning in the sense that the leftover, residual portion is growing, it must be true that everyone else is winning also.

Because the goal of financial management is to maximize the value of the stock, we need to learn how to identify those investments and financing arrangements that favorably impact the value of the stock. This is precisely what we will be studying. In fact, we could have defined corporate finance as the study of the relationship between business decisions and the value of the stock in the business.

A More General Goal

Given our goal as stated in the preceding section (to maximize the value of the stock), an obvious question comes up: What is the appropriate goal when the firm has no traded stock? Corporations are certainly not the only type of business; and the stock in many corporations rarely changes hands, so it's difficult to say what the value per share is at any given time.

As long as we are dealing with for-profit businesses, only a slight modification is needed. The total value of the stock in a corporation is simply equal to the value of the owners' equity. Therefore, a more general way of stating our goal is as follows: Maximize the market value of the existing owners' equity.

With this in mind, it doesn't matter whether the business is a proprietorship, a partnership, or a corporation. For each of these, good financial decisions increase the market value of the owners' equity and poor financial decisions decrease it. In fact, although we choose to focus on corporations in the chapters ahead, the principles we develop apply to all forms of business. Many of them even apply to the not-for-profit sector.

Finally, our goal does not imply that the financial manager should take illegal or unethical actions in the hope of increasing the value of the equity in the firm. What we mean is that the financial manager best serves the owners of the business by identifying goods and services that add value to the firm because they are desired and valued in the free marketplace.

THE AGENCY PROBLEM AND CONTROL OF THE CORPORATION

We've seen that the financial manager acts in the best interests of the stockholders by taking actions that increase the value of the stock. However, in large corporations ownership can be spread over a huge number of stockholders. This dispersion of ownership arguably means that management effectively controls the firm. In this case, will management necessarily act in the best interests of the stockholders? Put another way, might not management pursue its own goals at the stockholders' expense? In the following pages, we briefly consider some of the arguments relating to this question.

Agency Relationships

The relationship between stockholders and management is called an *agency relationship*. Such a relationship exists whenever someone (the principal) hires another (the agent) to represent his/her interests. For example, you might hire someone (an agent) to sell a car that you own while you are away at school. In all such relationships, there is a possibility of a conflict of interest between the principal and the agent. Such a conflict is called an agency problem. Suppose you hire someone to sell your car and you agree to pay that person a flat fee when he/she sells the car. The agent's incentive in this case is to make the sale, not necessarily to get you the best price. If you offer a commission of, say, 10 percent of the sales price instead of a flat fee, then this problem might not exist. This example illustrates that the way in which an agent is compensated is one factor that affects agency problems.

Management Goals

To see how management and stockholder interests might differ, imagine that the firm is considering a new investment. The new investment is expected to favorably impact the share value, but it is also a relatively risky venture. The owners of the firm will wish to take the investment (because the stock value will rise), but management may not because there is the possibility that things will turn out badly and management jobs will be lost. If management does not take the investment, then the stockholders may lose a valuable opportunity. This is one example of an *agency cost*.

More generally, the term agency costs refers to the costs of the conflict of interest between stockholders and management. These costs can be indirect or direct. An indirect agency cost is a lost opportunity, such as the one we have just described.

Direct agency costs come in two forms. The first type is a corporate expenditure that benefits management but costs the stockholders. Perhaps the purchase of a luxurious and unneeded corporate jet would fall under this heading. The second type of direct agency cost is an expense that arises from the need to monitor management actions. Paying outside auditors to assess the accuracy of financial statement information could be one example. It is sometimes argued that, left to themselves, managers would tend to maximize the amount of resources over which they have control or, more generally, corporate power or wealth. This goal could lead to an overemphasis on corporate size or growth. For example, cases in which management is accused of overpaying to buy up another company just to increase the size of the business or to demonstrate corporate power are not uncommon. Obviously, if overpayment does take place, such a purchase does not benefit the stockholders of the purchasing company.

Our discussion indicates that management may tend to overemphasize organizational survival to protect job security. Also, management may dislike outside interference, so independence and corporate self-sufficiency may be important goals.

Do Managers Act in the Stockholders' Interests?

Whether managers will, in fact, act in the best interests of stockholders depends on two factors. First, how closely are management goals aligned with stockholder goals? This question relates, at least in part, to the way managers are compensated. Second, can management be replaced if they do not pursue stockholder goals? This issue relates to control of the firm. As we will discuss, there are a number of reasons to think that, even in the largest firms, management has a significant incentive to act in the interests of stockholders.

MANAGERIAL COMPENSATION

Management will frequently have a significant economic incentive to increase share value for two reasons. First, managerial compensation, particularly at the top, is usually tied to financial performance in general and oftentimes to share value in particular. For example, managers are frequently given the option to buy stock at a bargain price. The more the stock is worth, the more valuable is this option. In fact, options are often used to motivate employees of all types, not just top management.

The second incentive managers have relates to job prospects. Better performers within the firm will tend to get promoted. More generally, those managers who are successful in pursuing stockholder goals will be in greater demand in the labor market and thus command higher salaries.

In fact, managers who are successful in pursuing stockholder goals can reap enormous rewards. For example, one of America's best paid executives in 2004 was Rueben

Mark, the CEO of Colgate-Palmolive for the past 20 years; according to Forbes magazine, he made $148 million in that year. By way of comparison, Mark made less than Mel Gibson and Oprah Winfrey ($210 million each) but more than Tiger Woods ($80 million). Over the period 2000–2004, Oracle CEO Larry Ellison was the highest paid executive, earning about $836 million. Dell CEO Michael Dell earned slightly less over the same period, only $526 million.

CONTROL OF THE FIRM

Control of the firm ultimately rests with stockholders. They elect the board of directors, who, in turn, hire and fire management. The fact that-stockholders control the corporation was made abundantly clear by Carly Fiorina's experience at HP, which we described to open the chapter. Even though she had reorganized the corporation, there came a time when shareholders, through their elected directors, decided that HP would be better off without her, so out she went.

An important mechanism by which unhappy stockholders can act to replace existing management is called a *proxy fight*. A proxy is the authority to vote someone else's stock. A proxy fight develops when a group solicits proxies in order to replace the existing board, and thereby replace existing management. For example, the proposed merger between HP and Compaq, which we mentioned in our chapter opener, triggered one of the most widely followed, bitterly contested, and expensive proxy fights in history, with an estimated price tag of well over $100 million.

Another way that management can be replaced is by takeover. Those firms that are poorly managed are more attractive as acquisitions than well-managed firms because a greater profit potential exists. Thus, avoiding a takeover by another firm gives management another incentive to act in the stockholders' interests. For example, in 2004, Comcast, the cable television giant, announced a surprise bid to buy Disney at a time when Disney's management was under close scrutiny for its performance. Not too surprisingly, Disney's management strongly opposed being acquired, and Comcast ultimately decided to withdraw, in part because of improvements in Disney's financial performance.

CONCLUSION

The available theory and evidence are consistent with the view that stockholders control the firm and that stockholder wealth maximization is the relevant goal of the corporation. Even so, there will undoubtedly be times when management goals are pursued at the expense of the stockholders, at least temporarily.

Stakeholders

Our discussion thus far implies that management and stockholders are the only parties with an interest in the firm's decisions. This is an oversimplification, of course. Employees, customers, suppliers, and even the government all have a financial interest in the firm.

Taken together, these various groups are called stakeholders in the firm. In general, a stakeholder is someone other than a stockholder or creditor who potentially has a claim on the cash flows of the firm. Such groups will also attempt to exert control over the firm, perhaps to the detriment of the owners.

FINANCIAL MARKETS

As indicated, firms offer two basic types of securities to investors. *Debt securities* are contractual obligations to repay corporate borrowing. *Equity securities* are shares of common stock and preferred stock that represent noncontractual claims to the residual cash flow of the firm. Issues of debt and stock that are publicly sold by the firm are then traded on the financial markets. The financial markets are composed of the money markets and the capital markets. Money markets are the markets for debt securities that will pay off in the short term (usually less than one year). Capital markets are the markets for long-term debt (with a maturity at over one year) and for equity shares. The term *money market* applies to a group of loosely connected markets. They are dealer markets.

Dealers are firms that make continuous quotations of prices for which they stand ready to buy and sell money market instruments for their own inventory and at their own risk. Thus, the dealer is a principal in most transactions. This is different from a stockbroker acting as an agent for a customer in buying or selling common stock on most stock exchanges; an agent does not actually acquire the securities.

At the core of the money markets are the money market banks (these are large banks mostly in New York), government securities dealers (some of which are the large banks), and a large number of money brokers. Money brokers specialize in finding short-term money for borrowers and placing money for lenders. The financial markets can be classified further as the *primary market* and the *secondary markets.*

The Primary Market: New Issues

The primary market is used when governments and corporations initially sell securities. Corporations engage in two types of primary market sales of debt and equity: public offerings and private placements.

Most publicly offered corporate debt and equity come to the market underwritten by a syndicate of investment banking firms. The *underwriting* syndicate buys the new securities from the firm for the syndicate's own account and resells them at a higher price. Publicly issued debt and equity must be registered with the United States Securities and Exchange Commission (SEC). *Registration* requires the corporation to disclose all of the material information in a registration statement. The legal, accounting, and other costs of preparing the registration statement are not negligible. In part to avoid these costs, privately placed debt and equity are sold on the basis of private negotiations to large financial institutions, such as insurance companies and mutual funds, and other investors. Private placements are not registered with the SEC.

Secondary Markets

A secondary market transaction involves one owner or creditor selling to another. It is therefore the secondary markets that provide the means for transferring ownership of corporate securities. Although a corporation is only directly involved in a primary market transaction (when it sells securities to raise cash), the secondary markets are still critical to large corporations. The reason is that investors are much more willing to purchase securities in a primary market transaction when they know that those securities can later be resold if desired.

DEALER VERSUS AUCTION MARKETS

There are two kinds of secondary markets: *dealer* markets and *auction* markets. Generally speaking, dealers buy and sell for themselves, at their own risk. A car dealer, for example, buys and sells automobiles. In contrast, brokers and agents match buyers and sellers, but they do not actually own the commodity that is bought or sold. A real estate agent, for example, does not normally buy and sell houses.

Dealer markets in stocks and long-term debt are called *over-the-counter* (OTC) markets. Most trading in debt securities takes place over the counter. The expression *over the counter* refers to days of old when securities were literally bought and sold at counters in offices around the country. Today, a significant fraction of the market for stocks and almost all of the market for long-term debt have no central location; the many dealers are connected electronically. Auction markets differ from dealer markets in two ways. First, an auction market or exchange has a physical location (like Wall Street). Second, in a dealer market, most of the buying and selling is done by the dealer. The primary purpose of an auction market, on the other hand, is to match those who wish to sell with those who wish to buy. Dealers play a limited role.

TRADING IN CORPORATE SECURITIES

The equity shares of most of the large firms in the United States trade in organized auction markets. The largest such market is the New York Stock Exchange (NYSE), which accounts for more than 85 percent of all the shares traded in auction markets. Other auction exchanges include the American Stock Exchange (AMEX) and regional exchanges such as the Pacific

Stock Exchange. In addition to the stock exchanges, there is a large OTC market for stocks. In 1971, the National Association of Securities Dealers (NASD) made available to dealers and brokers an electronic quotation system called NASDAQ (which originally stood for NASD Automated Quotation system and is pronounced "naz-dak").

There are roughly two times as many companies on NASDAQ as there are on NYSE, but they tend to be much smaller in size and trade less actively. There are exceptions, of course. Both Microsoft and Intel trade OTC, for example. Nonetheless, the total value of NASDAQ stocks is much less than the total value of NYSE stocks.

There are many large and important financial markets outside the United States, of course, and U.S. corporations are increasingly looking to these markets to raise cash. The Tokyo Stock Exchange and the London Stock Exchange (TSE and LSE, respectively) are two well-known examples. The fact that OTC markets have no physical location means that national borders do not present a great barrier, and there is now a huge international OTC debt market. Because of globalization, financial markets have reached the point where trading in many investments never stops; it just travels around the world.

Exchange Trading of Listed Stocks

Auction markets are different from dealer markets in two ways. First, trading in a given auction exchange takes place at a single site on the floor of the exchange. Second, transaction prices of shares traded on auction exchanges are communicated almost immediately to the public by computer and other devices. The NYSE is one of the preeminent securities exchanges in the world. All transactions in stocks listed on the NYSE occur at a particular place on the floor of the exchange called a *post.* At the heart of the market is the specialist. Specialists are members of the NYSE who *make a market* in designated stocks. Specialists have an obligation to offer to buy and sell shares of their assigned NYSE stocks. It is believed that this makes the market liquid because the specialist assumes the role of a buyer for investors if they wish to sell and a seller if they wish to buy.

SARBANES-OXLEY

In response to corporate scandals at companies such as Enron, WorldCom, Tyco, and Adelphia, Congress enacted the Sarbanes-Oxley Act in 2002. The act, better known as "Sarbox," is intended to protect investors from corporate abuses. For example, one section of Sarbox prohibits personal loans from a company to its officers, such as the ones that were received by WorldCom CEO Bernie Ebbers.

One of the key sections of Sarbox took effect on November 15, 2004. Section 404 requires, among other things, that each company's annual report must have an assessment of the company's internal control structure and financial reporting. The auditor must then evaluate and attest to management's assessment of these issues.

Sarbox contains other key requirements. For example, the officers of the corporation must review and sign the annual reports. They must explicitly declare that the annual report does not contain any false statements or material omissions; that the financial statements fairly represent the financial results; and that they are responsible for all internal controls. Finally, the annual report must list any deficiencies in internal controls. In essence, Sarbox makes company management responsible for the accuracy of the company's financial statements.

Of course, as with any law, there are compliance costs, and Sarbox has increased the cost of corporate audits, sometimes dramatically. Estimates of the increase in company audit costs to comply with Sarbox range from $500,000 to over $5 million, which has led to some unintended consequences.

For example, in 2003, 198 firms delisted their shares from exchanges, or "went dark." This was up from 30 delistings in 1999. For 2004, estimates of the number of companies that would go dark ranged from 134 to 250. Most of the companies that delisted stated that their reason was to avoid the cost of compliance with Sarbox. Some conservative estimates put the national Sarbox compliance tab at $35 billion in the first year alone, which is roughly 20 times the amount originally estimated by the SEC. For a large multibilliondollar revenue company, the cost might be.05 percent of revenues, but it could be 3 percent or so for smaller companies, an enormous cost.

A company that goes dark does not have to file quarterly or annual reports. Annual audits by independent auditors are not required, and executives do not have to certify the accuracy of the financial statements, so the savings can be huge. Of course, there are costs. Stock prices typically fall when a company announces it is going dark. Further, such companies will typically have limited access to capital markets and usually will have a higher interest cost on bank loans.

Foreign companies have also been affected. Lastminute, a British online travel group, and Lion Bioscience, a German software company, have already initiated the process to withdraw from U.S. exchanges. And it is not just smaller foreign companies that are considering delisting from U.S. exchanges. German conglomerate Siemens AG, with worldwide sales approaching $100 billion, is considering delisting, and the London Stock Exchange has reported that several companies have discussed going public on that exchange rather than list on a U.S. exchange, to avoid the compliance costs of Sarbox.

Stocks that trade on an organized exchange are said to be *listed* on that exchange. In order to be listed, firms must meet certain minimum criteria concerning, for example, asset size and number of shareholders. These criteria differ from one exchange to another. NYSE has the most stringent requirements of the exchanges in the United States. For example, to be listed on NYSE, a company is expected to have a market value for its publicly held shares of at least $100 million. There are additional minimums on earnings, assets, and number of shares outstanding. The listing requirements for non–U.S. companies are somewhat more stringent. As our nearby *The Real World* box discusses, listed companies also face significant costs arising from disclosure requirements. The market value of NYSE-listed stocks and bonds.

6

Industrial Banks: Assets and Liabilities

INTRODUCTION

This study attempts to find out behaviour of the banks with respect to their capital adequacy ratio dynamics, by decomposing the financial statements. We used information analysis of the balance sheet and a data set that spanned between 1998 and 2002, for twenty public sector banks. We found that information measures can explain banks' policy decisions on liabilities and assts reorganisation. Quantitatively, we found that proportional development took place, in both liabilities and asset items of the banks under different capital adequacy ratio values.

Evidences did show that banks reorganised their assets and liabilities to achieve higher capital adequacy ratios, but such reorganisation did not result from a planned action of the banks, except in certain isolated cases. We also found that the assets reorganisation was more pronounced than the reorganisation of the liabilities. The study points out that the Reserve Bank of India is justified in enhancing the normative minimum CAR from 8% to 9% effective from the year 2000. Indian banking has a rather chequered history. In the early days of independence, that is, during 1950s, the banking activities were restricted to certain selected towns and metropolis. Banking services in rural and semi-urban areas were virtually non-existent. With the establishment of the State Bank of India in 1955, some concerted attempt was made to provide banking services in the rural areas. It is after the nationalisation of the banks that a thrust was made to expand banking services in rural areas.

The banking resources were made available for meeting credit needs of the rural masses. Expanding banking services in hitherto unrepresented areas, financing agriculture and small-scale industries, setting up lead banks were some of the hallmarks of the new policy. In April 1980, six more banks were nationalised. An accelerated growth of banking activities took place and the banks became the major and dominant provider of the credit needs of the business and industry in the economy. Soon, however, expansion led to interplay of dysfunctional forces in the economy and the banks increasingly found themselves in an economically precarious position. The crisis was heightened during 1990s and some of the banks were on the verge of collapse. Since, the Central Government were the owners of the banks, fortunately there was no run on the deposits. Internationally, meanwhile, Basle Committee on Banking Supervision announced (July 1988) risk-based capital standards for the banks.

In India, recommendations of the Committee on Financial Sector Reforms were adopted and capital to risk-weighted assts norms were introduced for the banks from April 1992. It became mandatory for the banks to adhere to the minimum capital adequacy ratio of 8% from 1992 onwards. This ratio was raised to 9% from the year 2000. The banking sector reforms attracted attention of the researchers worldwide, including India. The studies were related to prediction of bank failures, effects and progress of sectoral reforms affecting banks, etc.

EARLIER STUDIES

Risk based capital standards are fairly recent phenomenon, while earlier studies are focussed on bank failures. One of the earliest researches was due to Secrist (1938), who used multivariate analysis to predict bank failures. Another noteworthy study was done by Meyer and Pifer (1970). Using paired sample technique and a sample of thirty-nine pairs of banks, solvent and failed during the period between 1948 and

1965, they constructed a linear regression model for the prediction of bank failures. The variables used were both dependent (dummy) and independent. Thirty-two financial measures were selected as independent variables. The model was successful in predicting approximately 80 percent of the sample banks, one to two years before failure. When the model was used to predict before three years or more, it performed poorly. Some of the variables that entered in the final regression equation are:

- Growth of consumer loan to total assets
- Coefficient of variation of total loans
- Errors in predicting cash and securities to total assets.

Subsequently, the research focus was turned towards investigation of banks behaviour vis-à-vis capital adequacy standards. Some of the researches in this direction were due to Haubrich and Watchel (1993), Hanscock, Laing and Wilcox (1995), Wall and Peterson (1995), Peek and Rosengren (1995), Jacques and Nigro (1997), Editz, Michael and Perraudin (1998), Rime (1998) and Furfine (2000). In all the above studies, evidences were documented to show that introduction of risk-based capital requirements did have influences over banks' lending decisions and change of their portfolio compositions. In India, researches in capital adequacy standards have been reported. In one such studies, Nachane, Narain, Ghosh and Sahoo (2000), using regression model and conditioning variables, designed to proxy bank's internal capital target, documented evidences that capital requirements significantly affect bank's capital ratio decisions.

However, to meet capital requirements approaching regulatory minimum, the banks did not significantly substitute high risk-weighted assets. They added, that profit played a dominant role in the adjustment of capital ratios and banks with higher levels of core capital could have been ploughing back their profits into reserves to raise overall capital levels. Importantly, they found no evidence to support the prevailing belief of shifting from loans to government securities for countering regulatory pressure. They concluded that capital adequacy requirement is an attractive regulatory instrument as it reinforces the stability of the banking system without apparently distorting lending choices of the banks. In another study by Nag and Das (2002) , mainly to investigate impact of imposition of capital requirement in the flow of bank credit, it was concluded that banks did shift their portfolio in a way that reduces their capital requirements. Using switching regression model and certain proxy measures, e.g., synthetic Index of Industrial Production, growth of non-SLR investments, they found a clear possibility of regulatory pressure acting as a controlling factor in the supply of credit to the commercial sector. Meanwhile, the regulatory system has been strengthened and it is of interest now to investigate what factors influence the banks' behaviour in a regime of falling interest rates added with healthy growth of deposits. This study, therefore, seeks to find out, whether there is any linkage in the reorganisation of capital, liabilities and assets of the banks, having different capital adequacy ratios.

Secondly, whether variations of capital adequacy ratios over time has any bearing on the liabilities and assets reorganisation of the banks. In order to investigate the banks' behaviour vis-à-vis variation of capital adequacy ratio over time, we used Informational Analysis. We reasoned that changes in balance sheet items of liabilities and assets effecting variations of capital adequacy ratio, would be better captured by the Information Analysis.

THE MODEL

The basic premise of the information theory is, that occurrence of an event may have several possibilities to which probabilities could be assigned. When information about the event is received these probabilities undergo changes. These changes in probabilities enable measurement of amount of information contained in the message.

Mathematically, the information function could be expressed as:

$$h(p) = -\log p \; ; \; 0 \leq p \leq 1. \qquad (1)$$

The function monotonically decreases from ∞ to 0, that is, infinite information, when probability is zero and no (zero) information, when probability of occurrence of an event is 1(one).

Extending the concept to n events, given by $E_1, E_2, \ldots, E_n$, with probabilities $p_1, p_2, \ldots, p_n$, we find that since one of the events is bound to occur, all the probabilities, $p_1, p_2, \ldots, p_n$ will sum to one. Now if the event E occurs, the amount of information in the message stating the occurrence of E is h (pi) and the expected information content of the message,

i.e., the entropy of the distribution with probabilities p_1, $p_2, \ldots, p_n$ is given by:

$$H(p_1, p_2, \ldots, p_n) = \sum_{i=1}^{n} p_i h(p_i) = -\sum_{i=1}^{n} p_i \log p_i ; \ p_i \geq 0, \ \sum_{i=1}^{n} p_i = 1 \text{ and} \quad (2)$$

$$p_i \log p_i = 0, \text{ when } p_i = 0$$

In the same way, the expected information content of a non-definite message can be evaluated and is given by the following expression:

$$I = \sum_{i=1}^{n} q_i \log q_i/p_i, \quad (3)$$

where, qi is the changed probability of the original robability pi, due to arrival of non- definite message in respect of event E.

The major constraint that is encountered in the application of information concept for the analysis of financial statements is the need to assign two sets of probabilities to all possible outcome, one before arrival of the message and the other, after it. If, for example, individual items of the balance sheet, like, fixed and current assets, capital and current liabilities are divided by their total; it would yield a set of non-negative fractions, which will sum to one. These fractions could then be regarded as probabilities, since the requirements of a probability distribution are the same, i.e., they are non-negative and sum to one. Statistically speaking, if the fixed assets yield a fraction denoted by 'p', then there is a probability of 'p' that a single rupee picked up at random from the balance sheet asset items would belong to fixed assets. Two sets of balance sheets would yield fractions that could be used as two sets of probabilities as mentioned above.

ASSETS AND LIABILITIES INFORMATION MEASURES

In the balance sheet, let us denote fractions of assets decomposition by p_i, i = 1, 2, ..., n (like p_1 = cash & balance with RBI, p_2 = balance with banks, money at call), etc., and let us also denote the corresponding fractions of a later period assets side of the balance sheet as q_i, i = 1, 2, ..., n, then the assets information measure I_A, would be:

$$I_A = \sum_{i=1}^{n} q_i \log q_i/p_i \qquad (4)$$

The details calculation of information measures of a sample bank is shown in Appendix A.

The assets information measures, as can be observed, reflect the variability of the individual asset items as contained in the two time-horizon balance sheets. The value of the measure will be zero, when the individual fractions of the two balance sheets items are identical, i.e., when $q_i = p_i$. The larger deviations of the two fractions (or the probabilities), would result in larger information measures. The measure would show the extent of deviations of the proportional development of the asset items. Higher and lower values would indicate relatively higher and lower reorganisation of the assets items between the two balance sheets. As Lev puts the decomposition of the firm's assets represents the end result of managerial policy with respect to resources allocation.

The assets information measures will therefore characterize, among other things, the degree of change in this policy'. Therefore, an examination of assets information measures of a bank, would bring out, the extent of change of managerial policy to counter regulatory pressure of achieving the normative capital ratio. Significance of information analysis can be traced out to the fact that variations of financial statement items over time duly reflect occurrence of significant event that are caused by planned as well as ad-hoc or non- planned actions of the management.

In the same way we can calculate liabilities information measures. The basic properties of this measure are same as that of the assets information measure. It would similarly indicate degree of deviation on proportional basis of the liabilities occurred during the period covered by the two balance sheets.

DATA SET

The data are collected from the Reserve Bank of India website and its related links. The individual websites of the public sector banks are also exploited to collect relevant data. The period covered spanned between 1998 and 2002. Due to paucity of data on the internet, analysis is done in respect of 20 public sector banks as given in Table I. We believe that analysis in respect of 20 banks would describe fairly accurately the entire profile of public sector banks in India. For the year 2002, the capital adequacy ratio cannot be obtained in respect of eleven banks.

The time horizon information measures, both for assets and liabilities, are calculated for all the referred years. Since the information measures are scale free, they are also calculated for several non-consecutive years.

The Table II shows the average information values under different capital adequacy ratio values and also the minimum and maximum values under the groups. Moreover, the capital ratios of the individual banks did not remain stable over time. The average values of information measures are calculated on period-to-period basis across switching capital adequacy ratio values. These are shown in Table III. Here, logarithm of base 10 is used to calculate expected information content. The unit of measurement is 'Hartley'. However, we would not mention it further in our study.

SUMMARY OF RESULTS

The average information measures under each category of capital adequacy ratio, show, different values between liabilities and assets time horizon measures. In each case, the average time horizon information measures in respect of liabilities, is always less than the average time horizon information of the assets. Even the highest and lowest values of information measure of the liabilities are systematically less than the highest and lowest information values of the assets. It shows that the assets side of the balance sheet has undergone more differential changes than the liabilities. Since, the information measure indicates variations in the items of financial statements over time, any high value would indicate higher variability, while it would show lower variability for low value. Acting on this premise, if we now examine the behaviour of the information measure, we could isolate a trend.

For instance, the average value of assets information measures for capital adequacy ratio of 7+ is 95.88×10^{-4} (henceforth the multiplier 10^{-4} will not be quoted), while 9+ capital adequacy ratio has an average value of 60.23. Since the banks, with 7+ capital adequacy ratio would be forced to take vigorous steps to reach the statutory minimum, there would be higher reshuffling of assets. The banks would also have to reallocate their liabilities in order to reach the normative minimum capital ratio. These efforts would obviously lead to greater variability amongst the various items of assets and liabilities over time and the effect of such variability would be captured in the information measure value. The veracity of the argument could be readily found when we calculate time horizon liabilities information measure. The average value of liabilities information measure for capital adequacy ratio (CAR) 7+ is 32.78, and thus supports our arguments. If we move on to examine behaviour of information values for other capital adequacy ratios, we find the average value of 77.51 for CAR 10+ and 37.60 for CAR 11+.

The reason for this difference is not difficult to comprehend. In case of CAR with magnitude 10+, the banks are very near to regulatory minimum level and they would more likely to reorganise their assets and liabilities vigorously, to stay above the stipulated minimum. If such an effort were exerted, it would increase variability of the items in assets and liabilities of the banks, which would finally result in higher information value. It may be further observed that, in both the liabilities and assets information measures, the average values for CAR 10+, are higher than those of category 9+ CAR. The question that arises at this stage, why the average value of information measures would be higher for 10+ CAR instead of 9+ CAR, since the banks with 9+ CAR would be more pro-active to increase the capital adequacy ratio. When we examine the individual information measures of the banks having 10+ CAR, the extreme assets information value is found to be 848.44, which is included in the calculation of the average.

If this extreme value is excluded from the samples, the average information value of the assets reduces to 32.16 and it fits well into our above hypothesis. In other words, banks having CAR of 9+ are in fact reorganising their total assets more actively than the banks with CAR 10+. Further, we find that the assets information measures of banks with CAR 11+ and CAR 12+ have values of 37.60 and 81.82 respectively.

These values are consistent, since the banks having CAR 11+ is reasonably well placed and the banks with the same CAR would like to stay stable at the same level. The banks with CAR of 12+ are once again growth-oriented banks, as they would concentrate more on to achieve optimal position. (This is not to suggest that CAR 12+ represents the optimal position. Further research in this regard is necessary.) Having reached this position, the banks would find little incentive to reorganise their total assets in a different manner and hence the information values would be low for the banks with CAR more than 12+.

Exactly the same behaviour is observed for the information measures of the banks with CAR 13+. The average value of assets information measure is 22.81, which is the lowest amongst all the average values of information measures under different capital adequacy ratios. However, when the difference between the values of above information measures is examined, it reveals that there is hardly any planned action that induces the change in the capital adequacy ratio values.

For instance, the difference between the assets information measures of CAR 12+ and CAR 13+ is approximately equal to the difference of the average values of the assets measure of CAR 7+ and CAR 11+. Similar identical differences could be found between CAR 9+ and CAR 13+ with that of CAR 10+ and CAR 11+. Moreover when we look at the minimum and maximum values of assets and liabilities information measures under different values of capital adequacy ratios, it is observed that such minimum and maximum values behave more or less in a random manner. It is, therefore, evident that the managerial actions to counter pressure of regulatory system are of unplanned in nature. Any planned action would have affected all the banks in the same way and effect of such actions would likely to have been same on all the banks leading to near identical information values. Wide divergence shows that no such planned action was taken by majority of the banks and the observed reorganisations of assets and liabilities of the individual banks were due to routine and sometimes unplanned management policy decisions.

It would be now of interest to examine, how the information measures behave when capital adequacy ratio changes over time. An examination of the average values of information measures in Table-III reveals, that the average values of the information measures are relatively higher when the capital adequacy ratio switches from a value of 10+ to 11+, with respect to average information values when the CAR hovers within 10+ region. The higher value shows that the banks exerted additional reorganisation effort to push the capital adequacy ratio to a higher level. This is consistent to our earlier findings that banks did reorganise their assets and liabilities to change their capital ratios.

Here also, we find that the average value of liabilities measures is lower than the average value of assets measures, signifying thereby, that the banks resorted to higher reorganisation of assets rather than capital and liabilities. The highest information value is seen in case of CAR switching values from 10+ to 12+, followed by CAR switching from 11+ to 12+. Since, additional effort would be required to push CAR to a magnitude of 12+, it shows near equal highest information values for both the above cases. In contrast, less effort is required to push the CAR from 12+ to 13+ and accordingly the information value is less in this case. However, behaviour of the measures for other switching values of the CAR cannot be explained with the above argument. The information values for CAR switching from 11+ to 13+ are 13.50 for liabilities and 36.09 for the assets, while CAR moving within 11+ range have nearly identical values, viz., 13.46 for liabilities and 31.60 for assets. It shows that banks hardly took any planned step to reorganise its assets and liabilities for the switching of the CAR. This phenomenon therefore suggests that, switching to higher value of CAR is possible without any planned managerial policy of reorganisation. The above findings are further supported when we examine the behaviour of information measures in a downward movement of CAR. The variability of the average values of liabilities measures cannot be explained by the above hypothesis for downward movement of CAR from 13+ to 12+ and from 11+ to 10+. The behaviour of measures for the CAR switching from 11+ to 7+ cannot be explained when compared against CAR switching from 12+ to 11+. It points to a clear possibility that banks although significantly changed their assets portfolio for adjustment of the CAR, but such efforts were not induced or planned but largely dependent on the perfunctory banking activities.

It is therefore observed that the information analysis is capable of explaining the behaviour of the banks in capital adequacy system regime. We find larger value of information measure when the capital adequacy ratio value is 12+. Such a large value shows that the banks reorganise their assets strongly at this level. Beyond this level, there is little incentive to change their status and the evidences in this regard are captured in information analysis.

However, the minimum and maximum information values describe some random characteristics and hence it is inferred that the banks do not resort to planned action to influence their capital adequacy structures. This view is further supported by the evidence of random behaviour of characteristic differences between information measures under different group of capital adequacy ratios. We also find that asset information measures are higher than the liabilities information measures, evidencing higher reorganisation of assets compared to capital and liabilities. Further evidences of random behaviour of information measures in upward and downward switching movements of

CAR, strongly point out that the banks are not induced or forced to take planned steps to attain targeted value of the capital adequacy ratio.

CONCLUSION

In India, capital standards for the banks have been introduced, in line with international practices, since 1992. Although a decade has passed, there are few researches in this direction to find out how banks adjust their normative capital ratios under the regulatory system. The purpose of the present study is to find out management behaviour with respect to their capital adequacy ratio dynamics, by decomposing the financial statements. We use information analysis of the balance sheet and a data set that spanned between 1998 and 2002, for twenty public sector banks.

We find that information measures can explain banks' policy decisions on liabilities and assets reorganisation. Quantitatively, we find that proportional development took place, in both liabilities and asset items of the banks under different capital adequacy ratio values. Evidences show that banks have reorganised their assets and liabilities to achieve higher capital adequacy ratios, but the evidences also point out such reorganisation do not result from a planned action of the banks, except in certain isolated cases. We have also found that the assets reorganisation is more pronounced than the reorganisation of the liabilities.

In other words, banks have resorted to reshuffling their assets differentially more than the proportional reorganisation of their capital and liabilities, during the referred period. The behaviour of both assets and liabilities information measures, is found to be largely random during investigation of period-to-period switching capital adequacy ratio values. It indicates that except in certain isolated cases, majority of the banks do not take deliberate steps to attain higher capital adequacy ratio. The study also points out that since there is little change in information measures of the banks at higher capital adequacy ratio level, the Reserve Bank of India is justified in enhancing the normative minimum CAR from 8% to 9% effective from the year 2000. This study foresees that there will not be any added difficulty if the capital adequacy ratio is raised further to 10% in near future.

Table: Average Information Values Under Different Capital Adequacy Ratio

Capital Adequacy Ratios	Average Information Value		Minimum Value		Maximum Value	
	Liabilities	Assets	Liabilities	Assets	Liabilities	Assets
7 or more but less than 8	32.78	95.88	5.8	55.1	59.75	136.66
9 or more but less than 10	2.13	60.23	1.73	19.64	2.53	143.21
10 or more but less than 11	16.51	77.51	1.47	3.67	93.39	848.44
11 or more but less than 12	22.54	37.6	2.98	2.26	96.64	203.26
12 or more but less than 13	24.31	81.82	1.19	8	67.52	296.58
13 or more but less than 14	9.38	22.81	0.95	9.85	16.78	33.3

• All the above values are expressed as : x 10^{-4} Hartley

WORRY ABOUT PUBLIC SECTOR BANKS

Since 2000, while public sector banks' (PSB's) assets have grown by 2.6 times to about $600 billion, they have reduced their workforce by about 3,00,000 employees in aggregate, suggesting a big improvement in productivity. Their profitability has increased from a return-on-assets of 0.47% to 0.79%, and their non-performing loans have come down from 7.9% to 0.94% during this period. They have also improved their capital adequacy ratio from 10.9% to 12%. Most of them have invested in technology and have an increasing proportion of their business being conducted on new core banking solution platforms, and as a group, they own 12,700 ATMs today. Many of them have undertaken major business restructuring exercises to improve their operations, and, as a segment, they are in better health today then they were seven years ago on almost all parameters.

The matter of being worried is that our democracy is real and our representatives are alive to their short-term political compulsions over a more distant greater good. This is true everywhere in the world and not limited to India. Political representatives will reflect the point of view of their political constituents because this is the basis of their election. This is independent of the political party in power.

Table III: Average Information Value and Switching Capital Adequacy Ratios

Capital Adequacy Ratio Switching Value		Average Value of Information Measure	
From	To	Liabilities (x 10-4 Hartley)	Assets
upwards			
10+	10+	13.41	32.59
10+	11+	17.94	61.22
10+	12+	17.33	100.38
11+	11+	13.46	31.6
11+	12+	11.51	99.3
11+	13+	13.5	36.09
12+	13+	13.77	57.43
downwards			
13+	12+	6.79	39.62
12+	11+	30.17	41.68
11+	10+	4.76	304.32
11+	7+	54.89	96.61

The only difference in India is that they can more directly influence the actions of PSBs. What I mean is that with elections around the corner, the good financial figures of banks are tempting. Recently, the composition of bank boards has changed. The representation of minority shareholders has been reduced. Political nominees have increased. Representatives from the RBI have been pulled out and government directors are starting to abstain from the management committees of the boards. It is not that any of the members on a board are good or bad, but it is clear they represent different interests. These interests may not be aligned with the commercial operations of the banks. The business cycle over the past seven years has been positive. Many sectors that had been struggling in 2000—steel, cement and sugar—are currently doing well. Many bank bad loans as a result are back in the black. But since last year, interest rates are rising on inflation concerns, the rupee is strengthening and capital inflows are so strong that economists worry about the "Dutch disease" afflicting India. The Economist warns people not to buy property in Mumbai. And many commentators worry about the coming softness in the US Economy. The intensely competitive Indian financial services market is set to see more competition. As one of the fastest growing Markets, foreign interest is high and the RBI is set to open the sector further in 2009. In a sense, it is the wrong time for pillage. Yet, exhortations to increase lending to agriculture, exports and the financially-excluded at capped interest rates are increasing at a time that interest rates are rising. At the same time, corridor talk about bad loan settlement at the behest of influential political brokers is increasing. Is the second coming that Yeats' so poetically wrote about close at hand? Do we see the tiger crouching?

There are silver linings, though, that gives hope. The FM is now reviewing PSBs against the operating metrics achieved by the best private sector banks. The ministry is supporting progressive managements, and defending them against the excesses of the political class. And most rewarding of all—Class III unions in bank after bank are becoming the most progressive and demanding votaries of change. They must all be supported by the press to ensure that the taxpayer and minority shareholders are not looted by a political class that has access to the till. On guard, all.

7

The Drawback of Financial System

The world over, the financial sector is faced with adjustment problems of facing up to rapid changes in the environment. The Indian financial system cannot be immune to this universal phenomenon. What we propose to do today is to discuss some of the problems of the Indian financial system and while recognising the progress made, we would attempt to address some of the hard issues in the reforms which do not seem to have easy solutions..

THE REAL PROBLEM

One of the fundamental problems which have all along afflicted the Indian economy is the lack of proper pricing of factor endowments. We are not here going into abstruse analytics but would merely set out certain issues in layman's language. In an increasingly integrated world economy nominal interest rate differentials need to reflect inflation rate differentials so that real rates of interest are equilibrated as between countries. To the extent that capital is more scarce in India, than say in most developed countries, one would expect real rates of interest to be higher in India. No one will ever wish to get into the cul-de-sac of how one should measure inflation, which interest rate to use and what time period to use. Suffice it to say that we in India have all along endeavoured to artificially keep down the cost of capital and this distortion has had serious repercussions on the viability of the Indian financial sector.

In a capital scarce economy we have used the interest rate mechanism to encourage the use of capital and discourage financial savings. Above all the government, as the biggest guzzler of resources, demanded and obtained resources at artificially low rates of interest. In such a milieu, a whole range of economic activity got generated based on an artificially low rate of interest. The Indian entrepreneur fitted in with the typical Hayekian entrepreneur, weak and excessively dependent on borrowered funds at low rates of interest. Like the Hayekian entrepreneur Indian industry found itself unable to adjust to a market related interest rate system and removal of the distortions in interest rates resulted in exposing the fragility of industry. More importantly, the overall policy thrust was on ensuring that financial intermediaries fully met the credit demands for "productive purposes" and, therefore, the felt need of the borrower gained primacy over the viability of the financial intermediary and the safety and security of the saver was put at a discount. What was most disconcerting was the fact that borrowers defaulted on loans without inviting any adverse action. Lest this sound like a denigration of the Indian system let me hasten to add that this was a world-wide phenomenon. In the context of the increasing fragility of the financial system, the world over, there emerged in the eighties the now famous Basle prudential norms.

With the requirement for proper asset classification, income recognition, provisioning and stipulations on minimum capital adequacy, large holes appeared in the balance sheets of banks requiring a rethinking on lending policies to reduce risks. In the worst cases major restructuring by way of recapitalisation, downsizing, mergers and in some cases closure of financial intermediaries become necessary. The Indian financial system also faced problems which took on a very different dimension. After three decades of a dirigiste regime the Indian financial system found it exceedingly hard to adjust to the sweeping changes in the international financial system.

With a monolithic public sector predominance in terms of ownership the emphasis was on carrying out the edicts set out and commercial decision taking, based on the viability of lending, took a backseat. Again, as ownership, regulation and borrowing became increasingly intertwined, regulatory forbearance become endemic. The level of non-performing assets of public sector banks in March 2000, as a proportion of advances, was estimated at 14.3 per cent gross and 7.4 per cent net which was very high as compared with other countries.

Despite all these adverse features the burden on the Indian fisc of recapitalisation of banks and financial institutions has been minimal at less than one per cent of GDP as compared with as large as 15 per cent in some extreme cases. The saving grace in the Indian system was the prohibitive reserve requirement for banks which, at the time of initiating the financial sector reforms, was as high as an average of 53.5 per cent. This, in a sense, minimised the cost of restructuring the Indian financial system. Again, another reason for the low fiscal burden in the Indian case is the possibility that at least, in some banks/institutions we are witnessing only the tip of the iceberg of non-performing assets.

IMPACT OF THE FIRST PHASE OF THE REFORMS

In the first phase of the reforms, which can be broadly identified as the period 1992-98, a number of measures were taken. First, the government on its part recognised the damage to the financial system of large automatic monetisation of the fiscal deficit and it entered into two historic supplemental agreements to phase out this obnoxious practice. Furthermore, government agreed to pay close to market related rates of interest on government paper.

More importantly, it bore the brunt of its responsibility as owner of public sector banks by recapitalising them to the tune of Rs. 20,000 crore. After this recapitalisation the government agreed to lower its holding in public sector banks to a minimum of 51 per cent.

Secondly, reserve requirements were brought down drastically from 53.5 per cent to 33 per cent. More particularly, the cash reserve ratio, which is the major drag on the banking system is now an average prescription of 8 per cent and with various exemptions the effective ratio is now only 7 per cent. Thirdly, significant steps were taken to develop the money, securities and forex markets.

Fourthly, prudential norms were introduced in a phased manner. Fifthly, the interest rates of banks and non-bank financial entities were, for all practical purposes, fully deregulated. Sixthly, the government backed off to a significant extent from behest lending and lending decisions were largely left to banks. Seventhly, serious attempts were made to deal with the legal and other infirmities which stood in the way of recovery of debts.

All these measures made up an impressive array of reforms but while acknowledging these positive steps there are a number of critical areas which require hard decisions. There is a need for a free and well structured debate to enable a broad consensus of support for the second generation financial sector reforms.

Emerging Structures in the Financial Sector

The banking system is still predominantly in the public sector which accounts for 80 per cent of the total. While a number of new well capitalised private sector banks have been set up they account for only 3 per cent of total deposits. Even under a best case scenario of new private sector banks growing at twice the pace of public sector banks, in five years the efficient Lilliputians would account for only 6 per cent of the banking system. While the new private sector banks would, hopefully, provide efficient service, the quality of the system as a whole will be largely determined by what happens to public sector banks. The All-India financial institutions (FIs) have provided yeoman service in the past but their raison d'exister is now under question. These institutions are increasingly moving into areas in the domain of banking and regulatory issues are coming to the fore in terms of the extensive debate on Universal Banking.

The non-bank financial companies (NBFCs) are indeed a motley crowd. At one extreme are the likes of Sundaram Finance which are well run efficient and responsible units and at the other extreme are the fly-by-night operators which violate the regulatory framework with impunity. The Reserve Bank of India (RBI) has been making commendable efforts in the recent period to ensure an element of order in the system. The mutual funds (MFs) are a set of institutions, quite apart from the others, but an insensate fiscal system has resulted in MFs giving torrid and grossly unfair competition to banks. We will come back to this issue when discussing the need for evolving a reasonably equitable financial architecture:

ISSUES IN SECOND GENERATION REFORMS

There is a popular misconception that there has been considerable soft- peddling on the second generation reforms. Such a view is unwarranted, unfair and unappreciative of the dimensions of the problems which are being tackled. It is necessary to go into the intracacies of the problems and to work out viable solutions in our milieu. This will require sensitising public opinion to ensure a better understanding of the need for adjustment and at the same time there is a need to assure all stakeholders that it is possible to work towards efficiency of operations without derailing the system.

TACKLING THE NPA PROBLEM

The NPAs of the banking system are reportedly in the region of Rs. 52,000 crore and it is clearly recognised that the drain on the system of such a large burden needs early resolution. It is expected that the one-time settlements for NPAs below Rs. 10 crore will be non-discretionary and uniform and a number of banks have focussed their energies on a one point agenda of recovery of loans.

It is recognised that recovery of NPAs is not an easy task and the sheer attrition of time results in an accretion to NPAs as loans are down-graded on the asset classification ladder. There is a general perception, reinforced by the global rating agencies, that actual NPAs are higher than indicated by the numbers as there is atleast anecdotal evidence of ever- greening and stipulation of weaker norms in India. Legal infirmities are by far the most formidable impediments to a strengthened banking system. The Andhyarujina Committee has recommended the creation of a new law granting statutory power of possession and sale of security directly to banks and FIs and creation of a new securitisation act which would confer legal sanctity to transfer of future receivables. Action on this front would be the most important measure in the second generation reforms.

GOVERNMENT OWNERSHIP OF BANKS

While Narasimham Committee-I had taken the stance that efficiency of operation was ownership neutral, Narasimham Committee-II indicated that predominant public ownership of banks is in conflict with efficiency of operations. Narasimhim-II advocated a reduction in the minimum public ownership from 51 per cent to 33 per cent and the government has formally announced the acceptance of this recommendation. Capital adequacy requirements would require that banks raise substantial amounts by way of fresh capital but the fisc is far too burdened to be able to provide the necessary resources.

This provides the rationale for reduction of the minimum public ownership of banks. Governor Dr. Bimal Jalan has indicated in his Administrative Staff College lecture in December 1999 that while the minimum public sector holding would be reduced to 33 per cent the public sector character of banks would remain unchanged. This has been misunderstood in some quarters to imply that inefficiencies in the system would be tolerated and that these banks would be strangulated by the overarching role of government. What Governor Jalan has set out is a pragmatic policy of meeting the additional capital requirements of banks by raising money from the capital market without a take over by predatory elements of these public sector banks for their narrow sectarian interests. This would ensure that while banks function on commercial terms the wider national interest would be taken into account and responsibility would not remain vague during the transition from predominant public ownership. It is hoped that the necessary legislative changes would be enacted in the current financial year.

Since the government is not willing to provide capital to these banks, only the relatively strong banks will be able to raise capital from the market and, therefore, those banks will grow at a faster pace than the weaker banks and the banking system would eventually become stronger. The other related issue is the track record of public sector banks which have gone to the market. The market's assessment of these stocks has been distinctly adverse. Most of these banks have gone to the market at inflated values and investors who have put their faith in these banks have been badly singed and they would not be gullible to put more of their resources into these banks. Banks must recognise the ground realities and build back credibility by entering the market at par or at a very modest premia. It may be contended that each bank has a dedicated set of captive investors drawn from loyal depositors. From the long-term interest of banks, however, it would be advisable for these banks to approach the market with defensible valuations. Banks which go to the market for their capital requirements will need to recognise that they will have to pay greater attention to the opinion of shareholders and banks would be able to raise capital from the market only if they give attention to creating shareholder value. This will require adequate ploughing back of profits into the reserves. In the first flush, as banks raised funds from the market, insufficient attention was paid to this aspect.

Apart from the three weak public sector banks, the Verma Panel identified six public sector banks which were showing signs of distress and were running high risk of slipping into the category of weak banks. What is of concern is some of these banks are bravely entering the market for raising capital and unless these banks show a vast improvement, shareholders faith in these banks could be belied and damage the credibility of public sector banks in the eyes of investors.

A recent report by Crisil has highlighted that while Indian banks are taking steps towards improved disclosures which meet the RBI regulatory requirements, Indian banks have a long way to go to come up to international best practices. A few banks are attempting to achieve international disclosure standards in the context of their plans to raise capital from international markets.

For the three weak banks the government has indicated that it would provide recapitalisation funds after being satisfied about the viability of the strategic action plans of these banks. This issue needs more detailed discussion and I would come back to this later on.

The fact that banks have started raising money from the capital market does not mean that the burden on the fisc of an eventual bailout would be any less. As Deputy Governor Dr. Y.V. Reddy has pointed out (in his lecture at the Bank Economists' Conference, December 1998), the experience the world over is that the fiscal burden is ownership neutral.

Prudential Norms

Based on the 1988 Basle Accord, prudential norms were introduced in India in 1992. Since then there has been a progressive move towards international norms. We do not need to be defensive but it is necessary to recognise that there are specific areas wherein our norms are clearly below the best international practices.

As against the international 90 days norm we still continue to use a criteria of 180 days plus 30 days past due for non-payment of principal and interest before we classify an account as sub-standard. Deputy Governor Shri S.P. Talwar has cogently argued that unless the underlying commercial and payments system moves to an improved settlement system it would not be feasible to shift the norms to one quarter in respect of past dues.

This is a chicken and egg problem and unless the RBI is stricter on the norms it is unlikely that the payments system would improve. It is important that we do not further delay the movement to a 90 days norm albeit, in a phased manner, say over 2-3 years. Continuing with the 180 days norms would be clearly indefensible.

The Basle Committee is in the process of developing A New Capital Adequacy Framework which would be more sensitive to the level of underlying economic risk. The 1988 Basle Accord had the disadvantage that various kinds of risks, such as interest rate risks and operational risks were not explicitly addressed and the earlier Accord provided an incentive for high-risk high-reward activity and encouraged regulatory arbitrage. In addition to the minimum capital standards taking into account the credit rating, the new norms give emphasis to supervisory oversight of capital adequacy at the individual bank level together with market discipline and better public disclosure.

The RBI has expressed reservations on relying on external rating agencies for assigning risk weights on exposures and has instead preferred greater reliance on domestic rating agencies and also the internal rating by banks themselves. The RBI has recognised that emerging economies would have considerable difficulty in adhering to the new Framework and has rightly argued that these countries will need a longer transition period.

In an increasingly integrated world we in India need to take cognisance of the fact that this time round the phasing in period will be much shorter than at the time of the Basle norms of 1988 and therefore concerted efforts should be made to first understand and then implement the new framework.

Narasimham-II had argued that with the difficulties that Indian banks would have with implementing international risk management guidelines it may be best to move to a 10 per cent capital to risk assets ratio (CRAR). Some observers have argued that raising the CRAR further, beyond the present 9 per cent, would be counterproductive in an already risk-averse Indian financial system.

The Bank of International Settlement (BIS) guidelines on risk management at the level of individual banks would be far too complex for Indian banks to operate in any meaningful manner. Risk management does not mean that a bank/financial institution merely employs a couple of technical personnel. Effective risk management is something which just cannot be delegated and the top management and the boards of banks/ institutions should be adept at risk management techniques.

It will take a new generation of top management to have a clear appreciation of risk management. In the interregnum, till a new generation of top management appears on the scene and can effectively deal with risks in a meaningful manner, it would be desirable to use the crude CRAR as an effective instrument by raising it to 10 per cent by say 2002. A further reason for increasing the CRAR to 10 per cent is that bank solvency is undermind as many risks are off the balance sheet. While an attempt is made to bring these risks under the umbrella of total risks a full coverage is not easily obtained and, therefore, there is merit in the raising of the present CRAR to 10 per cent. Where the new risk assessment models require sophisticated statistical techniques, it is necessary to develop a holistic approach wherein statistical models are combined with sound judgement.

While on the matter of risk management it is pertinent to mention that in the more recent period, the question of counterparty risk has come to the fore in the context of ring-fencing by the branches of certain foreign banks in India. If this issue really becomes a full fledged reality, in the context of the evolving international norms, it would be only appropriate for Indian banks to seriously reconsider their exposures on these banks.

ISSUES IN REGULATION/SUPERVISION

The regulators no doubt wish to believe that the regulations are now less on micro management and more by way of prudential norms with greater emphasis on internal controls. While the direction of change is welcome it is only if there is a comprehensive codification of the regulations that it would become clear as to how the system is operating. A codification would also provide a sharp focus on redundant regulations. The objective should be to ensure that regulation is light and supervision is scrupulously strict. Moreover, supervision should largely be in the nature of on- going disclosures by the supervised institution. Banks and others which are deposit taking institutions owe it to their depositors to provide relevant information on performance in simple language easily understood by depositors. The present disclosure standards in India can, by no means, be considered to be satisfactory. While stressing the need for greater disclosure, there should be legitimate protection for proprietal information. Adequate disclosure becomes particularly relevant as banks progressively base capital requirement on internal risk measures. Another important issue which needs attention is adverse action by the supervisor. It is not at all necessary to unleash a reign of terror. All that the supervisors needs to do is to take contemporaneous adverse action as soon as there are incipient signs of violation. On taking adverse action there should be comprehensive publicity. Sometimes supervisors fight shy of publicity because of fears of adverse action snow-balling into systemic problems.

This is a totally unwarranted fear. So long as adverse action is taken at the incipient stage of infringement the adverse action would be mild and there would not be a systemic fall out. When penalties are imposed, they should be widely publicised however small the penalties. Minimal, but timely, adverse action would alert all stakeholders viz. owners, depositors and employees and there would be early convergence to least cost remedial action.

The supervisor should, however, have the authority to require individual banks to operate at higher capital adequacy ratios in view of the higher perceived risks. Moreover, if the stipulated capital is not maintained the supervisor should take early action to remedy the situation and not wait till the situation deteriorates to a point of no return.

The legislative framework should be made a lot more flexible to give the regulatory/supervisory authority sufficient powers to adequately deal with rapid financial innovations. Furthermore, as internal controls develop and banks undertake fuller disclosures, the supervisory function should become more in the nature of a backstop and should concentrate on inspecting systems rather than individual transactions.

Ownership by the government / RBI of financial intermediaries impinges on regulatory/supervisory freedom of action because the close links result in a regulatory capture. Supervisory forbearance is probably the most dangerous aspect of this intertwining relationship and this is yet one more reason for divesting government ownership of financial intermediaries. In this context it is unconscionable for the RBI to put its nominee directors on the boards of banks. Sometimes it is argued that the RBI is passive and merely fulfils the legal requirement. In the interregnum, till the law is changed, the least the RBI could do is to atleast withdraw its front line A team from the boards of public sector banks. Translating this into specific action, no officer of the rank of Chief General Manager and above should be nominated to the board of a bank/institution.

The RBI is committed to implementing the BIS Core Principles for Effective Banking Supervision (1997). While most of the Core Principles are enshrined in the Indian legislative and regulatory framework, there are gaps in a number of areas wherein further progress is necessary before India can claim full compliance. One of the aspects of the Core Principles is that the supervisor should be neutral as between public and private sector institutions. There is an impression that in India we are stricter with public sector banks than private sector banks as public sector banks are subject to a lot more regulation; this erroneous impression emanates from the fact that the public sector banks are saddled with a lot more directions from the authorities than private sector banks. But, when it comes to a bank making losses there is unlimited forbearance in the case of public sector banks and it is this infirmity which is a major departure from adherence to the Core Principles.

A cardinal principle of sound regulation/supervision is that it should never be varied over the business cycle. It is entirely a monetary policy function to deal appropriately with the business cycle. Per contra, monetary policy should not be diluted to make it less costly for financial intermediaries to comply with prudential norms.

The regulator/supervisor has to ensure that a period of good macro economic performance does not create euphoria which results in a dropping of the supervisory guard to ignore prudential management. This is particularly important because of the old adage that bad loans are made in good times.

While in some countries regulation/supervision has been separated from the central bank there are some disadvantages in doing so. In a crisis it is the central bank which has to act and a central bank without hands on experience of banking organisations faces a tremendous handicap. Hence, at this stage of our financial development, there is much merit in keeping regulation/supervision within the RBI.

While on the issue of regulation and supervision it is necessary to recognise that the days when more administrative controls would restrict activity are clearly over. Thus regulators/ supervisors have to learn to work with, rather than against, market forces.

Future of Financial Institutions (FIs)

The future of financial institutions has been the centre of debate for the last two years. It should be clear to all that with the cessation of concessional resources and concessional lending and the blurring of short-term and long-term lending the question of continuing with the special status of FIs comes to the fore. Narasimham- II had set out that the FIs should either become banks or NBFCs. What is emerging is a cafeteria approach under which a FI can either itself become a bank or use the conglomerate approach and set up a banking subsidiary. The present environment is excessively permissive. There must be an incentive/disincentive system and FIs should be given a clear outer time frame by which they would have to become banks. The FIs are far too big to be allowed to function outside the regulatory framework for banks, and yet enjoy a favourite son status.

NON-BANK FINANCE COMPANIES (NBFCS)

A peculiar feature of the Indian financial system is the extensive system of non-bank institutions raising deposits. The NBFCs are a group of vastly different units from the best run financial units in the country to rampant and outright predatory elements. The RBI has all along had a difficult time reigning in obstreperous elements. There have, in recent years, been admirable efforts by the RBI to bring an element of order into the system. The shake out was to expected and sooner or later the permissive mushrooming of these companies had to stop. The well-run units should work closely with the regulator/ supervisor to develop strong self-regulatory organisations. No tears need be shed over the disappearance of poorly run units.

Ultimately, the regulatory/supervisory framework for banks and non-banks should converge and in such a scenario the well run NBFCs should be provided strong incentives to become banks. Over time, the asset side controls on the Residuary Non-Bank Companies should gradually become applicable to all NBFCs and the RBI should device special incentives for well run NBFCs to become banks.

Providing deposit insurance cover to the non-bank sector would be detrimental to the development of a strong financial sector as the stronger units would be subsidising the weaker units. Deposit insurance should, as at present, remain strictly restricted to banks. It is reported that consideration is being given to providing insurance for depositors in the corporate sector. If this is implemented it would be difficult to resist pressures to provide deposit insurance for NBFCs. While deposit insurance in the non-bank segment is being mooted as part of investor protection this would be a wrong signal to depositors. Such deposits carry a substantial risk and deposit insurance would give a false sense of security.

In the recent period there have been ominous noises about separating regulation/supervision of NBFCs from the RBI. In the last four years the RBI has performed magnificently in dealing with the NBFCs. It is not as if the RBI would wish to cling on to this function but the pertinent question is whether there can be any other organisation which can handle the regulation/supervision of the NBFCs better than the RBI.

To the extent the NBFC sector needs closer regulation/ supervision, the RBI's staff resources in this sphere need to be augmented and the RBI run Board for Financial Supervision could be split into two, one for banks and one for NBFCs but the important point is that the regulation/supervision of NBFCs should continue to be under the aegis of the RBI. In my view, separating the regulation/supervision of NBFCs from the RBI would be a serious mistake.

MUTUAL FUNDS

Developments in the area of mutual funds have had reverberations in the entire financial system. In the aftermath of the UTI imbroglio the government provided largesse to all mutual funds by making the income distributed by mutual funds totally tax free in the hands of the recipient. Earlier on, company dividends were also exempt from income taxation. This resulted in the income funds of mutual funds becoming extremely competitive vis-a-vis bank deposits, deposits of NBFCs and bonds of FIs. To assuage criticism of this exemption the government has imposed a 22 per cent tax on the dividend distributed by mutual funds. The rationale for exempting these incomes from income tax is based on the premise that double taxation should be avoided. While the tax on mutual funds and bank deposits is broadly equated at the macro level the system is iniquitous in that in the mutual funds sector the lower income holders subsidise the higher income holders. There has been a perceptible shift of bank deposits of longer maturities to mutual funds. In the longer run, continuing with this taxation system will progressively reduce the average maturity of term deposits of banks and generate serious asset-liability maturity mismatches. Moreover, it is against all cannons of distributive justice. Individual measures to tackle a specific problem can have a systemic fall out. Hence a holistic view should be taken to avoid such distortions.

Corporate Governance in the Financial Sector

The issue of governance in the Indian financial sector has received benign neglect essentially because of the predominant role of government. With the changing role of government, issues of governance are coming to the fore. The quality and character of management of banks and financial institutions should develop as the first line of defence and no system of regulation/supervision can be a substitute for good management. In the present system there is a total obfuscation between the role of management and the role of managers. In the public sector financial system management vests with the government and the top officials are merely the managers acting at the beckoning of government.

There has been considerable discussion about the need for greater autonomy of financial intermediaries and a concomitant of this is greater transparency and increased responsibility for banks and institutions. As the government gradually reduces its overarching role in the running of public sector banks, the boards of banks and top management will have to take on a significantly greater role in decision taking. The powers of the board, the structure and formation of the boards, the role and functions of the Chairman and the Chief Executive Officer will all need to be examined in some detail. While banks at present have the comfort of governmental control the dilution of such control can lead to a crisis of governance.

The boards of banks, top management as well as the supervisory authority need to recognise that there must be a fine balance between risk models and judgement based on experience. Moreover, mere reliance on heavier regulation and supervision is not a solution and in fact intensification of supervisory oversight can undermine market discipline and increasingly, there will need to be more reliance on market forces and less on the supervisory authority.

In this context internal governance of banks will gain primacy. Enhanced transparency in disclosures is reflective of good corporate governance and it gives credibility to banks' financial statements.

While transparency, per se, is highly desirable it cannot be the be all and end all of corporate governance in the financial sector. In any effective system of corporate governance in the financial sector, the board of directors would have to device relevant strategies and be fully responsible for the working of the organisation. The board of directors should be subject to a considerable degree of accountability. Suppression of facts or misinformation should be made a criminal offence. The directors should be duly elected by the shareholders. To ensure that unsuitable persons are not on the boards of banks it is not necessary to take away the voting rights of shareholders. The regulator/supervisor should have the power to use the standard fit and proper criteria to ensure that the boards of banks are appropriately manned.

The issue of corporate governance in the financial sector is much more complex than in other sectors. The depositor, as a stakeholder, should get precedence over the shareholder who has much less at stake in a bank. The real challenge in the Indian system is not merely how quickly banks migrate out of the public sector but how banks are governed in an optimal manner. There are no parallel models to draw on and corporate governance in the Indian financial sector will need to chart its own course.

There have been so many Committees and Working Groups to examine specific issues but for some reason we do not seem to be giving sufficient attention to issues of governance in the context of change in government ownership in the financial sector. The time is apposite to give early attention to this matter.

Offshore Banking

The feasibility of allowing offshore banking to develop has been debated for the last 30 years. This is an idea whose time has past. In today's internationally integrated world it no longer makes sense to have a mere offshore financial pocket. In the inexorable march towards international financial integration the authorities should prepare the Indian system for meaningful integration and not be content with off-shore pockets which in any case cannot be separated from the rest of the financial system in these days of complex financial transactions.

WEAK BANKS

It is now over two years since Narasimham-II was submitted and nine months have passed since the Verma Panel report on weak banks. The government has rightly maintained confidence in the banking system by categorically indicating that no weak public sector bank would be closed down. This is indeed a very appropriate response but now serious thought has to be given to what to do with the three weak public sector banks. Discussions and debate on the weak bank dates back to as far back as 1988. Had these banks merely allowed the natural attrition of staff through retirement during the 1990's the weak banks would not have had any problems of excess staff. The time has come to close the debate and to take decisive action.

The government appears inclined to set up a Financial Restructuring Authority (FRA) to deal with the problems of these banks, which is a positive step. It would be highly desirable to set up the FRA as part of the RBI infrastructure rather than create a new institution and a predictable turf war.

The weak banks have been asked to submit their strategic action plans to pull themselves out of their difficulties. All the three banks have submitted plans based on a step up in the rate of growth of deposits and advances and it is reported that all these proposals have been rejected.

The authorities have also rejected the concept of narrow banking which has been a time tested concept, the world over, under which weak banks reduce their exposure to risk assets and invest their resources in government securities. The authorities do not favour narrow banking despite the clear evidence that a number of Indian public sector banks pulled themselves out of problems precisely using the strategy of narrow banking. The fact of the matter is that in the Indian context, on a risk adjusted basis, the return on government securities is higher than on bank lending. This would clearly show that it is best for weak banks to slowdown lending.

The government would be well advised to avoid the recapitalisation route as it is a bog from which the government would not be able to extricate itself. Providing largesse for the three weak banks would encourage the six potentially weak banks identified by the Verma Panel to put out their bowls to receive the government's munificence.

It would be best to let the three weak banks use a bootstraps operation to come out of their problems. The problems of these banks are mind boggling and it is necessary to take all possible steps to remedy the position : sell overseas offices to other Indian banks, sell real estate, sell branches in areas where these banks do not enjoy a competitive advantage and reduce staff by a rigorously enforced ban on fresh recruitment.

Rather than considering very ambitious VRS schemes these banks should endeavour to reduce their staff by 6 per cent per annum as opposed to a natural attrition rate of 3 per cent per annum through retirements. Whatever be the strategy adopted it would take these weak banks at least a decade to reconstruct their balance sheets and it is totally unrealistic to expect a turnaround in a year or two. Let us hope that the authorities are able to pull it off with an alternative strategy through what that viable strategy would be is yet to be revealed.

Here one can readily concede that the advocacy of narrow banking has failed to convince the government, the RBI, the weak banks, economists and the public at large. So what are we left with?

When the financial policies of the present period are evaluated, in a historical perspective, the RBI and the government would be indicted for their inaction in devising an effective strategy for weak banks.

Bureaucratic brilliance of equivocation can be no substitute for hard action. The problem of weak banks is not a uniquely Indian phenomenon. It has been tackled elsewhere and it has to be tackled in India. This is the most crucial issue, and the future course for the Indian financial system is essentially contingent on what is done regarding weak banks. If the authorities fail to take action a Pro bono publico (for the public good) has to speak up.

HUMAN RESOURCE DEVELOPMENT, TECHNOLOGY, INDUSTRIAL RELATIONS AND CUSTOMERS SERVICE

HRD, technology, IR and customer service are the four pillars of the banking system of the future. Each of these issues deserves a full fledged and exclusive examination and any meaningful assessment of the financial sector without taking cognisance of these vital matters would be incomplete. On these issues the public sector banking system has operated as a monolith.

Continuing such an approach will be sub-optimal and competitive forces will eventually result in the stronger elements unleashing themselves from the drag of the weaker elements. At the present time these are sensitive issues which create tensions but they need urgent attention. An early resolution of these dilemmas would be in the interest of all concerned.

CONCLUSION

Financial crises the worldover have revealed that weaknesses in financial systems and their supervision contribute to macro instability. The prescription therefore is the strengthening of the financial system. Not only is stronger supervision necessary but the discipline of the market needs to be reinforced. Corporate governance needs to be strengthened and bankruptcy legislation made more robust. With rapid technological changes, the leaders in innovation would claim the best business. Banks and financial institutions which resist change would, like dinosaurs, become extinct. The financial system would need to be guided by three requirements viz. transparency, rigorous norms and appropriate incentives. It is hoped that in the years to come the Indian financial system would face upto these challenges

8

The Hidden Agenda

Sixteen years back present prime minister, then as finance minister piloted the economic reforms to align Indian economy with the global market controlled by eight developed countries in the world with USA having significant share, reflected in its huge share of 32 percent of the global GDP.

The compelling reason for so called reforms has its origin in the destablisation of the fixed parity in the exchange rates of currencies in the year 1973 by replacing it with floating rates. That was a time when USA came to face financial deficit internally and in external trade and that trend is persisting.

In the meanwhile, faced with the problem of stagnation and stagflation the USA commenced the exercise of creation of wealth by creating assets resorting to unrestricted speculative activities in the financial sector. These developments imposed burden on the developing countries in the area of international trade and to overcome the same the panacea prescribed by the world bank and the IMF are mainly deregulation of market, privatisation of public sector – both manufacturing and services and less governance by the governments on economic issues and abandonment of governance in social sectors. The total deregulation of the financial sector and the agenda of privatisation of public sector bank is part and parcel of the said reform policy.

The rulers of our country during the early years of reforms were hesitant on the agenda of privatisation and government after government declared that profit making public sector undertakings will not be privatised. It was consistently emphasised that public sector banks will not be privatised. In fact, learning the lesson from the South East Asian Economic crisis causing collapse of the banks suffering from capital inadequacy and reserves, the Indian government augmented the capital of public sector banks by pumping Rs 20000 crores which with their widespread network of branches could safeguard the stability of banking system. So much so, that they gained the capacity to merge with them almost 10 private sector banks which collapsed during the ongoing reform period. By such mergers, the depositors' interest and security of job of the employees have been protected and safeguarded.

This amazing performance of the public sector banks has become an eye sore and the World Bank, IMF, WTO are constantly pressurising the Indian government to fully deregulate the financial sector and privatise the public sector banks. While such pressurising continues, multinational banks operating in our country obtained or snatched concessions tantamount to imposing deregulation which enabled them to capture increasing share in the assets of the industry which now amounts to 8 percent and another 4 percent off balance sheet which is borrowings from their head offices.

By such mechanism their volume of business is far in excess of the liabilities in India. Further, resorting to excessive service charges and on one pretext or the other denying interest on savings accounts of the customer and containing the cost in wages by resorting to multiple unfair labour practices, the operating costs are brought down enabling them to increase profitability to about 4 percent i.e. profit ratio to assets, while in public sector banks that ratio is hardly 1 percent which is at par with the profitability of banks in developed countries. This situation has arisen because the government does not apply the banking policy to the foreign banks which are given freedom to pursue their own super profits motivated business policies. In no developed country, host banks are subjected to such discrimination and in fact migrant banks from other countries are put under strict regulations to follow prescribed banking policies. Another breach of regulation is that while foreign banks are permitted to open 12 branches per year, by installing hundreds of ATMs throughout India and through their financial subsidiaries, significant retail and consumer banking business are transacted. Citibank alone beside branches have now more than 150 outlets under the guise of Citi financial company. As against this, the application for licence to open a branch in New York made by SBI, ICICI Bank are pending for over two years.

Reforms and deregulations are applicable only to developing countries. Their markets are to be kept open and free for being exploited by the developed countries. Create crisis after crisis and the last target is banking and financial sector. The events of past 20 years reveal that in Latin American countries and East European countries their banks are fully under the control of foreign multinational banks having significant ownership in the capital and assets. Bank acquisitions globally accounted for $ 2.5 billion between 1991-1995, increased to $ 55.5 billions between 1996-2000 and by 2005 it has shot upto $ 123.5 Billion. Consequently in 2005 the share of foreign banks in banking business in Argentina was 48 percent valued at $ 31 billion being 20 percent of that country's GDP.

In Brazil the share is 27 percent valued at $ 107 billion which is 20 percent of its GDP. In Bulgaria the share is 80 percent valued at $ 13 billion, i.e. 49 percent of its GDP. In Chile the share is 42 percent valued at $ 35 billion which is 37 percent of its GDP. In Czech Republic the share is 96 percent valued at $ 99 billion which is 92 percent of the GDP. In Mexico the share is 82 percent valued at $ 342 billion which is 51 percent of its GDP. In Poland the share is $ 68 Billion valued at $ 105 billion accounting 43 percent of GDP of that country.

Multinational banks and their financial subsidiaries resort to retail trading and other services which enables them to earn huge income and profits. This is the prize of the deregulation of the banking sector and liberalisation of the financial sector and hailed as universal banks, which is often commended by the finance minister, and for this purpose he propagates merger of public sector banks and their disinvestment.

Disinvestment opens the gate for eventual privatisation and this route must be opposed. Instead, the alternative of issuing of bonds and preference shares should be encouraged. No individual or institution should be permitted to hold beyond 5 percent of the shares. Already foreign institutional investors are holding sizeable shares in public sector banks as also in the major new private sector Indian banks, as could be seen from the table hereunder:

Foreign Investments in Capital of Banks

Name of the Bank	No. of Shares As on 31.03.2004	% to Paid up Capital	No. of Shares As on 31.03.2006	% to Paid up Capital
Public Sector Banks				
Andhra Bank	2,15,77,223	5.39	8,40,30,646	17.32
Bank of Baroda	4,75,40,615	16.14	73,33,56,892	20.13
Bank of India	2,37,64,900	4.86	6,44,68,034	13.19
Canara Bank	4,36,00,569	10.63	7,49,35,787	18.27
Corporation Bank	1,10,83,135	7.72	1,44,47,387	10.07
Indian Overseas Bank	11,31,795	0.20	9,49,49,445	17.42
Oriental Bank of Comerce	2,53,75,968	13.17	4,97,68,926	19.86
Punjab National Bank	2,96,25,795	11.16	6,32,47,778	20.00
State Bank of India	6,01,97,755	11.43	6,25,03,693	11.87
Syndicate Bank	36,83,407	0.78	6,37,89,100	13.51
UCO Bank	6,25,000	0.07	1,45,71,873	1.82
Union Bank	5,39,07,074	11.71	10,06,13,918	19.91
Vijaya Bank	2,19,71,273	5.06	6,94,62,629	16.02
Private Sector Banks				
Centurian Bank	76,73,437	5.37	27,75,78,001	21.67
Federal Bank	10,65,637	4.80	1,83,15,281	27.53
HDFC Bank	7,67,38,812	27.02	10,22,08,872	32.71
ICICI Bank	28,33,78,082	38.63	41,48,16,138	46.63
Indusind Bank	1,36,76,792	4.70	3,75,20,769	12.90
ING Vysya Bank	46,45,021	20.53	1,55,02,328	17.03
Jammu & Kashmir Bank	77,12,696	15.90	1,45,49,707	29.99
Karnataka Bank	18,98,653	4.68	2,29,13,805	18.88
Karur Vysya Bank	9.19,613	5.10	29,43,356	16.35
Kotak Mahindra Bank	94,35,947	7.92	6,45,43,383	20.93
UTI Bank	3,31,63,474	14.27	9,69,84,197	34.87

The financial subsidiaries of foreign banks have a big hand in these investments and at appropriate time they will make their presence felt in many Indian banks probably after 2009, whereafter under WTO rules these foreign banks could acquire 74 percent shares of Indian private banks. Our government has acted magnanimously by permitting this cap already. In the same spirit the government intend to amend the Banking Regulation Act to do away with the restriction of voting rights to maximum 10 percent. These rules and regulations are protected and preserved in the developed countries. The moot question is then why developing countries including India are being pressurised to change. The answer is simple when we see what has happened in Latin America and the East European countries. The foreign multinational banks' objective is to acquire the local banks – private and public.

The banking policy pursued by Indian government has encouraged the foreign banks to step up pressure. In the meanwhile, situations are created permitting the foreign banks and their financial subsidiaries to indulge in trading and services to increase their income and profits. They are exempted from social banking and agricultural credit. These burdens are put solely on the public sector banks, sapping their income and profits. If this adverse playing field continue, they will be rendered week and face the risk of being acquired by foreign banks who with 8 percent market share in the business are already earning $ 36 billion i.e. Rs 162000 crores. The 4 percent share appropriated through their subsidiary, financial companies could be another $ 18 Billion i.e. 81000 crores of rupees.

This disturbing banking policy must be changed. Rules and regulations applicable to public sector banks must be applied to all the banks. Existing common regulations for payment of interest on savings account should be governed by common rules ensuring uniform implementation. In the same manner, common rules should govern service charges. Foreign banks should not be permitted to establish financial subsidiaries since such subsidiaries are being used as banking and trading companies. The globally prevalent regulation of capping on ownership of shares and voting rights as it exists now in India should not be disturbed. Disinvestment must be stopped once for all and alternate mechanism of issuing bonds and preference shares ought to be adopted to strengthen the capital base.

Each Public Sector Bank should further expand by opening new branches since household savings are increasing significantly as can be seen from more than 32 percent increase in bank deposits and demand for credit is about 80 percent of deposits. These measures will go a long way in strengthening public sector banks and the agenda of privatisation will have natural death. The bank employees movement is duty bound not only to save public sector banks but also overall economic interest of the country and large majority of the people.

FINANCIAL INCLUSION IN INDIA

Microlending: Current Industry Trends

In the Indian context, microfinance is no longer the purview of development institutions. While the rhetoric of development has been retained, banks have embraced it as an extremely profitable business, for two reasons.

First, Indian banks are required to lend a certain percentage (currently 40%) into priority areas – called priority sector lending – which includes agriculture, SMEs, and government securities. Compared to returns on government bonds of 6-7%, MFI lending provides returns of 10-14%. Banks, therefore, have expanded investments in these areas.

Second, microfinance lending - as it is currently practiced- is simply not very risky. In the absence of individual credit assessments, MFIs lend to groups or through referral, leading to repayment rates of 95% or more. Banks then get the best of both worlds - higher rates of return with very low risk.

The result is massive expansion in microlending. ICICI Bank, the largest private bank in India, had 1.2 million microfinance clients in 2005 and a portfolio of $227 million. A year later, ICICI has multiple partnerships and 3 million clients, targeting 25 million in 3 years. Other banks, such as ABN

Amro, and YES Bank have smaller but still sizable operations that generate goodwill benefits for their entire operations (both featured on FT's sustainable banking awards last year).

Public sector banks usually operate as integrated micro-lenders, creating self-help groups (SHG) to which they disbursing loans directly rather than through an intermediary. Private sector banks, by contrast, operate through a partnership model, contracting with existing MFIs to function as the bank's retail arm to acquire and manage micro-clients. In return, MFI's retain a percentage of the interest earned on loans. Many MFIs are now financially independent of such funds, but high effective rates (of over 30%) have also led to a regulatory backlash.

Mismatch between Credit and Deposit Growth

This expansion of rural credit tracks a more general expansion of retail credit in India. In 2006, non-food credit expanded by over 30%, up from a growth rate of 28.8% in the 3 years prior. Simultaneously, the share of retail credit in overall credit stood at 46% in 2005-06, up from 6.4% in 1990-91.

Interestingly, this growth has not been accompanied by growth of deposits, particularly in rural areas. As a result: Banks have been financing much of the incremental credit expansion by unwinding their surplus investments in government securities. What deposit growth that has been observed is, moreover, concentrated in the larger cities...[this] could also mean that financial inclusion may have suffered.

The implications of this mismatch are important to understand some of the constraints faced by an expanding microbanking industry. In the absence of deposit growth banks face a liquidity problem which limits further credit expansion. This problem is evident in recent policy changes to reduce the statutory liquidity ratio (SLR) of Indian banks.

In other words, the banking system will be expected to increasingly provide larger quantum of funds to existing and emerging enterprises. And without adequate deposit growth, however, credit expansion might not be sustainable over the medium-term, without putting immense pressure on real interest rates and impacting the overall stability of the financial system.

Financial Inclusion: Consequences and Benefits

The preceding discussion does not distinguish between rural and urban markets. However, the expansion of financial services to all sections of society (financial inclusion) is important, in order to leverage development and growth benefits. There are obvious reasons to encourage such financial inclusion and deepening:

Countries with low levels of income inequality tend to have lower levels of financial exclusion, while high levels of exclusion are associated with the least equal ones. In Sweden, lower than two per cent of adults did not have an account in 2000...[while] in Portugal, about 17 per cent of the adult population had no account of any kind in 2000.

The Gini index for Sweden was 24, and for Portugal 37 in 2001 (lower is better). Sweden ranked 119, and Portugal 59 in income inequality in 1996. At the macro-level a well-developed and widespread financial system accelerates growth "through expansion of access to those who do not have adequate finance themselves."

In its absence, the sources of finance available to individuals and enterprises are limited. The McKinsey Quarterly reports that companies in emerging markets demand further development of financial systems, and remain limited in their ability to access external finance. This results in fewer economic activities being financed, resulting in lower growth potential. Further, financial exclusion is self-propagating and limits growth prospects:

It is the incumbents who have better access to financial services through relationship banking. Moreover, incumbents also finance their growth through internal resource generation. Thus...growth is constrained to the expansion potential of incumbents.

At the individual, micro-level, however, the consequences of financial exclusion are very different. Exclusion results in a susceptibility to cash flow disruptions, inability to benefit from interest rates, and lack of long-term financial security and planning through saving opportunities.

It is very important to note the distinction between the enterprise level macro benefits and the individual micro benefits, as the two are often confused in development literature. In the former, the benefits of inclusion are productivity and higher trend growth. These are benefits commonly ascribed to microfinance, yet microfinance as it is currently practiced is targeted not at enterprises but at individuals. The benefits that accrue therefore are smoothening consumption and safeguarding assets from major disruptions (e.g. disease, natural disaster). Recent studies seem to suggest as much.

Policy Responses to Financial Exclusion

Despite the massive growth in micro-credit mentioned previously, Dr. Mohan expresses serious concern over financial exclusion in India, backing those concerns with data. For instance, spatial distribution of banking services indicates that rural credit, deposits, and offices as a share of overall services decreased between 1996 and 2005, with most expansion restricted to metropolitan areas.

There are two obstacles to greater financial inclusion. The first is simply commercial. Transaction costs for both banks and clients remain high, particularly in disbursing credit, which is essentially a high cost, distributed business. Further, interest rates remain high in the absence of structured credit assessments. The second obstacle is policy requirements such as know your customer (KYC) procedures that limit the geographical reach of financial services beyond physical bank branches. Yet, the importance of financial inclusion becomes important, particularly in the context of doubling agricultural productivity, targeted for India's 11 five year plan. Consequently, the RBI has moved to enforce multiple policy and industry changes:

1. Banks have been asked to voluntarily make available a 'no-frills' account, and all printed bank material has to be made available in regional languages.

2. KYC procedures have been simplified for low income groups.
3. Significantly, since January 2006 banks can provide a full range of banking services through 'business facilitator and correspondent' (i.e. MFI partnership) models. Previously, MFIs could only provide credit, but not open bank accounts.
4. The Credit Information Bureau Act, 2006, will eventually establish a credit bureau that makes available credit histories of individuals and small businesses. This should lower risk for banks, in extending credit further.

CONCLUSIONS

This has been an inordinately long post, but an eye-opening one. Most microfinance literature has seen credit expansion as an end in itself, with productivity benefits magically accruing from such expansion. This discussion, however, debunks that belief without denying the importance of microcredit. However, microcredit must be part of micro-banking, which must be seen as a viable and important business within the financial sector.

Contrary to popular belief, the reach of microfinance in India remains limited. Both market and policy reforms are necessary in order to correct this, expand microcredit, and sustain it through deposit growth. The resulting industry and policy moves may prove important for other countries on a similar trajectory.

9

Vigilance in Industrial Financing Banks

Vigilance is emerging as an important aspect of successful management today. If eternal vigilance is the price of liberty, eternal alertness is the price of vigilance. The scandal of Enron and its reflection in the functioning of Anderson has highlighted the international level, how if there is lack of vigilance, it may be possible still to build a successful enterprise but it will collapse like a house of cards one day. The non-performing assets of the Indian banking system which is estimated to be anywhere between 58000 to 70000 crores is again a reflection of moral hazard and in quite a few cases, lack of vigilance. Below is a statement of a senior authority who took charge of CVC and comes to the following conclusions.

One of the problems generally raised about the public sector banks is the role of the CVC and whether CVC comes in the way of effective decision making in the banks. In fact, after taking over as the CVC, one of the first steps I did within three months of my taking over was to bring out a Separate Chapter in the Vigilance Manual for the Banks. I think, this Separate Chapter had, at least, raised the requisite confidence in the minds of the banking community that so long as they follow prudential banking norms, they have nothing to fear from vigilance. In fact, to give double assurance to the public sector bank employees, we also created, under the chairmanship of a retired Deputy Governor of the Reserve Bank, the Advisory Board on Bank Frauds. The performance of the Board has, at least, shown that even though legally the CBI is not obliged to go by any directions given by any agency so far as investigation of criminal cases are concerned, they have respected the advice of the Advisory Board. In the year 1999, 14 cases were referred to of which in 7 cases the Advisory Board said that investigation need not be carried out and this was complied with the CBI. Another major area is the culture of blackmail which prevailed in many public sector undertakings. The order of the CVC of 29 th June 1999 that no action to be taken on anonymous / pseudonymous petition is a measure which would give confidence to the honest people in the banking sector. I also get complaints sometime that in spite of this order, anonymous petitions are being inquired into. If this is so, it is totally against the CVC guidelines and, at least, the banks concerned should not blame the CVC for honest officers being harassed on the basis of the inquiry started by the anonymous complaints. In fact, the Chief Vigilance Officers must be courageous enough to bring to the notice of the CMDs in case there is insistence on inquiring into anonymous / pseudonymous petitions. The IBA also mentioned about this. We have reiterated our instructions of 29.6.99. If there are still cases of violation, the CVC can take up the issue with the organisations concerned.

Based on the experience of last three years and the points raised by IBA, the following decision has been taken to amend the Chapter on Banks: Every bank has evolved a system of credit audit / inspection for non-borrowal / borrowal accounts under which they are subjected to close scrutiny. This audit / inspection would scrutinize pre-sanction appraisal, documentation and disbursement of the loans / advances and post sanction follow up. If any irregularity is missed out by auditors / inspectors in the first audit / inspection, it is reasonable to expect that the remaining undetected irregularities will be detected in the second audit / inspection and necessary disciplinary proceedings initiated against the concerned officials in the follow up action. Normally, the second audit / inspection would be completed within 3-4 years. The Commission has accordingly approved the proposal that no disciplinary proceedings will ordinarily lie against any official for any lapse not detected within two successive audit / inspection of the same account or 4 years from the date of event, whichever is later. In case any irregularity is detected subsequent to the second audit / inspection the auditors / inspectors concerned will be held accountable and be liable for disciplinary proceedings. This time limit will not apply to cases of (i) frauds, (ii) other criminal offences or (iii) lapses where malafide are inferable.

In addition, we also have the Advisory Board on Bank Frauds which has in the last three years has considered various cases. The CBI even though is legally entitled to decide on its own, has been honouring the recommendations of the Advisory Board. The vigilance function should also be looked upon not from a negative point of view but from a positive point of view. If eternal vigilance is the price of liberty, eternal alertness is the price of vigilance. Eternal alertness can make the banks ensure that they do not lose financially. After all, many a time the frauds are committed by insiders. I have heard a banker say that they are more worried about the dedicated worker than the sincere worker. The sincere bank worker comes to the office at 9 o'clock, works the whole day and goes back whereas the dedicated worker not only works for long hours, he does not take leave also. Only when he falls sick or he is not able to come to the office, some of the frauds which he might have been committing over the years come to light. Even in the era of information technology, organisations like KPMG who study such frauds point out that the majority of the frauds are committed by insiders. Probably because of the nature of the work, a majority of this fraud is also not publicised.

Sometime back the CVC made a study on the vigilance cases of the banks which have been referred to the CVC. The highlights are as follows: The present study further shows that the psychosis if it exists at all is without basis; first, only 18.47% of the officers appear to come with the Commission's jurisdiction (44,525 out of 2,41,120 officers). The number of individuals whose cases were reported during 1999, works out to paltry 2.08%. Out of this figure, the number of officers who may reasonably be expected to end up with a major penalty would be only about 251 or about .58% of the statistical universe.

This is surely too small a figure for creating any psychosis. Secondly, the Commission tendered advice in only those cases where the Banks concerned were themselves convinced that lapses had occurred. The Commission's role was limited to tendering advice.

Finally, there was an overall agreement to the extent of 93% between the Commission and the Banks on the further course of action to be taken. 134 cases were referred back to the Commission for reconsideration; the Commission agreed to the Bank's point of view in 60% of these cases. After such reconsideration proposals, there appeared to be 97% agreement between the Bank and the Commission as to the future course of action to be adopted. These facts do not appear to suggest that the Commission has been over-zealous in the performance of its functions or interfered in the commercial decision making of banks. It is, however, concerned, as the Banks themselves should be, over the lack of professional skills reflected in the cases that were referred to it.

The CVC has also taken the initiative to rate organisations in terms of the Probity Perception Index (PPI) based on three factors. The first is the Vigilance Intensity Index (VII). This is based on the vigilance cases with the CVC as well as the complaints received against the organisation. The second is the meta perception (M) of the organisations themselves who have been asked to rate themselves in a scale of 1 to 10 – 1 being the most corrupt and 10 being the least corrupt.

Field studies to be made by selected NGOs after following a transparent process in five cities of Delhi, Mumbai, Calcutta, Chennai and Guwahati about the perception of probity in the top 20 of the Vigilance Intensity Index is the third factor. The Probity Perception Index will contain the inputs of Vigilance Intensity Index, the meta perceptions as well as the results of the study. The advantages of such an exercise are the following:

(i) There will be informed debate about the level of corruption in different organisations.

(ii) It will provide an incentive for the organisations which are perceived to be more corrupt to improve themselves.

This happened, for example, in the urban administrative offices of Bangalore in response to the report card and Bangalore Administration produced by the Public Affairs Centre, headed by Dr. Samuel Paul.

(iii) It also provides an annual exercise where the organisations do introspection, identify areas of corruption and take follow up action. In fact, apart from meta perception, the CVC has also asked the organisations to do this introspection and launch programme for fighting corruption.

(iv) It also provides a message to the rest of the world that India is serious of fighting corruption and also provides hopefully a healthy competition among various organisations to improve their performance in the Probity Perception Index.

So far as the CVC and the banks are concerned, the CVC should be looked upon not as an organisation that discourages decision making. In fact, we appreciate the sensitive nature of the work being done by the banks and therefore we came up with the separate chapter on the banks. We have further created assurance by setting up of the Advisory Board on Banks Frauds. We have also ensured that the honest officers do not become victim of blackmail. Looking to the Indian banking industry as a whole, the main problem is that of non- performing assets. I have been arguing that non-performing assets can be effectively brought down if there is greater transparency in the system. I hope, on the suggestions made by the CVC in late 1998, the practice of the banks at least exchanging information about wilful defaulters of more than Rs.25 lakh is in practice.

In fact, there is need for amending the Banking Secrecy Act and publish the names of the defaulters just as CVC published the names of the charged officers in the web site. Such a transparency will ensure that unscrupulous and influential people do not exploit out banking system.

The same logic would also apply to the Sick Industries Companies Act. It is originally the Act which was drawn on the basis of an experience in Germany where when a company loses its capital, it becomes the property of that creditors. In our country, on the other hand, the SICA in the initial years operated in such a way that the industries were afraid of being a reference made to the BIFR.

Subsequently, they have discovered in the BIFR that there is a convenient alibi available for getting away with their responsibility. The Finance Minister announced in the Budget Speech of 2001-2002 that the SICA will be abolished but apparently no action has been taken. There is no reason why this should not be done without further delay.

That brings me to the need for strengthening the legal framework of our banking system like we should be able to have on the model of the United States laws relating to four closure and Chapter 11 proceedings so that the banks are able to perform effectively. Unfortunately, our banking system especially the public sector are the legacy of the vestitudes of the policies followed in the past and it is high time that we come out of this legacy by making our banks operate in conditions similar to the global environment. In fact, the observations made by the Shri Krishnamurthy, Chairman, State Bank of India in the Indian Banks' Survey of Financial Express of December 2001 is worth noting.

Shri Krishnamurthy says: "Who created this operating environment. First, you had loan melas then waivers. Then we are chased to our non-performing assets. You ask banks to be all things to all people and then you see that there are NPAs and that recapitalisation is bad. Let me tell you that recapitalisation is a price that we have to pay for what we did all along".

While NPAs may be one aspect of the banking scene today, equally important is the role which the banks will play in the years to come. If more and more multinational banks are coming and operating in India, what will happen to our Indian banks? It is interesting that in the Financial Express survey of 2001, among the top ten banks listed in terms of performance, there is only one public sector bank namely, the Corporation Bank at rank 9. Other ranks are CITI Bank, IDBI Bank Ltd., Dovish Bank, Hong Kong and Shanghai Banking Corporation Ltd.,

Standard Chartered Bank, Bank of Tokyo Mitsubishi Ltd., Development Bank of Singapore Ltd., HDFC Bank Ltd.

With the greater liberalisation of the banking sector, how are our banks going to survive? One approach I find is some of the financial institutions have started talking about universal banking. One of the important features of the last year was the VRS which has tried to reduce the wage bill.

Universal banking on the one hand to cover a wider range of risks and at the same time reducing the wage bill may be two strategic step which probably other banks also would consider. But then the question arises about the role of the size of a bank in the emerging global scene. If greater liberalisation in the financial sector means that we will see large banks, particularly multinational banks come and operate in a more aggressive way in our country, what is going to be the future of the banks of Indian origin?

Perhaps strategic thinking among the Indian banks themselves under the auspices of Indian Banks' Association may be required so that at least for the next three to five years the Indian banks have a broad strategy which they can adopt and survive in the new environment.

In this context, I must complement the banks for taking seriously the CVC's directive to computerise at least 70% of their business. Today, I understand 74% of the business of all the public sector banks has been computerised. We should now aim for not branch wise but bank wide computerisation. Bank wide computerisation with the capacity to focus on the customer and develop a culture of customer focus services mindset is perhaps needed in today's context for facing the future.

Sumantra Ghoshal, Gita Piramal and Christopher Bartlett in their book have shown the way of about what Indian companies must do to become world class. We are today in a state of "satisfactory underperformance". What we need is radical change. To borrow the words of the authors, the problem of Indian industry "lies in a corporate disease called satisfactory underperformance. It is a pervasive disease – we have confronted it in companies all over the world. It is a disease that is very easy to catch – indeed, finding a way to avoid it is the difficult part".

The dynamics of satisfactory underperformance is also traced by the authors. By luck, chance or foresight and courage, a company develops an effective and successful business strategy. The strategy fits the market demands, and matches the company's strengths. As a result, the company becomes highly competitive, with growth and profits as the ensuing rewards. With growth and profits come recognition and celebration. Top managers of the company start seeing their face on the covers of business journals. The Harvard Business School writes a case on their success. Soon they start believing all that is being said of them – they are the best. It is their brilliance that caused it all.

They go on the lecture circuit to tell others how they did it, despite great odds. With growth comes the perceived need for better control. After all, if they did it all, then they must continue to do it all, to protect the success and build on it. As the company becomes bigger, to do it all they need support to collect all the information, to bring all the important choices and decisions to them. So, they hire layers of staff, as instruments to leverage their own brilliance in the expanded organisation. The staff joins the business press in telling them how good they are, and it all becomes a positive reinforcement cycle. Being the best gives these managers the right to be arrogant, not only with their subordinates, but also with customers and suppliers: 'Why make a fuss if some little thing goes wrong? Don't you understand what a privilege you have, dealing with the best?' External arrogance and a focus on internal control soon stifle all initiative and enthusiasm at the operating levels of the company. Those who can manage the politics progress, those who side with customers or employees or raise uncomfortable questions are seen as obstacles and are soon sidelined or, better still, pushed overboard. Compliance and fear take over from enthusiasm and passion. Gradually the company slips first into satisfactory underperformance and, finally, into acute crisis.

I wonder whether such free thinking has been done by our banks either at the individual level or even collectively under the auspices of the IBA so that new ideas are explored and new strategies worked out.

Ultimately, in the emerging environment two aspects become important. One is the aspect of better corporate governance and the second is innovativeness and developing competitive edge through imagination. So far as better corporate governance is concerned, what is needed is ensuring that there is transparency in the system of decision making and this transparency in would lead to accountability, and accountability will be to the shareholders and stakeholders. The basic for good corporate governance would be to see that the decision making is ethical. In this context, I would invite attention to the book, 'The Power of Ethical Management' by Norman Vincent Peale and Kenneth Blanchard. They prescribe a three-way test to decide whether your action is ethical or not.

The first test is "Is it legal?" If decision taken is not legal, it is not ethical. The second test is, "Is it fair?" Being fair means that it provides equal advantage / disadvantage to the parties concerned. If it favours any particular party, to that extent it is not fair and therefore it is not ethical. The third is, what I would call, the eleventh commandment test. Cynics say that there are ten commandment in the Bible but there is eleventh commandment, "Thou Shall Not". You can violate all the ten commandment but "Thou Shall Not Be Found Out". The third test is, if the decision taken is known publicly in the media, will you feel ashamed? This is a basic test for propriety so that when we take decisions in the banking sector, we ensure that the decisions are all ethical.

The significance of ethics in the context of competitiveness has been highlighted by many successful managers. I would mention three. This is what Jack Welch, the management icon of the 20th century says:

> *"Excellence and competitiveness are totally compatible with honesty and integrity. The A student, the four-minute miler, the high-jump record holder – all strong winners – can achieve those results without resorting to cheating. People who cheat are simply weak".*

> *"A professor gave a hypothetical case to his business school students. He said, 'If you were running a business for a larger company and were about to book a $50 million order, but to do so, you had to deposit $1 million in a Swiss bank account to an agent, would you do it? Approximately 40 per cent to 50 per cent said they would. I was shocked! Shocked! I told the students someone was teaching them the wrong things. This was not one of those cases where you had to interpret the law; this was a simple bribery case".*
>
> *"In the end, your integrity is all you've got".*

Shri Narayana Murthy of Infosys who underlined the principle of Infosys while addressing the Students at Wharton School of Business is worth noting:

> *"The Infosys value system can be captured in one line– the softest pillow is a clear conscience. A company's value system is the guiding light in its hours of darkness. It builds confidence, peace of mind, and enhances enthusiasm during tough times. The importance you attach to your value system is reflected in the cost you are willing to incur for your belies and convictions. At Infosys, we have stood firm whenever our value system was tested. We knew that talking short cuts that compromise our values would be detrimental. One of my strongest beliefs is that corporations have an important duty to contribute to society. No corporation can sustain its progress unless it makes a difference to its context".*

Azim Premji of Wipro, who as built a world class institution, said that in building a world- class institution, five factors are important. These are:

i. Vision

ii. Values

iii. Innovation

iv. Leadership

v. Social Commitment

We therefore find that successful managers face competition have not given up on the ethical and the value dimension. Corporate governance only emphasises this aspect. That still leaves the second important aspect I said in the context of imagination. This will mean that we must be able to get the best out of every individual in an organisation. Here again, I would invite attention to what Jack Welch says about human productivity. "The world of the 1990s and beyond will not belong to 'managers' or those who can make the numbers dance. The world will belong to passionate, driven leaders – people who not only have enormous amounts of energy but who can energize those whom they lead." "I simply dislike the traits that have come to be associated with 'managing' – controlling, stifling people, keeping them in the dark, wasting their time on trivia and reports. Breathing down their necks. You can't manage self-confidence into people. You have to get out of their way and let it grow in them by allowing them to win, and then rewarding them when they do.

The word manager has too often come to be synonymous with control – cold, uncaring, button-down, passionless. I never associate passion with the word manage, and I've never seen a leader without it." "Somebody who can develop a vision of what he or she wants their business unit, their activity to do and be. Somebody who is able to articulate to the entire unit what the business is, and gain through a sharing of discussion – listening and talking – an acceptance of the vision. And [some on] who then can relentlessly drive implementation of that vision to a successful conclusion." "Too often we measure everything and understand nothing. The three most important things you need to measure in a business are customer satisfaction, employee satisfaction, and cash flow. If you're growing satisfaction, your global market share is sure to grow, too. Employee satisfaction feeds you productivity, quality, pride and creativity. And cash flow is the pulse –the key vital sign of a company."

GE Leaders always with Unyielding Integrity

Create a clear, simple, reality based customer focussed vision, and are able to communicate it straightforwardly to all constituencies Reach, set aggressive targets, recognize and reward progress, while understanding accountability and commitment Have a passion for excellence, hate bureaucracy, and all the nonsense that comes with it Have the self confidence to empower others and behave in a boundaryless fashion; believe in and are committed to workout as a means of empowerment, are open to ideas from any where Have, or have the capacity to develop, global brains and global sensitivity, and are comfortable building diverse and global teams Have enormous energy and the ability to energize and invigorate others, stimulate and relish change and not be frightened or paralysed by it, see change as an opportunity, not a threat Possess a mindset that drives quality, cost and speed for a competitive advantage "Growing productivity must be the foundation of everything we do. We've been chasing it at GE for years. We once thought we could manage it into business operations, with control and hierarchies and vinyl books with charts. All we did was stifle people, sit on them, slow them up, and bore them to death. In the early 80s we fell in love with robots and automation and filled some of our factories with them as our employees looked on sullenly and fearfully. It didn't work.

We now know where productivity – real and limitless productivity – comes from. It comes from challenged, empowered, excited, rewarded teams of people. It comes from engaging every single mind in the organisation.

When a business becomes productive it gains control of its destiny." "Productivity is not the squeezing our of a rag. Productivity is the belief that there's an infinite capacity to improve anything."

"What we have done has barely scratched the surface. It turns out that there is, in fact, unlimited juice in that lemon. The fact is, this is not about squeezing anything at all; it is about tapping an ocean of creativity, passion, and energy that as far as we can see, has no bottom and no shores."

"Just as surely as speed flows from simplicity, simplicity is grounded in self confidence. Self confidence does not grow in someone who is just another appendage on the bureaucracy... whose authority rests on the bureaucracy..... whose authority rests on little more than a title..... people who are freed from the confines of their box on the organisation chart, whose status rests on real world achievement.... Those are the people who develop self confidence to be simple, to share every bit of information available to them, to listen to those above, below and around them, and then move boldly.

Ultimately, therefore, we can succeed if we practice the standard advice given in the Taitreya Upanishad. Let us come together. Let us enjoy together. Let our strengths come together. Let us move from darkness to light. Let there be no poison of misunderstanding or hatred. That way is the path to progress.

CAUSES FOR NON-PERFORMING ASSETS IN PUBLIC SECTOR BANKS

Public Sector Bank Suspense (PSB Suspense)

As already mentioned, Pay and Accounts Office of a Ministry / Department is placed in account with a branch of Reserve Bank or a Public Sector Bank nominated for the Ministry / Department. Similarly, a Cheque Drawing Officer of a Ministry / Department is also placed in account with a branch of the same Bank.

Public Sector Banks are now conducting Government business on behalf of the Reserve Bank of India who is the official banker of the Central Government. When a cheque is issued in payment of a bill, the amount is normally debited to the final head of account. At the close of the month the paid bills or vouchers are posted in the compilation sheet and the net amount of payment is tallied with the total amount of cheques delivered during the month. After this is done, the net amount of cheques delivered during the month is credited to the head "8670-Cheques and Bills-102 PAO Cheques." In case of cheques issued by the cheque drawing officers, the total amount of cheques drawn during a month is credited to the head '8670-Cheques and Bills-103 Departmental Cheques'. Offices/Departments which are required to follow the Public Works / Forest System of accounts credit the amount so arrived at to the head '8782 Cash Remittances etc.-102 Public Works Remittances 103 Forest Remittances' as the case may be, in their monthly account. Whenever a cheque is encashed by a Public Sector Bank, it initially pays the amount from its own cash balance and then claims reimbursement from the Central Accounts Section (CAS), RBI Nagpur which maintains the account of each Ministry/Department. Similarly, when Government receipts are paid into a Public Sector Bank, it passes on the proceeds to the Central Accounts Section, RBI, Nagpur. As there is a time lag for a Government transaction carried out by the bank to get reflected in Government cash balance the minor head 'Public Sector Bark Suspense' is operated in Government books to account for the transactions awaiting settlement.

The dealing branches of Public Sector Banks send the daily scrolls of receipts/payments in duplicate to the Focal Point Branch alongwith challans/paid cheques. The Focal Point Branch consolidates the transactions PAO-wise and prepares a main scroll in triplicate and sends two copies of the main scroll alongwith the original of the daily receipts/payments scrolls received from the dealing branches together with challans/paid cheques to the Pay and Accounts Office. The aggregate of receipts/payments are to be incorporated in a Daily Memo by the Focal Point Branch and it sends the same to the Link Cell of the bank at Nagpur which settles the amounts with the RBI, CAS, Nagpur.

The receipt scrolls attached to the main scrolls are to be examined by the Pay and Accounts Office to ensure that the challans enclosed actually pertain to the Pay and Accounts Office concerned and the receipts recorded in the scroll tally with the amount shown in the challans. Similarly, the payment scrolls attached are also to be examined to ensure that the paid cheques are those which are issued by the Pay and Accounts Officer or by the Cheque Drawing Officer functioning under him and that the amount of payments recorded in the scroll tallies with the amount shown on the paid cheque.

The Pay and Accounts Officer will ensure that error-free Main Scroll is verified and duplicate thereof returned to the Focal Point Branch. Any discrepancy in the Main Scroll is to be got rectified by personal contacts. After this verification, the totals of the payments and receipts of the main scroll are to be entered date-wise in columns 2 and 3 respectively in the Register of PSB Suspense/RB Deposits in Form CAM-17 indicating date of the main scroll in column 1 ibid.

Separate pages/folios are to be used for entering scrolls pertaining to the office of the Pay and Accounts Officer and for each Cheque Drawing Officer, one page being used for total consolidated account of the Focal Point Branch. The total for the month is to be struck separately for payment scrolls and receipt scrolls.

After verifying the total amounts of receipts/payments as noted in the 'Register of Public Sector Bank Suspense/R.B. Deposits' on the basis of daily main scrolls, necessary transfer entry will be prepared by the Pay and Accounts Officer to adjust the amounts of payments in his books as under:-

(-) Cr. 8670 - Cheques and Bills

102 PAO Cheques

or

103 Departmental Cheques

(as the case may be)

To

8658—Suspense Accounts

108 Public Sector Bank Suspense. Cr

In case of offices following the Public Works/Forest Divisional system of accounts, the amount of paid cheques will be adjusted as under:

(-) Cr. 8782-Cash Remittances etc.

102 Public Works Remittances

or

103 Forest Remittances

(as the case may be)

Cr. 8658—Suspense Accounts

108 Public Sector Bank Suspense

So far as the amounts of receipts are concerned, the challans are posted under final receipt heads of accounts or minus debited to the advance or salary head under which the payment was originally debited in the compilation sheet as per classification recorded in the challans. The total amount of receipts is then arrived at and after verifying the monthly total under column 3 of the 'Register of PSB Suspense' is debited to the head '8658—Suspense Accounts 108—PSB Suspense'.

After the close of the month, 'the Focal Point Branch sends to the Pay and Accounts Office four copies of "Date-wise Monthly Statement (DMS)" based on the verified daily Main Scrolls by the 3rd of the following month. This statement is to be checked with reference to the gross receipts/payments worked out in CAM 17 with reference to daily Main Scrolls. Two copies of the DMS are returned to the Focal Point Branch by the 7th of the following month. The duplicate copy of the DMS is sent to the Principal Accounts Office.

The Pay and Accounts Office also receives Monthly computerised (Put-through) Statement from SBI GAD or link cell of the other Public Sector Banks at Nagpur showing the amounts of receipts/payments settled with RBI, CAS, Nagpur. The Pay and Accounts Office checks the entries therein with reference to the figures in the DMS.

After verifying the figures of computerised statement of credit/debit settled with the RBI, CAS, Nagpur by the SBI GAD or link cell of other Public Sector Banks with the Date-wise Monthly Statement received earlier from the Focal Point Bank, the Pay and Accounts Office has to reconcile the figures as in its books with the figures appearing in the put-through statement. For this purpose a 'Monthly Reconciliation Analysis' has to be prepared in the form as per 'Annexure I'. The Pay and Accounts Office is responsible for any difference appearing in Part 'A' of the Analysis. For discrepant items appearing in serial (vi) (b) of Part 'C' and transactions other than those appearing in Serial (vi) (a) of Part 'C', it has to contact the Focal Point Branch to ensure that the rectification is carried out and the item has been put through by the Focal Point Branch through the GAD/Link Cell in the subsequent month positively. The grand total of Serial (vi) (a) and (vi) (b) is tallied with the closing balance shown against serial (v) of Part 'C'.

The Pay and Accounts Office has also to maintain a 'Register of amounts put through', with the RBI, CAS, Nagpur separately for receipts and payments as in Part I of Annexure II. Normally, all the amounts except those relating to the last 3-4 days of the month will be put through/settled with RBI, CAS, Nagpur in the same month. The items of last 3-4 days are expected to be put through/settled in the first few days of the subsequent month. In case it is seen while closing the register of subsequent month, that some balance of a month is outstanding the Focal Point Branch will immediately be contacted for remedial action.

The Pay and Accounts Office has also to maintain a Register showing the progressive position of amounts to be put through/ settled with RBI, CAS, Nagpur as in Part II of Annexure II separately for receipts and payments.

The Pay and Accounts Office prepares a statement of monthly reconciliation between the figures as in 'Datewise Monthly Statement' and the amounts booked under '8658—Suspense Accounts—108 PSB Suspense' in Annexure III. Proper explanations/reasons for the difference with reference to the 'Datewise Monthly Statement' are given in the statement. Action taken for clearance of difference is also given therein. A copy of the monthly reconciliation statement is sent by the Pay and Accounts Office alongwith the monthly account to the Principal Accounts Office.

Verification of the amounts put-through/settled with the RBI, CAS, Nagpur with the figures of the DMS and preparation of 'Monthly Reconciliation Analysis' will throw light on the amount of reimbursement claimed in excess by the bank. A statement in Annexure IV is sent by the Pay and Accounts Office to the Principal Accounts Office for reporting excess put through to the Controller General of Accounts as per instructions issued on the subject.

In order to keep a watch over the clearance of balances under the suspense head, a 'Broad-sheet of PSB Suspense' is also maintained by the Pay and Accounts Office in the Form as per Annexure V separately for Debits (receipts) and Credits (payments). The clearance of the head 'PSB Suspense' is however, done by the Principal Accounts Office on receipt of a monthly statement of closing balances (CAS-122) from RBI, CAS Nagpur. The amount of debits/credits cleared from 'PSB Suspense' shall be intimated to the concerned Pay and Accounts Office by the Principal Accounts Office for maintaining the Broadsheet of PSB Suspense. The Pay and Accounts Office also works out the age-wise analysis of balances in Annexure VI (supported by amount put-through/settled with RBI, CAS, Nagpur). The statement received from RBI, CAS, Nagpur shows the details of payments and receipts for which settlement had been effected between the Public Sector Bank and the RBI, CAS, Nagpur. This statement also includes the details by RBI, CAS, Nagpur on the basis of advices issued by the Principal Accounts Office. After verification of this balance statement, the Principal Accounts Office has to prepare the following Transfer Entry:-

Payments settled between PSB and RBI, CAS, Nagpur

(-) Cr. 8658-Suspense Accounts

108-PSB Suspense

To

8675-Deposits with Reserve Bank

101-Central-Civil Cr.

Receipts settled between the PSB and RBI, CAS, Nagpur.

Dr. 8675-Deposits with Reserve Bank

101-Central Civil

To

8658-Suspense Accounts

108, PSB Suspense (-)Dr.

The balances outstanding on the credit and debit side after deducing the above adjustments for a month under the minor head 'PSB Suspense' separately would indicate the amounts paid by the Public Sector Bank which have not been got recouped by it during the month itself and the amount of receipts collected by the Public Sector Bank which it has not credited to RBI, CAS, Nagpur before the end of the month respectively. A close watch has to be kept on the clearance of balances (both credit and debit) under the minor head 'PSB Suspense' to ensure that actual settlement between the Public Sector Banks and Central Accounts Section of Reserve Bank of India at Nagpur is conducted within the minimum possible time; otherwise the cash balances of the Government as reflected in the books of the RBI would give an erroneous picture of cash balance of the Government of India with the Reserve Bank of India.

PROCEDURE IN CASE OF CENTRAL BOARD OF EXCISE AND CUSTOMS.

(a) *Receipt of Revenue:* The receipt scrolls are prepared by the bank in triplicate major head wise. The serial number in the scroll is recorded on the right hand top corner of all copies of challans to facilitate identification. Each day's scrolls are also given running serial number separately for each major head for the financial year. The dealing branch sends the scrolls together with challans arranged serially to the Focal Point Branch for onward transmission to the Pay and Accounts Office. The quadruplicate copies of challans are also sent duly bound and serially arranged.

(b) *Refund of Revenue:* At the headquarters of each Collectorate one branch of the selected bank is authorised to make payment of refunds on cheques (marked Revenue Refunds and Rebates) issued by the Divisional Officer. The paying branch prepares in quadruplicate separate major head-wise scrolls (marked Refunds, Rebates and Drawbacks). Two copies of the scrolls with paid cheques are sent to the Focal Point Branch and the third copy of scroll is sent to the Divisional Officer.

(c) *Action in Focal Point Branch:* It prepares major head-wise daily main scroll in triplicate and sends two copies of the scrolls to the Pay and Accounts Office of the Collectorate alongwith the original copy of receipt payment scrolls and challans and paid cheques received from the dealing branches. The major head-wise quadruplicate copies of challans duly arranged Rangewise are sent to the nominated Range Officer.

(d) *Accounting Adjustment:* The Pay and Accounts Office adjusts the receipts in its account under the concerned heads by contra debit (bank wise) to head 8658—Suspense Accounts—108 PSB Suspense Bank— "X" (name of the bank). Similarly, in case of payment of refund cheques the amount is credited bank-wise to the head 'PSB Suspense Bank—"X". It maintains a separate register of 'PSB Suspense' for each bank concerned with the work of Revenue Account' and posts therein each day's receipts payments. The Link Cell prepares in respect of each Pay and Accounts Office (i.e. Collectorate) a statement in quadruplicate of receipts and payments put through to RBI, CAS, Nagpur. The monthly statement as got verified by the RBI, CAS, Nagpur is sent to the Principal Chief Controller of Accounts, Central Board of Excise and Customs by the latter and a copy is also sent to the Focal Point Branch. Another copy is sent to Pay and Accounts Office direct. On receipt of the statement from RBI, CAS, Nagpur, Principal Chief Controller of Accounts, Central Board of Excise and Customs clears the head "PSB Suspense—Bank—'X' by transfer to the head '8675 Deposits with Reserve Bank—101 Central-Civil'.

PROCEDURE IN CASE OF CENTRAL BOARD OF DIRECT TAXES

(a) *Receipt of Taxes:* The receipt scrolls are prepared major head-wise in quadruplicate. A running serial number for each financial year is given to the scrolls for each major head. The dealing branch also prepares a summary of receipts indicating total receipts under all major heads for the day. The branch then sends three sets of scrolls /challans, the first set containing original scroll and original challan intended for Designated Officer; the second set containing duplicate copies of scrolls and challans meant for the Zonal Accounts Officer and the triplicate copy of scroll and the summary of receipts meant for the Nodal Branch with a forwarding letter to the Nodal Branch.

(b) *Income Tax Refund Orders (ITROs):* Only the authorised Income Tax Officer (ITO) can issue the ITRO on the authorised bank. In case of refund orders upto Rs. 1000 two foils of relative refund orders are issued to the assessee. In case of refund of Rs. 1000 and above, the ITO will issue one foil to assessee and simultaneously refund advice in duplicate will be sent to the paying branch. The ITRO and refund advice bear the same number and the payment is made en the strength of refund advice. The paying branch prepares the scrolls major head-wise in quadruplicate. The scrolls are made into sets similar to the sets relating to receipts except that instead of challans, the paid refund orders/advices are attached to the scrolls. Besides, the set meant for Designated Officer does not contain the refund order in case of refunds of Rs. 1000 and above. However, in these cases a copy of the refund advice is sent to him.

(c) *Action in Nodal Branch:* On receipt of sets of scrolls with challans/paid instruments the Nodal Branch prepares daily main receipt/payment scrolls in triplicate Designated Officer/major head-wise. The scrolls are given running serial numbers for each financial year. The receipt scrolls together with original branch bank scrolls and challans and similarly the payment scrolls together with ITROs are sent in duplicate to the Zonal Accounts Office on day to day basis. Another set of receipt scrolls containing original challans and payment scrolls together with refund advice for refund of Rs.1000 and above and paid ITROs upto Rs.1000 is sent to the Designated Officer bi-weekly. The Nodal Branch also records a certificate on the main scroll sent to Zonal Accounts Office/Designated Officer to the effect that necessary advice has been sent to the Link Cell at

Nagpur. It also maintains a Register to record daily receipts and payments reported to it by branch banks under various major heads. Two copies of the Register (kept in perforated form) are furnished to the Zonal Accounts Office with the relevant scrolls etc. Nodal Branch is required to prepare a Daily Memo on the basis of entries in the above Register and sends it on daily basis to the Link Cell at Nagpur.

The Nodal Branch also prepares each month ZAO-wise monthly statements in quadruplicate indicating date-wise receipts/payments reported to the Zonal Accounts Office earlier and sends 3 copies to the Zonal Accounts Office for verification. The third copy is sent by the Zonal Accounts Office to the Principal Chief Controller of Accounts, Central Board of Direct Taxes. On receipt of the verified copy, the same is passed on to Link Cell by the Nodal Branch after keeping necessary note in the office copy.

(d) *Accounting Adjustments:* The Link Cell at Nagpur checks the Daily Memos received from the Nodal Branch and passes on the same to RBI, CAS, Nagpur for settlement. On the basis of the Daily Memos received from Link Cell, RBI, CAS, Nagpur generates daily input statements and furnishes two copies thereof to Link Cell for confirming the figures. For the purpose of final reconciliation of transaction with the concerned Zonal Accounts Office and Link Cell, the RBI, CAS, Nagpur generates monthly statement and furnishes the same to Zonal Accounts Office and the Link Cell of the bank. It also sends a monthly analysis indicating major head-wise receipts/ refunds etc. to Principal Chief Controller of Accounts, Central Board of Direct Taxes.

The Zonal Accounts Office on receipt of the monthly statements of receipts and payments from the Nodal Branch carries adjustments in its books by per conra debit and credit to the head '8658—Suspense Accounts—108—PSB Suspense'. The minor head 'Receipts awaiting transfer to other minor heads' is operated initially under various receipt major heads. The above minor head is cleared by transfer of the amounts to the concerned minor heads on receipt of account from the Designated Officer. On receipt of major head-wise monthly statement from the RBI, the Principal Chief Controller of Accounts, Central Board of Direct Taxes clears the above suspense head by minus debit/ minus credit by per contra debit and credit to the head '8675— Deposits with Reserve Bank—101 Central-Civil'.

DEPOSITS WITH RESERVE BANK

The general banking business of the Central Government is conducted by the Reserve Bank of India. Ministries and Departments of the Central Government operate on such branches of the Reserve Bank and or the Public Sector Bank, as have been, or may be nominated by the Reserve Bank as its agents for handling the receipt and payment transactions of a particular Ministry or Department.

The Central Accounts Section of Reserve Bank of India at Nagpur keeps a complete account of receipts and payments (including inter-Government adjustments and adjustments inter-se of Defence, Railways and Posts) in respect of Central Government. It maintains individual accounts of each Ministry / Department of the Central Government and of Union Territory administrations having separated accounts offices and sends a monthly statement, taking into account all cash transactions in all the branches and agencies of the Bank and the adjusting transactions in its own books to their Principal Accounts Offices with such supporting details as may be prescribed by Government from time to time. Beside keeping the Ministry/ Department-wise accounts, the Central Accounts Section also acts as a general clearing house for the adjustment of such transactions between the Central and State Governments as may be specified by the Central Government.

As will be clear from adjustments shown in para above, all receipts of Central Government are finally debited to the head '8675 Deposits with Reserve Bank—101 Central-Civil' and all payments on its behalf are finally credited to the above head. The net position of credit or debit under the above head during the year is reflected by the Principal Accounts Office of each Ministry/Department in the Statement of Central Transactions.

The cash balance of Central Government (including Railways, Defence, Posts & Telecommunications) is worked out by Controller General of Accounts by transferring the net transactions shown under "8675 Deposits with Reserve Bank" to "8999—Cash Balance—102 Deposits with Reserve Bank," and reflected accordingly in the Union Government Finance Accounts.

10

Banking Sector Reforms: After and Before

The strategy of planned economic development required huge development expenditure, which was met through Government's dominance of ownership of banks, automatic monetization of fiscal deficit and subjecting the banking sector to large pre-emptions – both in terms of the statutory holding of Government securities (statutory liquidity ratio, or SLR) and cash reserve ratio (CRR). Besides, there was a complex structure of administered interest rates guided by the social concerns, resulting in cross-subsidization. These not only distorted the interest rate mechanism but also adversely affected the viability and profitability of banks by the end of 1980s.

There is perhaps an element of commonality of such a 'repressed' regime in the financial sector of many emerging market economies. It follows that the process of reform of financial sector in most emerging economies also has significant commonalities while being specific to the circumstances of each country. A narration of the broad contours of reform in India would be helpful in appreciating both the commonalities and the differences in our paths of reforms.

CONTOURS OF BANKING REFORMS IN INDIA

First, reform measures were initiated and sequenced to create an enabling environment for banks to overcome the external constraints – these were related to administered structure of interest rates, high levels of pre-emption in the form of reserve requirements, and credit allocation to certain sectors. Sequencing of interest rate deregulation has been an important component of the reform process which has imparted greater efficiency to resource allocation. The process has been gradual and predicated upon the institution of prudential regulation for the banking system, market behaviour, financial opening and, above all, the underlying macroeconomic conditions. The interest rates in the banking system have been largely deregulated except for certain specific classes; these are: savings deposit accounts, non-resident Indian (NRI) deposits, small loans up to Rs.2 lakh and export credit. The need for continuance of these prescriptions as well as those relating to priority sector lending have been flagged for wider debate in the latest annual policy of the RBI. However, administered interest rates still prevail in small savings schemes of the Government.

Second, as regards the policy environment of public ownership, it must be recognised that the lion's share of financial intermediation was accounted for by the public sector during the pre-reform period. As part of the reforms programme, initially, there was infusion of capital by the Government in public sector banks, which was followed by expanding the capital base with equity participation by the private investors.

The share of the public sector banks in the aggregate assets of the banking sector has come down from 90 per cent in 1991 to around 75 per cent in 2004. The share of wholly Government- owned public sector banks (i.e., where no diversification of ownership has taken place) sharply declined from about 90 per cent to 10 per cent of aggregate assets of all scheduled commercial banks during the same period. Diversification of ownership has led to greater market accountability and improved efficiency. Since the initiation of reforms, infusion of funds by the Government into the public sector banks for the purpose of recapitalisation amounted, on a cumulative basis, to less than one per cent of India's GDP, a figure much lower than that for many other countries. Even after accounting for the reduction in the Government's shareholding on account of losses set off, the current market value of the share capital of the Government in public sector banks has increased manifold and as such what was perceived to be a bail-out of public sector banks by Government seems to be turning out to be a profitable investment for the Government.

Third, one of the major objectives of banking sector reforms has been to enhance efficiency and productivity through competition. Guidelines have been laid down for establishment of new banks in the private sector and the foreign banks have been allowed more liberal entry. Since 1993, twelve new private sector banks have been set up. As already mentioned, an element of private shareholding in public sector banks has been injected by enabling a reduction in the Government shareholding in public sector banks to 51 per cent. As a major step towards enhancing competition in the banking sector, foreign direct investment in the private sector banks is now allowed up to 74 per cent, subject to conformity with the guidelines issued from time to time.

Fourth, consolidation in the banking sector has been another feature of the reform process. This also encompassed the Development Financial Institutions (DFIs), which have been providers of long-term finance while the distinction between short-term and long-term finance provider has increasingly become blurred over time. The complexities involved in harmonising the role and operations of the DFIs were examined and the RBI enabled the reverse-merger of a large DFI with its commercial banking subsidiary which is a major initiative towards universal banking. Recently, another large term-lending institution has been converted into a bank. While guidelines for mergers between non-banking financial companies and banks were issued some time ago, guidelines for mergers between private sector banks have been issued a few days ago. The principles underlying these guidelines would be applicable, as appropriate, to the public sector banks also, subject to the provisions of the relevant legislation.

Fifth, impressive institutional and legal reforms have been undertaken in relation to the banking sector. In 1994, a Board for Financial Supervision (BFS) was constituted comprising select members of the RBI Board with a variety of professional expertise to exercise 'undivided attention to supervision'. The BFS, which generally meets once a month, provides direction on a continuing basis on regulatory policies including governance issues and supervisory practices. It also provides direction on supervisory actions in specific cases. The BFS also ensures an integrated approach to supervision of commercial banks, development finance institutions, non-banking finance companies, urban cooperatives banks and primary dealers.

A Board for Regulation and Supervision of Payment and Settlement Systems (BPSS) has also been recently constituted to prescribe policies relating to the regulation and supervision of all types of payment and settlement systems, set standards for existing and future systems, authorise the payment and settlement systems and determine criteria for membership to these systems. The Credit Information Companies (Regulation) Bill, 2004 has been passed by both the Houses of the Parliament while the Government Securities Bills, 2004 is under process. Certain amendments are being considered by the Parliament to enhance Reserve Bank's regulatory and supervisory powers.

Major amendments relate to requirement of prior approval of RBI for acquisition of five per cent or more of shares of a banking company with a view to ensuring 'fit and proper' status of the significant shareholders, aligning the voting rights with the economic holding and empowering the RBI to supersede the Board of a banking company.

Sixth, there have been a number of measures for enhancing the transparency and disclosures standards. Illustratively, with a view to enhancing further transparency, all cases of penalty imposed by the RBI on the banks as also directions issued on specific matters, including those arising out of inspection, are to be placed in the public domain.

Seventh, while the regulatory framework and supervisory practices have almost converged with the best practices elsewhere in the world, two points are noteworthy. First, the minimum capital to risk assets ratio (CRAR) has been kept at nine per cent i.e., one percentage point above the international norm; and second, the banks are required to maintain a separate Investment Fluctuation Reserve (IFR) out of profits, towards interest rate risk, at five per cent of their investment portfolio under the categories 'held for trading' and 'available for sale'. This was prescribed at a time when interest rates were falling and banks were realizing large gains out of their treasury activities. Simultaneously, the conservative accounting norms did not allow banks to recognize the unrealized gains. Such unrealized gains coupled with the creation of IFR helped in cushioning the valuation losses required to be booked when interest rates in the longer tenors have moved up in the last one year or so.

Eighth, of late, the regulatory framework in India, in addition to prescribing prudential guidelines and encouraging market discipline, is increasingly focusing on ensuring good governance through "fit and proper" owners, directors and senior managers of the banks. Transfer of shareholding of five per cent and above requires acknowledgement from the RBI and such significant shareholders are put through a 'fit and proper' test.

Banks have also been asked to ensure that the nominated and elected directors are screened by a nomination committee to satisfy 'fit and proper' criteria. Directors are also required to sign a covenant indicating their roles and responsibilities. The RBI has recently issued detailed guidelines on ownership and governance in private sector banks emphasizing diversified ownership. The listed banks are also required to comply with governance principles laid down by the SEBI – the securities markets regulator.

PROCESSES OF BANKING REFORM

The processes adopted for bringing about the reforms in India may be of some interest to this audience. Recalling some features of financial sector reforms in India would be in order, before narrating the processes.

First, financial sector reform was undertaken early in the reform-cycle in India.

Second, the financial sector was not driven by any crisis and the reforms have not been an outcome of multilateral aid.

Third, the design and detail of the reform were evolved by domestic expertise, though international experience is always kept in view.

Fourth, the Government preferred that public sector banks manage the over-hang problems of the past rather than cleanup the balance sheets with support of the Government.

Fifth, it was felt that there is enough room for growth and healthy competition for public and private sector banks as well as foreign and domestic banks.

The twin governing principles are non-disruptive progress and consultative process. In order to ensure timely and effective implementation of the measures, RBI has been adopting a consultative approach before introducing policy measures. Suitable mechanisms have been instituted to deliberate upon various issues so that the benefits of financial efficiency and stability percolate to the common person and the services of the Indian financial system can be benchmarked against international best standards in a transparent manner. Let me give a brief account of these mechanisms.

First, on all important issues, workings group are constituted or technical reports are prepared, generally encompassing a review of the international best practices, options available and way forward.

The group membership may be internal or external to the RBI or mixed. Draft reports are often placed in public domain and final reports take account of inputs, in particular from industry associations and self-regulatory organizations. The reform-measures emanate out of such a series of reports, the pioneering ones being: Report of the Committee on the Financial System (Chairman: Shri M. Narasimham), in 1991; Report of the High Level Committee on Balance of Payments (Chairman: Dr. C. Rangarajan) in 1992; and the Report of the Committee on Banking Sector Reforms (Chairman: Shri M. Narasimham) in 1998.

Second, Resource Management Discussions meetings are held by the RBI with select commercial banks, prior to the policy announcements. These meetings not only focus on perception and outlook of the bankers on the economy, liquidity conditions, credit flow, development of different markets and directions of interest rates, but also on issues relating to developmental aspects of banking operations.

Third, we have formed a Technical Advisory Committee on Money, Foreign Exchange and Government Securities Markets (TAC). It has emerged as a key consultative mechanism amongst the regulators and various market players including banks.

The Committee has been crystallizing the synergies of experts across various fields of the financial market and thereby acting as a facilitator for the RBI in steering reforms in money, government securities and foreign exchange markets.

Fourth, in order to strengthen the consultative process in the regulatory domain and to place such a process on a continuing basis, the RBI has constituted a Standing Technical Advisory Committee on Financial Regulation on the lines similar to the TAC.

The Committee consists of experts drawn from academia, financial markets, banks, non-bank financial institutions and credit rating agencies. The Committee examines the issues referred to it and advises the RBI on desirable regulatory framework on an on-going basis for banks, non-bank financial institutions and other market participants.

Fifth, for ensuring periodic formal interaction, amongst the regulators, there is a High Level Co- ordination Committee on Financial and Capital Markets (HLCCFCM) with the Governor, RBI as the Chairman, and the Heads of the securities market and insurance regulators, and the Secretary of the Finance Ministry as the members.

This Co-ordination Committee has authorised constitution of several standing committees to ensure co-ordination in regulatory frameworks at an operational level.

Sixth, more recently a Standing Advisory Committee on Urban Co-operative Banks (UCBs) has been activated to advise on structural, regulatory and supervisory issues relating to UCBs and to facilitate the process of formulating future approaches for this sector. Similar mechanisms are being worked out for non-banking financial companies.

Seventh, the RBI has also instituted a mechanism of placing draft versions of important guidelines for comments of the public at large before finalisation of the guidelines. To further this consultative process and with a specific goal of making the regulatory guidelines more user-friendly, a Users' Consultative Panel has been constituted comprising the representatives of select banks and market participants.

The panel provides feedback on regulatory instructions at the formulation stage to avoid any subsequent ambiguities and operational glitches.

Eighth, an extensive and transparent communication system has been evolved. The annual policy statements and their mid-term reviews communicate the RBI's stance on monetary policy in the immediate future of six months to one year. Over the years, the reports of various working groups and committees have emerged as another plank of two-way communication from RBI.

An important feature of the RBI's communication policy is the almost real-time dissemination of information through its web- site. The auction results under Liquidity Adjustment Facility (LAF) of the day are posted on the web- site by 12.30 p.m the same day, while by 2.30 p.m. the 'reference rates' of select foreign currencies are also placed on the website. By the next day morning, the press release on money market operations is issued.

Every Saturday, by 12 noon, the weekly statistical supplement is placed on the web-site providing a fairly detailed, recent data-base on the RBI and the financial sector. All the regulatory and administrative circulars of different Departments of the RBI are placed on the web-site within half an hour of their finalization.

Ninth, an important feature of the reform of the Indian financial system has been the intent of the authorities to align the regulatory framework with international best practices keeping in view the developmental needs of the country and domestic factors. Towards this end, a Standing Committee on International Financial Standards and Codes was constituted in 1999.

The Standing Committee had set up ten Advisory Groups in key areas of the financial sector whose reports are available on the RBI website. The recommendations contained in these reports have either been implemented or are in the process of implementation. I would like to draw your attention to two reports in particular, which have a direct bearing on the banking system, viz., Advisory Group on Banking Supervision and Advisory Group on Corporate Governance.

Subsequently, in 2004, we conducted a review of the recommendations of the Advisory Groups and reported the progress and agenda ahead. What has been the impact?

These reform measures have had major impact on the overall efficiency and stability of the banking system in India. The present capital adequacy of Indian banks is comparable to those at international level. There has been a marked improvement in the asset quality with the percentage of gross non- performing assets (NPAs) to gross advances for the banking system reduced from 14.4 per cent in 1998 to 7.2 per cent in 2004.

The reform measures have also resulted in an improvement in the profitability of banks. The Return on Assets (RoA) of the banks rose from 0.4 per cent in the year 1991-92 to 1.2 per cent in 2003-04. Considering that, globally, the RoA has been in the range 0.9 to 1.5 per cent for 2004, Indian banks are well placed.

The banking sector reforms also emphasized the need to review the manpower resources and rationalize the requirements by drawing a realistic plan so as to reduce the operating cost and improve the profitability. During the last five years, the business per employee for public sector banks more than doubled to around Rs.25 million in 2004.

CONTINUITY, CHANGE AND CONTEXT

We lay considerable emphasis on appropriate mix between the elements of continuity and change in the process of reform, but the dynamic elements in the mix are determined by the context. While there is usually a consensus on the broad direction, relative emphasis on various elements of the process of reform keeps changing, depending on the evolving circumstances. Perhaps it will be useful to illustrate this approach to contextualising the mix of continuity and change. The mid-term review in November 2003, reviewed the progress of implementation of various developmental as well as regulatory measures in the banking sector but emphasised facilitating the ease of transactions by the common person and strengthening the credit delivery systems, as a response to the pressing needs of the society and economy. The annual policy statement of May 2004 carried forward this focus but flagged major areas requiring urgent attention especially in the areas of ownership, governance, conflicts of interest and customer-protection. Some extracts of the policy statement may be in order:

"First, it is necessary to articulate in a comprehensive and transparent manner the policy in regard to ownership and governance of both public and private sector banks keeping in view the special nature of banks. This will also facilitate the ongoing shift from external regulation to internal systems of controls and risk assessments.

Second, from a systemic point of view, inter-relationships between activities of financial intermediaries and areas of conflict of interests need to be considered.

Third, in order to protect the integrity of the financial system by reducing the likelihood of their becoming conduits for money laundering, terrorist financing and other unlawful activities and also to ensure audit trail, greater accent needs to be laid on the adoption of an effective consolidated know your customer (KYC) system, on both assets and liabilities, in all financial intermediaries regulated by RBI. At the same time, it is essential that banks do not seek intrusive details from their customers and do not resort to sharing of information regarding the customer except with the written consent of the customer.

Fourth, while the stability and efficiency imparted to the large commercial banking system is universally recognised, there are some segments which warrant restructuring." The annual policy statement for the current year reiterates the concern for common person, while enunciating a medium term framework, for development of money, forex and government securities markets; for enhancing credit flow to agriculture and small industry; for action points in technology and payments systems; for institutional reform in co-operative banking, non-banking financial companies and regional rural banks; and, for ensuring availability of quality services to all sections of the population.

The most distinguishing feature of the policy statement relates to the availability of banking services to the common person, especially depositors.The statement reiterates that depositors' interests form the focal point of the regulatory framework for banking in India, and elaborates the theme as follows: "A licence to do banking business provides the entity, the ability to accept deposits and access to deposit insurance for small depositors. Similarly, regulation and supervision by RBI enables these entities to access funds from a wider investor base and the payment and settlement systems provides efficient payments and funds transfer services. All these services, which are in the nature of public good, involve significant costs and are being made available only to ensure availability of banking and payment services to the entire population without discrimination".

The policy draws attention to the divergence in treatment of depositors compared to borrowers as: " ... while policies relating to credit allocation, credit pricing and credit restructuring should continue to receive attention, it is inappropriate to ignore the mandate relating to depositors' interests. Further, in our country, the socio-economic profile for a typical depositor who seeks safe avenues for his savings deserves special attention relative to other stakeholders in the banks".

Another significant area of concern has been the possible exclusion of a large section of population from the provision of services and the Statement pleads for financial inclusion. It states: "There has been expansion, greater competition and diversification of ownership of banks leading to both enhanced efficiency and systemic resilience in the banking sector. However, there are legitimate concerns in regard to the banking practices that tend to exclude rather than attract vast sections of population, in particular pensioners, self-employed and those employed in unorganised sector. While commercial considerations are no doubt important, the banks have been bestowed with several privileges, especially of seeking public deposits on a highly leveraged basis, and consequently they should be obliged to provide banking services to all segments of the population, on equitable basis." Operationally, it has been made clear that RBI will implement policies to encourage banks which provide extensive services while disincentivising those which are not responsive to the banking needs of the community, including the underprivileged.

The quality of services rendered has also invited attention in the current policy. I quote further, "Liberalisation and enhanced competition accord immense benefits, but experience has shown that consumers' interests are not necessarily accorded full protection and their grievances are not properly attended to. Several representations are being received in regard to recent trends of levying unreasonably high service/user charges and enhancement of user charges without proper and prior intimation. Taking account of all these considerations, it has been decided by RBI to set up an independent Banking Codes and Standards Board of India on the model of the mechanism in the UK in order to ensure that comprehensive code of conduct for fair treatment of customers are evolved and adhered to".

It is essential to recognise that, while these constitute contextual nuanced responses to changing circumstances within the country, the overwhelming compulsion to be in harmony with global developments must be respected and that essentially relates to Basel II.

Basel II and India

RBI's association with the Basel Committee on Banking Supervision dates back to 1997 as India was among the 16 non-member countries that were consulted in the drafting of the Basel Core Principles.

Reserve Bank of India became a member of the Core Principles Liaison Group in 1998 and subsequently became a member of the Core Principles Working Group on Capital. Within the Working Group, RBI has been actively participating in the deliberations on the New Accord and had the privilege to lead a group of six major non-G-10 supervisors which presented a proposal on a simplified approach for Basel II to the Committee. Commercial banks in India will start implementing Basel II with effect from March 31, 2007. They will adopt Standardised Approach for credit risk and Basic Indicator Approach for operational risk, initially. After adequate skills are developed, both at the banks and also at supervisory levels, some banks may be allowed to migrate to the Internal Rating Based (IRB) Approach.

Let me briefly review the steps taken for implementation of Basel II and the emerging issues. The RBI had announced in its annual policy statement in May 2004 that banks in India should examine in depth the options available under Basel II and draw a road-map by end-December 2004 for migration to Basel II and review the progress made at quarterly intervals. The Reserve Bank organized a two-day seminar in July 2004 mainly to sensitise the Chief Executive Officers of banks to the opportunities and challenges emerging from the Basel II norms.

Soon thereafter all banks were advised in August 2004 to undertake a self-assessment of the various risk management systems in place, with specific reference to the three major risks covered under the Basel II and initiate necessary remedial measures to update the systems to match up to the minimum standards prescribed under the New Framework. Banks have also been advised to formulate and operationalise the Capital Adequacy Assessment Process (CAAP) within the banks as required under Pillar II of the New Framework.

It is appropriate to list some of the other regulatory initiatives taken by the Reserve Bank of India, relevant for Basel II.

First, we have tried to ensure that the banks have suitable risk management framework oriented towards their requirements dictated by the size and complexity of business, risk philosophy, market perceptions and the expected level of capital.

Second, Risk Based Supervision (RBS) in 23 banks has been introduced on a pilot basis.

Third, we have been encouraging banks to formalize their capital adequacy assessment process (CAAP) in alignment with their business plan and performance budgeting system. This, together with the adoption of RBS would aid in factoring the Pillar II requirements under Basel II.

Fourth, we have been expanding the area of disclosures (Pillar III), so as to have greater transparency in the financial position and risk profile of banks.

Finally, we have tried to build capacity for ensuring the regulator's ability for identifying and permitting eligible banks to adopt IRB / Advanced Measurement approaches.

As per normal practice, and with a view to ensuring migration to Basel II in a non-disruptive manner, a consultative and participative approach has been adopted for both designing and implementing Basel II. A Steering Committee comprising senior officials from 14 banks (public, private and foreign) has been constituted wherein representation from the Indian Banks' Association and the RBI has also been ensured. The Steering Committee had formed sub-groups to address specific issues. On the basis of recommendations of the Steering Committee, draft guidelines to the banks on implementation of the New Capital Adequacy Framework have been issued. Implementation of Basel II will require more capital for banks in India due to the fact that operational risk is not captured under Basel I, and the capital charge for market risk was not prescribed until recently. Though last year has not been a very good year for banks, they are exploring all avenues for meeting the capital requirements under Basel II. The cushion available in the system, which has a CRAR of over 12 per cent now, is, however, comforting.

India has four rating agencies of which three are owned partly/wholly by international rating agencies. Compared to developing countries, the extent of rating penetration has been increasing every year and a large number of capital issues of companies has been rated. However, since rating is of issues and not of issuers, it is likely to result, in effect, in application of only Basel I standards for credit risks in respect of non-retail exposures. While Basel II provides some scope to extend the rating of issues to issuers, this would only be an approximation and it would be necessary for the system to move to rating of issuers. Encouraging rating of issuers would be essential in this regard. In this context, current non-availability of acceptable and qualitative historical data relevant to ratings, along with the related costs involved in building up and maintaining the requisite database, does influence the pace of migration to the advanced approaches available under Basel II.

Above all, capacity building, both in banks and the regulatory bodies is a serious challenge, especially with regard to adoption of the advanced approaches. We in India have initiated supervisory capacity- building measures to identify the gaps and to assess as well as quantify the extent of additional capital which may be required to be maintained by such banks. The magnitude of this task, which is scheduled to be completed by December 2006, appears daunting since we have as many as 90 scheduled commercial banks in India.

CONCLUDING OBSERVATIONS

In the current scenario, banks are constantly pushing the frontiers of risk management. Compulsions arising out of increasing competition, as well as agency problems between management, owners and other stakeholders are inducing banks to look at newer avenues to augment revenues, while trimming costs.

Consolidation, competition and risk management are no doubt critical to the future of banking but governance and financial inclusion would also emerge as the key issues for a country like India, at this stage of socio-economic development.

Bibliography

Ahluwalia, Montek S.: *"Reforming India's Financial Sector: An Overview"*, OUP, New Delhi, 1999.

Bhagwati, Jagdish: *India in Transition: Freeing the Economy*, Oxford, Clarendon Press, 1993.

Campbell, J.Y., Lo, A.W.: *The Econometrics of Financial Markets*, Princeton University Press, 1996.

Dhingra, C.: *The Indian Economy: Resources, Planning, Development, and Problems*, Delhi, Sultan Chand, 1983.

Eleanor B. Steinberg and Joseph A. Yager: *New Means of Financing International Needs: Possible Sources of Finance*, Washington D.C.: The Brookings Institution, 1978.

Gerald, K.: *The Less Developed Countries in the International Economy*, Cambridge, Cambridge University Press, 1975.

Hart, Oliver: *Firms, Contracts, and Financial Structure*, Clarendon Press, Oxford, 1995.

Jha, P.R.: *Agriculture and Economic Development*, New Delhi, Ashish, 1988.

MacKinley, A.C.: *The Econometrics of Financial Markets*, Princeton University Press, 1996.

Ottomar, H.: *Distribution of Stock of Money*, Effingham, London, 1892.

Paul, Kegan : *Money and the Mechanism of Exchange*, Oxford, London, 1890.

Raj, K.N.: *New Economic Policy*, Delhi, Oxford University Press, 1986.

Seligman, E. R. A. : *Currency Inflation and Public Debts*, New York, 1922.

Wolfe, J.N.: *Value, Capital and Growth*, Chicago, Edinburgh University Press. 1968.

Index

❑❑❑